BUDDHISM AND ABORTION

Buddhism and Abortion

Edited by

Damien Keown

UNIVERSITY OF HAWAI'I PRESS
HONOLULU

© 1999 Damien Keown: Selection and Editorial Matter, Introduction and Chapter 10
© 1999 Macmillan Press Ltd.: Chapters 2–9

Published in North America by
UNIVERSITY OF HAWAI'I PRESS
2840 Kolowalu Street
Honolulu, Hawai'i 96822

First Published in the United Kingdom by
MACMILLAN PUBLISHERS LTD
Houndmills, Basingstoke, Hampshire, RG21 6XS
ENGLAND

This book is printed on paper suitable for recycling and
made from fully managed and sustained forest sources.

Printed in Great Britain

Library of Congress Cataloging-in-Publication Data
Buddhism and abortion / edited by Damien Keown.
p.   cm.
Includes bibliographical references and index.
ISBN 0–8248–2107–6 (alk. paper). — ISBN 0–8248–2108–4 (pbk. :
alk. paper)
1. Abortion—Religious aspects—Buddhism.   I. Keown, Damien,
1951–   .
HQ767.38.B83B83   1998
294.3'56976—dc21   98–6079
                                                                          CIP

A mis hermanos

Contents

Part Three

Acknowledgements

Thanks are due to the following, without whose assistance the volume could not have appeared in its present form: Princeton University Press for permission to use material in chapter five adapted from *Liquid Life: Abortion and Buddhism in Japan* by William R. LaFleur; the Daeyang Research Fund of Sejong University which kindly provided funding for research by Frank Tedesco in 1995 which led to chapter seven; Canisius College, Buffalo, New York, for supporting research leading to chapter eight by James McDermott with a Summer Grant and Supplemental Research Grant from the Faculty Research Fund.

On a personal note there are many individuals and institutions I would like to thank. The Religious Studies Program at Pennsylvania State University provided a travel grant which allowed me to present chapter ten at a seminar there in November 1995. The chapter was previously given as a paper at Bristol University, Department of Theology and Religious Studies, in October 1995 and I am grateful to staff and students at both institutions for their comments. I am also grateful to the Spalding Trust which generously funded a one year visiting research fellowship at Clare Hall, Cambridge for 1996-7 which allowed me to complete the editing much sooner than would otherwise have been possible. I also wish to record my appreciation of the efforts made by the contributors, who worked hard to produce the chapters contained herein in the face of other pressing commitments. It has been a pleasure to work with such learned and co-operative colleagues.

Finally, thanks are due to Jason Lyon for proofreading the final draft and to Tim Farmiloe and Charmian Hearne of Macmillan for seeing the volume through to publication.

Contributors

Robert Florida is Professor of Religion and Dean of Arts at Brandon University, in Brandon, Manitoba, Canada. He has published several articles on Buddhist ethics and is active in a cross-cultural health care ethics research team involving Canadian and Thai universities and health professionals.

Cleo Odzer is a researcher and Webmaster for Daytop Village in New York. Her published works include *Patpong Sisters, Goa Freaks*, and the forthcoming *Virtual Spaces*.

Pinit Ratanakul is Director of the Center of Human Resources Development, Mahidol University, Bangkok. He is the author of *Bioethics, An Introduction to the Ethics of Medicine and Life Sciences*, and has published widely on medical ethics from a Thai Buddhist perspective.

William R. LaFleur is Professor of Japanese and the Joseph B. Glossberg Term Professor of Humanities at University of Pennsylvania. His many publications include *Liquid Life: Abortion and Buddhism in Japan*, and *Buddhism: A Cultural Perspective*.

Elizabeth G. Harrison is an Assistant Professor in the Department of East Asian Studies at the University of Arizona in Tucson, Arizona. She has published several articles on memorial services for dead children in Japan and is currently completing a collaborative book-length manuscript on the same topic with Professor Bardwell Smith of Carleton College, Northfield, Minnesota, USA. She is also pursuing historical research on Buddhist sermons in Japan.

Frank Tedesco teaches at Sejong University in Seoul, Korea. He is a researcher in contemporary social issues, bioethics and religion in Asia. He is an adviser to the Korean National Commission for UNESCO and other NGOs.

James P. McDermott is Professor and Chair in the Department of Religious Studies, Canisius College, Buffalo, New York. He is the author of *Development in the Early Buddhist Concept of Kamma/Karma.*

James Hughes is a sociologist, bioethicist, and Assistant Director of Research at the MacLean Center for Clinical Medical Ethics, University of Chicago.

Damien Keown is Senior Lecturer in Indian Religion at Goldsmiths College, University of London. His published works on ethics include *The Nature of Buddhist Ethics* and *Buddhism & Bioethics.* He is co-editor (with Charles S. Prebish) of the *Journal of Buddhist Ethics.*

1

Introduction

Damien Keown

Abortion is arguably the most controversial and divisive moral issue of modern times. For the past three decades, arguments both for and against abortion have been mounted by groups of all kinds, from religious fundamentalists to radical feminists and every shade of opinion in between. Rather than mutual understanding, however, the result has been the polarisation of opinion and the deepening of entrenched positions which now seem further apart than ever. All too often argument has given way to violent action resulting in death and serious injury.

In the face of this deadlock a new perspective is urgently required. Buddhism is an ancient tradition which over the centuries has refined its distinctive beliefs and values in the course of a long interaction with the major cultures of Asia. As Buddhism continues to engage the attention of the West, the time is now opportune for its views on abortion to be heard. Moreover, many seem willing to listen. Courses on contemporary ethics are increasingly adopting a comparative perspective, and there is clearly a desire to explore beyond the Western tradition, without necessarily rejecting its immense contribution. Specialist studies, such as the present volume, which explore the way in which non-Western ethical traditions respond to specific moral dilemmas are now beginning to address this need.

This book is intended to interest a broad interdisciplinary readership. The subject of abortion cuts across many academic disciplines, including law, ethics, medicine, philosophy, religion and

1

the social sciences. Readers who approach the subject from the discipline of Buddhist Studies may find the book helpful as an introduction to the particular ethical issues raised by abortion. Ethicists and others already familiar with the facts, statistics and arguments surrounding the abortion debate may find that the book provides useful comparative material. For the latter group, it may also serve as an introduction to Buddhism, since several of the chapters contain explanatory material by way of a prologue to the main discussion.

Another constituency the volume may interest is practising lay Buddhists, who may have a keen but not specialized interest in the subject, and be searching for a broader and more objective analysis than is available from popular literature (such little as exists) or religious teachers. Finally, aside from the various academic specialists and Buddhist practitioners, the contents should interest an informed general readership, since the topic is among the most widely debated of modern times. The issues raised by abortion are universal and touch the lives of men and women everywhere. In this respect Buddhists are no different to anyone else, and the Buddhist perspective should be readily comprehensible to anyone who has reflected on the abortion issue. There are, however, important differences between Buddhism and Western thought with respect to their philosophical presuppositions about the nature of human life and its destiny—belief in rebirth is one obvious example. Different emphases and nuances among the various Buddhist cultures give matters an added complexity.

The term 'Buddhism' (a word coined by Westerners in the 1830s) is little more than a label for a vast and complex religious and philosophical tradition which spans many Asian cultures as well as being established in the West. A rough estimate puts the number of Buddhists worldwide at something in the region of 500 million, including several million in the United States, Europe and Australia. It thus seems fair to speak of 'American Buddhism' or 'Western Buddhism' just as we speak of 'Japanese Buddhism' and 'Tibetan Buddhism'. Naturally, many Westerners who have adopted Buddhism hold views on abortion which are influenced both by their own culture and the more traditional beliefs and values of Buddhism. The answer to the questions raised by the issue of abortion will therefore depend in large part on what we understand by the terms 'Buddhist' and 'Buddhism', a matter on which there is no clear agreement. You may get very different answers depending on which Buddhists you ask, a point which will become clear in the following chapters.

In recent decades the subject of abortion has generated an enormous literature spanning diverse fields of knowledge. In spite of this, however, the topic remains virtually unexplored from a Buddhist perspective. Compared to the ink which has been spilled on the subject in the West, students of Buddhism—whether in the West or Asia—have left the topic almost untouched. To date only one monograph has been published on the subject—I refer here to Professor William LaFleur's acclaimed study of the cultural history of abortion in Japan—*Liquid Life: Abortion and Buddhism in Japan*, published in 1992.[1] The subject is also discussed along with other issues in medical ethics in my *Buddhism & Bioethics*.[2] Aside from these two volumes there is a limited amount of periodical literature, most of which concerns Japan,[3] and little information is available on abortion elsewhere in Buddhist Asia.

The present volume complements the literature currently available by including three chapters on Japan, but also supplements it significantly by introducing alternative cultural perspectives. Most of what has been published on the subject to date has been written by the authors whose work is brought together here for the first time. In the following nine chapters consideration is given to early textual sources, contemporary practice in both Theravāda and Mahāyāna Buddhist countries, and philosophical arguments both for and against abortion in terms of Buddhist beliefs and values. Only one of the chapters (chapter five) has appeared in print before, and then in a rather different form. The remaining chapters were commissioned specially for this volume, and many contain original research data which is not available elsewhere.

Format

The book is divided into three parts. Parts One and Two may be thought of as area studies which focus on south and east Asia respectively. Part Three is concerned with textual and normative issues.

Part One consists of three chapters which provide perspectives on abortion in Thailand, a country where Buddhism is the state religion. The first chapter, by Robert Florida, provides an introduction to aspects of traditional Buddhist ethics which bear upon abortion before turning to the contemporary situation in Thailand. He makes a point which strikes many observers, namely the apparent reluctance of those in positions of religious authority within Buddhism to take a position on controversial moral questions. The profile of the Buddhist establishment on questions of this kind could scarcely be lower (this applies not only to Thailand), and in many respects their pronouncements and public statements seem geared to a bygone age rather than the needs of today.

Florida provides useful information on the legal regulation of abortion in Thailand as well as statistics on the number of abortions performed per annum. Somewhat surprising for a country in which Buddhism—a religion renowned for its respect for life—is the state religion, abortions are running at some 50 per cent higher than the number in the USA for the equivalent number of citizens. 'Thailand', he writes, 'essentially has therapeutic abortion on demand'. 85 per cent or more of abortions are obtained by married women who appear to use it as a means of birth control. Florida refers to an estimated 300,000 abortions per year, the majority of which are illegal. While only an estimate, the figure represents an increase of two thirds on the annual total for the United Kingdom (Thailand has a population of 60 million, one or two million higher than the United Kingdom). Opinion polls in Thailand also reveal a paradox: while most Thais regard abortion as immoral, a majority also believe the legal grounds for obtaining it should be relaxed.

Cleo Odzer provides a glimpse into abortion in the lives of Thai women involved in prostitution and the sex-tourist industry in Bangkok. For three years between 1987–90 she traced the lives of 51 prostitutes, following eleven of them closely. Her study reveals a pronounced androcentric bias in Thai society which leaves many women socially and economically dependent on men. Many of the women saw their gender itself as the result of bad karma, an attitude arguably perpetuated by Buddhist teachings. Somewhat surprisingly, although a large number of the prostitutes became pregnant during the term of the study, and knew how to obtain abortions, none of them did so. The reasons for this seem to include their higher-than-average incomes, which enabled them to support a child, and also a desire to avoid further bad karma and perhaps create good karma by raising a son who might become a monk. A somewhat unexpected conclusion from the first two chapters, therefore, is that while married women in Thailand regularly seek abortions, prostitutes do not.

Further information on Thailand is provided by Pinit Ratanakul, whose chapter rounds off the section. Ratanakul provides further information on traditional Buddhist and Thai religious attitudes to abortion, before discussing it in the context of genetic abnormalities and AIDS. Factoring these difficult issues into his discussion, Ratanakul proposes a possible Buddhist 'middle way', which takes a moral stand on the middle ground, allowing abortion to be seen in some situations as 'the lesser of evils in the grey light of human reality'.

Part Two shifts the scene from the Theravāda Buddhism of south Asia to the Mahāyāna Buddhism of north Asia. Of the three chapters in this section, two are devoted to Japan and one to Korea. The first chapter, by William LaFleur, is adapted from his study of abortion in Japan, *Liquid Life*. The book explores the cultural history of abortion in depth, but the historical material has been omitted from this chapter in favour of an emphasis on the contemporary situation and an exploration of traditional beliefs about fetal life. The chapter draws frequent comparisons and contrasts with the abortion debate in the West, and commends the Japanese response as one from which the West might learn.

Central to the contemporary Japanese experience is the phenomenon of *mizuko kuyō*, a memorial service held for aborted children. This recent development allows women who have had an abortion, along with their families, to acknowledge publicly what was done, and to offer an apology to the deceased child. LaFleur unravels the complex symbolism of the service and discusses some of the issues and problems it has given rise to. The rate of abortion in Japan has been very high in recent years, perhaps peaking at over a million before decreasing in the last few years as the Pill has become more easily available.

While LaFleur decodes the cultural form of the service; the following chapter by Elizabeth Harrison explores its personal dimension. Up to now, the voice of the women who have the service performed has not been clearly heard. Why do they do it, and what do they feel it achieves for them? Based on research using questionnaires and taped interviews, Harrison's chapter provides a fascinating glimpse into the way the *mizuko kuyō* ritual is perceived by its lay participants. This perspective is usefully contextualized by juxtaposing it with the contrasting construction placed upon the ritual in promotional literature and in the media, and by Buddhist clergy.

The final paper in this section provides the first academic exploration of abortion in Korea from a Buddhist perspective. Korea provides an interesting comparison with Japan. Both countries have a very high rate of abortion, but in Japan it is legal (since 1948) whereas in Korea, it is not. Before turning to the topic of abortion, however, Tedesco provides a useful introduction to Buddhism in Korea, a field which has been neglected in Buddhist studies. He also provides invaluable factual information on the political, legal, and social issues which have influenced contemporary attitudes to abortion. Annual figures of between one and two million are quoted for this country, which has a population of around 46 million. Over a quarter of the population are Buddhists, which makes them the majority religious group. Statistics quoted by Tedesco reveal that Buddhists are slightly more likely to have abortions than other segments of the population.

As elsewhere in Asia, the voice of Buddhism has been little heard on the abortion question. Tedesco notes 'Buddhists have been mute regarding the issue of abortion in Korea, at least until the last few years'. In 1985, an anti-abortion movement began to gain ground following the publication of a book by the Venerable Sŏk Myogak, a Buddhist monk of the Chogye order. His book, entitled *My Dear Baby, Please Forgive Me!* quickly became popular, and readers began to demand rites and services for aborted children similar to the Japanese *mizuko kuyō* service, although distinctively Korean in form. Other Korean Buddhist leaders have echoed the clear pro-life message of the book. A Buddhist nun, the Venerable Sŏngdŏk, has since 1991 organized long ceremonial meetings for the spirits of aborted babies. So far, however, few practical alternatives are available for women who seek an alternative to abortion. There are only nine facilities available nationwide for unwed mothers: four are run by Catholics, three by Protestants, one by the

Salvation Army, and one by a private social welfare organization. None is run by Buddhists. Although Buddhist scriptures have much to say about compassion, there would seem to be a lack of follow-through in practice where social welfare issues are concerned.

The three chapters in Part Three are concerned with determining or establishing normative positions based on textual and other evidence. In formulating a Buddhist response to abortion, a crucial question is clearly: What do the early scriptural sources have to say on the matter? James McDermott examines the Pali Canon—the earliest surviving corpus of Buddhist scripture—along with a number of other influential primary and secondary sources. These sources are unequivocal in regarding abortion as gravely wrong, and a breach of the First Precept against taking life. It is clear from these texts that individual human life was thought to begin at conception, and that to cause intentional injury to a child in the womb, as in the case of abortion, was considered as serious a breach of the First Precept as killing a child already born. McDermott cites stories which depict the evil karmic consequences which follow an abortion. The section of the early canon in which abortion receives most attention is the Vinaya, or monastic code, and McDermott explores some of the complex questions which arise from the case-histories and judgements found there. This early material contains vital information on key questions relevant to abortion, such as when life begins, early ideas on embryology, notions regarding the moral status of fetal life, early techniques of abortion, the use of abortifacient drugs and preparations, and so forth.

But how relevant are the ancient scriptures to the problems posed by abortion today? In advancing 'A Western Approach' to abortion in the following chapter, James Hughes suggests that the Buddhist attitude has never been to follow scripture slavishly, but 'to continually adapt the Dharma to new audiences'. Thus while texts may form part of the dialogue, they cannot be allowed to be the dominant voice. For one thing, their conclusions may be based on information which has been shown to be inaccurate in the light of scientific discoveries, and for another they may embody attitudes which are now simply out of date.

Hughes suggests that Buddhism contains a variety of different 'moral logics', and that it is a matter of choosing the right one in each case. Suggesting that 'clear and defensible distinctions can be made between fetuses and other human life', he finds the moral logic of utilitarianism persuasive in the context of abortion, although tempered by the requirements of a 'virtue ethic' which takes into account the mindset of the actors. Abortion may therefore be allowable where the intention is compassionate and the act achieves the best outcome for all concerned. Hughes concludes his chapter with the text of a service devised by an American Zen Buddhist group, the Diamond Sangha, which can be performed on the death of an unborn child.

The concluding paper, by the editor, addresses directly a question which has come up several times in the collection, namely whether Buddhism can offer the West a solution to the abortion deadlock. The chapter considers the notion of the 'middle way' in Buddhism and its relevance to ethical dilemmas. It argues that the concept of the 'middle way' cannot be applied to the abortion debate to generate a liberal or moderate stance which would allow abortion in the way some commentators envisage. The roots of the proposal for a compromise are traced to Japan and the 'liberal' Buddhism of the West, and appear to lack a foundation in the early Indian tradition. The chapter suggests instead that early Buddhist teachings are consistently 'pro-life' in orientation, and concludes with a critique of some contemporary alternative readings.

Gaps

As editor, I am all too aware of the gaps in the coverage of the subject in this volume. Although south and east Asia are represented, there is nothing on Tibet. Moreover, why three chapters on Thailand, and nothing on Sri Lanka or Burma? What about Laos, Cambodia, and Vietnam, not to mention China? Again, although the views of women are quite well represented in the following pages, no explicitly feminist perspective on abortion is offered. I regret these shortcomings, which are essentially a reflection of the lack of research to date into the subject. The deeper reason for the gaps which remain is that in the academic study of Buddhism ethical issues have been neglected, just as they have by the tradition itself. Intellectual attention has been channelled instead into other fields which, while undeniably fascinating in themselves, have little obvious relevance to to the problems of everyday life. As Steven Covey has observed, some issues are important and others are urgent, but few are both.[4] I hope this book will demonstrate that the ethical challenges confronting Buddhism are both urgent and important, and that others will be encouraged to undertake the research needed to supply what is missing here.

Notes

[1] William R. LaFleur *Liquid Life: Abortion and Buddhism in Japan* (Princeton: Princeton University Press, 1992). This has since been supplemented by Helen Hardacre *Marketing the Menacing Fetus in Japan* (Berkeley, Los Angeles and London: University of California Press, 1997) which appeared while the present volume was in press.

[2] Damien Keown *Buddhism & Bioethics* (London: Macmillan, and New York: St Martin's Press, 1995).

[3] R.E. Florida, 'Buddhist Approaches to Abortion', *Asian Philosophy*, 1991, 1, 1:39-50. For further details of the literature on this subject see James J.Hughes and Damien Keown 'Buddhism and Medical Ethics: A Bibliographic Introduction', *Journal of Buddhist Ethics* 1995 2:105-124.

[4] Steven R. Covey, A. Roger Merrill, Rebecca R. Merrill *First Things First* (London: Simon and Schuster, 1994).

2

Abortion in Buddhist Thailand

Robert E. Florida

Introduction

During my visit to Thailand in January 1994, Bangkok authorities were scandalized by the discovery of thirty-four aborted fetuses beside a main road leading from Bangkok to Ayutthya.[1] They were presumed to come from one of the estimated one hundred illegal abortion clinics found along that route. Abortion, as we will see later, is legal only under certain controlled circumstances in Thailand. However, in this case, as in so many aspects of life in Thailand, what the law prescribes is not necessarily the actual practice. Nonetheless, the authorities announced their resolve to see that the law would be enforced.

Abortion is a very contentious public issue in the United States, Canada and parts of Europe. It is debated on all levels, from screamed insults and slogans on placards to the most learned philosophical and theological reflections. There is a very sophisticated body of serious scholarship on all sides of the question, including theological positions that reflect centuries of systematic work. In Thailand also, abortion is a serious reality, but it is much less openly discussed. Contemporary Buddhist thinkers and scholars of Buddhism in Asia and in the West, mostly laymen and laywomen, are beginning to address bioethical issues systematically, but the field is relatively new and open. In Thailand, the discussion has mainly been by politicians and medical people, and theological issues have very little weight in the public debates.

In this chapter, I will first present some of the basic principles of Buddhist ethics in order to place the abortion issue in its proper context. Then I will discuss the situation in Thailand. My research is based on a review of the literature and on interviews and field observations made in Thailand in the period from 1989 to the present.[2]

Some Buddhist Ethical Principles

Let us begin with some basic Buddhist principles to put the question of abortion in wider context. First, anything that exists exists only in relationship with everything else that exists. That is, nothing has independent self-being. You and I—anything that is—exist only as the result of temporary, contingent causal relationships with other similarly changing, unsubstantial, suffering beings.

The wise person who sees the contingency and interdependence of all beings is moved to compassion by their foolish and frenzied grasping driven by selfish desire. Practically, wisdom leads to selfless action for the sake of others. Thus *prajñā,* or wisdom, and *karuṇā*, or compassion, are the two major Buddhist ideals, the first relating to the realm of ultimacy and the second to the world of day to day existence. Without ultimate wisdom one will be defective in *upāya* or skilful means for helping others. Witless compassion, the bungling attempt to do good without the wisdom to effect it, is extremely dangerous.

Moral behaviour in Buddhist systems, then, is not an absolute in itself—it is a means towards a religious end, the transcendence of those selfish cravings which bind all beings to an unending round of suffering. Accordingly all moral acts are understood either to be *kuśala karma*, skilful deeds which are beneficial to self and others, or *akuśala karma*, unskilful deeds which harm self and others. In Thai popular Buddhism, *kuśala karma* is 'making merit,' which can be achieved through ethical behaviour, generosity (especially to the *sangha*), and rituals.

Everything in the phenomenal world is relative. Human behaviour, therefore, is to be judged not on an absolute scale of good and evil but rather on a relative scale of skilful and unskilful. Skilfulness, of course, is understood in regard to the ascent of the paths of Lord Buddha out of this world of suffering.

The precepts of morality laid down by the Buddha also are thus not absolute commandments. They are clearly understood as 'rules of training' which the individual undertakes in order to advance along the religious path. In fact, so little are they absolute commandments, that the precepts have been used since the earliest days of the Buddhist community as temporary vows, freely assumed by individuals for specified lengths of time. A lay meditator, for example, might undertake to follow the rule of training to abstain from the misuse of sensual pleasures for the period of a retreat. The relativity of the precepts is further demonstrated by the fact that there are traditionally five for the ordinary person, eight for the advanced laity, and two hundred and twenty seven for Thai monks. The five most basic precepts are:

> I undertake to observe the rule
> to abstain from taking life;
> to abstain from taking what is not given;
> to abstain from sensuous misconduct;
> to abstain from false speech;
> to abstain from intoxicants as tending to cloud the mind.[3]

Note that the form of these precepts shows that they are understood to be personal commitments or practical guidelines to be undertaken provisionally as steps on a religious path. They are not absolute divine commandments which must be obeyed. Dr Hema Goonatilake, a Theravādin Buddhist from Sri Lanka makes this point very well:

> It is ... to be understood that precepts are rules of training and not commandments from God, the Buddha or anyone else. It is only an undertaking by one, to oneself, if one is convinced that it is a good practice to observe.[4]

This fundamental difference of attitude towards the nature of the basic religious laws of human life underlies and helps to explain, in my opinion, many of the differences and misunderstandings that arise between Eastern and Western people.

On the level of relative truth, one's deeds or karma obey fixed laws of causality which determine one's destiny. Basically the moral consequences of an act are determined by the will or motivation (*cetanā*) of the actor. If the will behind an act is driven by greed, hatred or delusion, which Buddhists understand as the three poisonous roots of selfish craving, then the act is *akuśala* or unskilful.

It works like this—every act involves body, speech and mind working in conjunction. Mind starts a train of activity, and if mind is motivated by greed, hatred or delusion, then the speech and bodily activity which follow are doomed to be unskilful. Unskilful acts always have negative consequences for the actor and generally for the recipient of the act. The precepts are designed to provide guidelines for skilful activity and when followed will minimize negative karmic consequences. From the Buddhist vantage point of the middle way, there are two basic errors one could fall into on this issue. If one denies the reality of karmic consequences, one has adopted the nihilistic extreme view, which tends towards antinomianism. The eternalistic extreme view takes moral rules as absolute, resulting in inflexible dogmatic positions.

Application to Abortion: Buddhist Embryology

From the very earliest days, the theory of co-conditioned causality, or *pratītyasamutpāda*, the teaching that every thing in the universe is interrelated with every other thing, was interpreted embryologically.[5] Ignorant, selfishly motivated acts in our past lives establish the karmic foundations or preconditions that give rise to our rebirth in another life. The third link in this process (*vijñāna*) was described by Vasubandhu, a great Buddhist commentator of the fourth or fifth century CE, as the physical and mental components of a living being at the moment of conception, that is, the moment of reincarnation.[6]

What all this boils down to is that traditionally Buddhists have understood that the human being begins at the instant of conception, when sperm, egg and *vijñāna* come together. Contemporary Buddhist ethicists, such as Taniguchi, maintain this point of view—'there is no qualitative difference between an unborn fetus and a born individual'.[7] R.H.B. Exell of the Siam Institute of Technology, in a recent article, attempts to understand modern science and technology from the point of view of Buddha's original teachings. After considering the quality of life of the human fetus from the modern scientific view, he concludes, 'These observations suggest that abortion should be regarded as killing a separate human being, not just removing a part of the mother'.[8]

Indeed, modern embryological research confirms the Buddhist teaching that a separate, co-dependent human life begins at the moment of conception. The first sentence of K.L. Moore's *The Developing Human: Clinically Oriented Embryology* clearly and succinctly makes the point that 'development is a continuous process that begins when an ovum is fertilized by a sperm and ends at death'.[9] Dr Moore does not, of course, mention the *vijñāna* or venture a judgement on whether or not this means that abortions are unskilful acts in the Buddhist sense.

On the other hand, the traditional Buddhist belief about the nature of the environment and the quality of the life of the fetus is very different from the prevailing modern Western view. Most of us Westerners seem to imagine that the fetus lives a peaceful, blissful life, floating without a care in the warm protective environment of the womb. The Buddhist idea is quite the opposite. I quote from *Three Worlds According to King Ruang*, written by a great king of the Sukhothai Era in the fourteenth century. It closely follows the Pali scriptures and their commentaries and is an extremely influential source for traditional Thai thought.[10]

> The baby has great trouble while it is in the mother's abdomen: the place is extremely revolting and disgusting; it is damp and full of bad smells caused by the eighty broods of worms and parasites that live there ... [T]hese worms and parasites are all mixed up in the mother's abdomen and cover the body of the fetus like a skin disease ... [B]lood and lymph run down all over its body, dripping at all times; the baby is like a monkey who, when it rains, sits in the hollow of a tree clutching its fists in a sluggish and dejected way.[11]

As to abortion, since the fetus is understood to be a living being, the first precept against taking life obviously applies. Buddhaghosa, a fifth century Theravāda commentator who is still very influential in Thailand and other countries today, has an extensive commentary on this precept:

> I undertake to observe the rule to abstain from taking life ...
> 'Taking life' means to murder anything that lives. It refers to the
> striking and killing of living beings. ...'Taking life' is then the
> will to kill anything that one perceives as having life, to act so as
> to terminate the life-force in it, in so far as the will finds expres-
> sion in bodily action or in speech. With regard to animals it is
> worse to kill large ones than small. Because a more extensive ef-
> fort is involved. Even where the effort is the same, the difference
> in substance must be considered. In the case of humans the kill-
> ing is the more blameworthy the more virtuous they are. Apart
> from that, the extent of the offence is proportionate to the inten-
> sity of the wish to kill.[12]

Generally speaking, then, abortion is a serious unskilful act as it involves violence with the intent to kill against a fetal human being.

Buddhaghosa's ancient opinion here supports Exell's contemporary common sense comment that, 'if the criterion of causing suffering is to be taken as a measure of how bad the karma is, then killing a young embryo would appear to be less bad than killing a well developed fetus'.[13] There are good clinical reasons to agree, and morally it is somehow intuitively obvious that the earlier an abortion the better. In the medically rare situation of a conflict between the life of the mother and of the fetus, Buddhaghosa's reasoning would justify sacrificing the latter as it is a very much smaller being than the mother. In the cases of pregnancies which harm the health of the mother without threatening her life, or which would create socio-economic hardships, there is no clear answer.[14] If it were possible to have a reliable quantification of the harm that would accrue to the mother if she had the child compared to the harm that would be done in the abortion, it might be possible to justify the abortion. However, since there is no such measure, the first precept and Buddhist tradition strongly suggest that abortion would be an unskilful act.

So far we have looked at abortion primarily from the outside, as an objective act, so to speak. However, from the Buddhist view, it is the internal aspect of an act, the motivation, that primarily determines the karmic nature or morality of an act. It would seem that, again, abortion involves several grievous errors.[15] Greed, hatred and delusion, the three root drives of unskilful men and women, seem to apply all too well to abortion decisions. Greed, that is, passionate attachment, would lie behind persons' considering only their own interests or pleasures in the situation. It would also solidify the notion that an 'I' owned the fetus and could do with it what 'I' would. Hatred would motivate one to strike out to eliminate the perceived cause of discomfort, the fetus. Delusion might cloud one's understanding and lead to denial that the fetus is a living being. It also could result in a condition of apathy where one, avoiding responsibility for oneself, followed advice to terminate the pregnancy. Underlying these three 'poisons' of greed, hatred, and delusion are even more fundamental errors. The three poisons arise through lack of insight into the interconnectedness of all beings, a misguided sense of difference between I and other. When *prajñā* is so lacking, then so too *karuṇā* or compassion will also fall short, and *upāya* or skilful means will not be conspicuous.

In light of co-conditioned causality, the moral consequences of abortion do not only concern the relationship between the pregnant woman and the fetus. Abortion also entails physical and mental trauma to the woman and has karmic consequences on the technicians, advisors, friends and family involved. Somewhat surprisingly, Buddhists also consider the karmic effect of an abortion on the fetus itself:

> Having just experienced the trauma of death and the terrifying uncertainty of the intermediate state, at last he has found a point upon which his energies can focus. When the consciousness is abruptly cut loose again, the effect may well be to accentuate feelings of fear and insecurity which will make an unfavourable rebirth more likely.[16]

Thus the unskilfulness of an abortion is increased because it steals away a rare opportunity to be reborn as a human being, the only status where one can advance spiritually.

The moral seriousness of abortion is illustrated in the *Three Worlds According to King Ruang*, where a special variety of female hungry ghost, a very unfortunate rebirth, is described:

> [They] are generally naked and have a strong and revolting odor coming from every part of their bodies. There are lots of flies swarming all over them and eating them, making holes in their

bodies. Their bodies are very skinny ... and [they] cannot find anything to eat.[17]

Twice a day they give birth to seven babies and each time, driven by their terrible hunger, gobble them down. They find themselves in this woeful state as a result of having been abortionists in past lives and having uttered a falsified oath of innocence. Abortion is also mentioned in other texts as one of the three special offences for women that lead to unfortunate rebirths. The other two are to treat her husband, or her husband's relatives, with contempt.[18]

Additionally, frequently, one is led to consider abortion because of some previous error in regard to the precept concerning sexuality, which as explained by Buddhaghosa is:

> 'I undertake to observe the rule to abstain from sensuous misconduct.' ... The offence is the more serious, the more moral and virtuous the person transgressed against. Four factors are involved: someone who should not be gone into, the thought of cohabiting with that one, the actions which lead to such cohabitation, and its actual performance. There is only one way of carrying it out: with one's own body.[19]

Sensuous misconduct leads to an awkward pregnancy, which leads to abortion being contemplated. One unskilful act tends to lead to another as long as one lives unmindfully.

This leads us back to the religious context of this discussion. What Buddhists aim to do is to perfect themselves by following the path that the Buddha blazed for them. It involves replacing unwholesome roots of action, namely the selfish drives of greed, hatred, and delusion with wholesome motives: loving-kindness, compassion, joy for others and equanimity. Similarly, the first precept, which is expressed negatively as abstention from taking life, has a positive form as well, 'with deeds of loving kindness, I purify my body'.[20] The application to abortion is obvious.

Morality, meditation, and wisdom constantly work together in this path of *prajñā* and *karuṇā*. From this point of view any pregnancy could be taken as an opportunity to help one perfect selfless compassion. Dr Pinit Ratnakul, one of Thailand's leading thinkers in bioethics, closes his first book with a very fine reminder of the high religious ideals of the 'voluntary sacrifice of one's claims or rights' that are at the heart of Buddhism and Christianity.[21] At any rate, whatever one does, one's acts will ripen, with those skilful acts that are beneficial to self and others bearing good fruit while those unskilful acts that harm self and others yielding bad fruit.

It should also be mentioned that contraception, if the methods used do no harm to fetus or the lovers, is considered to be skilful means.[22] Obviously, then, from the Buddhist point of view, preventing unwanted pregnancies is far better than terminating them.

Abortion and Buddhism in Thailand[23]

A. Religious and Ethical Issues

In Thailand most of the research on abortion has been medical,[24] and I have found only a very few scattered statements in publications by monks and official religious spokesmen on the issue. In large part, I believe this is a reflection of the Thai traditional attitude that monks as world renouncers should be above the ordinary earthy concerns of those who remain enmeshed in day to day life. Monks are to serve as exemplars and as purified fields of merit for individuals and the nation by devoting themselves to studying the Buddhist scriptures, performing rites and public service such as education, and (for a few) dedicating themselves to meditation. Thus most monks have little reason to pay close attention to contemporary social issues—indeed, such concerns can lead to difficulties with government and *sangha* officials. Furthermore, their form of intellectual discipline, the minute study and memorization of ancient texts, does not encourage critical reflection on the modern world.

One of the things that impresses me about the learned books and sermons produced by the official *sangha* today is that they hardly seem aware of the twentieth century. Take, for example, the recent book, *Plan of Life*, which was written by a leading monk, dedicated to Her Majesty Queen Sirikit on her sixtieth birthday in 1992, commended by the Supreme Patriarch of Thailand, and published jointly by a prestigious foundation, an Air Chief Marshal, and a Buddhist university.[25] This book is an inspirational review of Pali texts and traditional commentaries, but almost completely

ignores the modern realities of Thai life. It is very interesting that a
plan of life published in 1992, for all practical purposes, could
have appeared in 1792.

Please note that this is not particularly meant as a criticism of
the Thai Buddhist establishment. Perhaps the greatest service that
Thai Buddhism can provide to the modern world is to preserve its
pure traditions. Of course, there is a real danger that if the *sangha*
does not effectively address current concerns, Thai youth and the
modernized section of the population, which is increasingly in
charge of the way the country is developing, will simply find Buddhism irrelevant. Indeed, sometimes it is already difficult to discern
traditional religious ideals in contemporary practices, and one
hears constant complaints that the young know very little about
their own religion. This dilemma of Thai Buddhists, how to maintain their ancient and noble tradition while also being relevant and
effective as Buddhists today, is obvious in the issue of abortion.

One high *sangha* official, in an oral communication to one of
my informants, said that abortion clearly entails a violation of the
first precept against the taking of life, and is therefore always a sin
and out of the question for those who live as monks in the religious
world. However, most of us live in another world, the ordinary
secular realm, which has different requirements. For example, in
the secular world we think that capital punishment is necessary,
and the monks will accept it to the extent that they will sermonize
and comfort the condemned person and the executioner, but would
never do the actual killing. Similarly, the monks will eat food prepared from living beings, but will never act as a butcher, and will
consecrate soldiers but never go to war. Thus the *sangha* may tolerate abortion while never encouraging it.

In fact, as Acharn Passano, the Abbot of Wat Pah Nanachat,
brought to my attention, the regulations that minutely govern the
life of the monk include arranging or encouraging an abortion under the rule against taking human life, one of the four most serious
offences that result in expulsion from the *sangha* with no possibility of reinstatement in the current lifetime. The Thai handbook of
monastic rules makes it very clear that the rule applies in this
case—'By the body of a human being is meant that which appears
in the womb of the mother at the time of conception, lasting until
the time of death'.[26] Acharn Passano noted that there really was no

reason for the *sangha* leadership to make special public statements about abortion as what they must say is both cut and dried and well known by everyone. He went on to add that Buddhist morality is a personal undertaking, not something imposed from without, and that abortion is therefore a personal moral dilemma which every one must decide for herself or himself. What monks must uphold in these matters, he said, is very clear, but standards for monks and for lay people are very different. Nonetheless, abortion is 'basically unskilful action'.

Professor Siralee Sirilai of the Faculty of Social Sciences and Humanities at Mahidol University, Bangkok, points out that the main Buddhist criterion for moral decision-making is whether or not the act has wholesome motivation. A skilful deed should work against greed, hatred, and delusion, and thus will be for the good of self and others. However, there are also secondary criteria such as 'wholesome-unwholesome, usefulness-unusefulness, trouble-untrouble, admirability-blameworthiness'.[27] She thinks that for the world renouncers, only the first criterion can be taken into account, but that for the Buddhist layperson the secondary can also come into play. Therefore, in some circumstances, abortion could perhaps be morally permissible.

The Buddhist community in Thailand is divided on the abortion issue. Some leaders like Major General Chamlong Srimuang, a leading figure in Thai democracy, one time political head of Bangkok, and a dedicated lay Buddhist who observes eight precepts, are firmly opposed to any liberalization of the abortion law, basing their position on the absolute sanctity of life in the Buddhist tradition.[28] It is perhaps worth noting that when General Chamlong was mayor of Bangkok, very little was done to suppress the illegal abortion clinics and quacks. Others, including some monastic leaders, take a much more global view, pointing out that in Buddhist morality the intent of the action has much to do with the karmic result of the act. Therefore, in some cases, for example when the mother's life is endangered by the pregnancy, abortion could be a skilful act. Dr Pinit Ratnakul's study *Bioethics*, while it does not offer a complete Buddhist discussion on the abortion question, looks at issues in subtle and complex ways. While the precept against killing counsels against easy abortion decisions, many factors have to be taken into account in coming to a skilful judgement.

B. Buddhist Factors in Thai Abortion Law

While Thailand has enshrined religious toleration in its constitution and in the hearts of its people, over ninety per cent of Thais are Theravāda Buddhists; and the laws and customs of the country are both consciously and unconsciously informed by Buddhist principles. Since these principles recognize the fetus as a human being from the moment of conception and take the precept against killing as the primary one,[29] one would not expect to find abortion on demand permitted in Thai law. In fact the current law, the Penal Code of 1956, specifies strict penalties: three years in prison or a fine of 3,000 baht or both, for a woman who causes an abortion for herself or who procures one from another party. The penalty for the abortionist is greater, five years or 5,000 baht or both. If the woman is injured or killed in the process, the penalties are much more severe.[30]

However, therapeutic abortions, those performed by qualified medical practitioners, are permitted in two circumstances: first, if 'it is necessary for the sake of the woman's health' and, second, if the pregnancy is the result of rape.[31] Since 'woman's health' is not defined, the medical practitioner has a great deal of freedom in deciding when to perform therapeutic abortions. I was surprised to see in the *Bangkok Nation* on Friday June 4 1993, a medical expert Dr Withoon Ungrapathan quoted as saying, 'Thai law regards abortions as illegal for whatever reasons they are committed'. He is very wrong indeed.

As to rape, which is the second circumstance under Thai law that legitimates abortion, it would seem to me that, strictly speaking, even though the outrage of rape involves both violence and sexual misconduct, there is not adequate dharmic grounds for an abortion, since abortion always involves violence against human life. One unskilful act does not justify another. The point is to break the chain.

If one looks at official figures, abortion would appear to be a very rare phenomenon in Thailand. Only five therapeutic abortions per year were reported in the 1960s.[32] However, as so often is true in Thailand, what is officially reported is not necessarily what is actually happening. There have been several major studies that attempt to determine the scope of abortion practice in the Kingdom.[33]

While the numbers do not exactly coincide from study to study, they all confirm that the abortion rate in Thailand is rather high, probably in the range of around 300,000 per year, or at a rate of 37 abortions per 1,000 women of childbearing age.[34] To compare with other countries, some other rates for the same period were: Canada 11.1, Hungary 35.3, Japan 22.6 officially, but probably between 65 and 90, Singapore 44.5, USA 24.2, and USSR an incredible 181.[35]

In the latest hospital study done in Thailand, published in 1987, 17 per cent of the abortions surveyed were therapeutic, that is, performed by physicians in hospitals, and the remainder were illegal abortions.[36] However, in fact, the proportion of medically performed abortions done under good clinical conditions is probably greater than this study shows because many are done in private clinics, government and NGO clinics, and doctors' offices. Since private services are expensive and public services are concentrated in Bangkok and other major cities, 'the majority of abortion-seeking women are still economically forced to choose low cost services from unqualified practitioners'.[37] Some of the illegal abortionists offer relatively clean and safe services, but many of them are appalling, resulting in many deaths and severe complications in one third of the cases.[38] The two most popular methods for illegal abortions are uterine massage and the introduction of a fluid into the cervical canal.

Judging from many conversations with Thais, including some in medical fields, it would seem that most believe abortion is primarily a problem for single women who have misbehaved and who wish to conceal their sexual activity because premarital virginity is highly valued and unwed mothers are disgraced. Furthermore, it is thought that abortion is an urban problem primarily because traditional morality is said to be weaker in the cities than in the country. However, the reality is far different. The latest study (1987) shows that 'the majority of illegal abortion clients were married women employed in agricultural work'.[39] Ninety-one per cent of the therapeutic abortions and eighty-five per cent of the illegal ones were obtained by married women.[40] A study published in 1975 found a high degree of acceptance of abortion among country women 'because it has been the traditional means to birth control in rural areas'.[41] This was born out in a study done in North East Thailand, published in 1981, which found a very high illegal abortion rate there of 107 per 1,000 rural women between the ages of 15 and 44.[42]

There have been many opinion polls taken on the issue of abortion in Thailand.[43] None of them asked questions relating directly to Buddhist beliefs, but indirectly all the results seem to reflect the marked dissonance between Thai religious theory, which judges abortion to be an unskilful violation of Buddhist principles, and Thai practical reality, which is that abortion is very common. In one study (1978), for example, the majority of the respondents believed that abortion is an immoral act, yet they also thought the law should be liberalized to allow it on socioeconomic grounds and to broaden the medical reasons.[44]

Encouraged by the overwhelming support to widen the grounds for therapeutic abortions, reformers made several attempts in the 1970s and 1980s to have the law changed in Parliament.[45] Some Buddhist leaders, including Major General Chamlong Srimuang, who was then Governor of Bangkok, in alliance with Roman Catholics, led the fight against this legal change. Nothing got through Parliament. Delayed by religious opposition, various reform bills failed to work their way through the system before governments were dissolved, whether through parliamentary procedure or by military takeover.

Currently there seems to be little interest in abortion law reform. Former activists are worn out and, in fact, the law is a dead letter. The latest study shows that therapeutic abortions were performed for social reasons in 77 per cent of the cases for single women and for socio-economic reasons for 70 per cent of the married women, while 16 per cent of the married women gave contraceptive failure as the reason. Only 14 per cent of the abortions performed for unmarried women and 5 per cent for married women were for the reasons allowed by law—rape and threats to maternal health.[46] No medical practitioner has ever been prosecuted under the current law,[47] so there is little incentive to change it. As Dr Suporn put it, 'We operate the Thai way—we do what we think that we should do'.[48]

For the women who can afford it, and who can find a cooperative doctor or who have access to certain public clinics, Thailand essentially has therapeutic abortion on demand. From interviews I note that there is a wide range of personal responses by medical people to the question of abortions. Some have quite lucrative abortion businesses in private institutions. On the other extreme, I know practitioners who refuse to perform abortions, because of their firm Buddhist scruples—they also will not refer patients for abortions or even inform them that they are possible. Some physicians make it a rule not to charge for abortions, so they will not be tempted to profit from a morally dubious act, and strictly limit the number they will perform. It is all very personal. Hospital abortion policies, and the policies of departments within hospitals, depend on what the Director believes. If he or she is opposed to abortions altogether or for certain reasons, then they are banned. As usual in Thailand, the situation is not very simple, but of course, simple things are not so interesting.

Thai Buddhist Religious Responses to Abortion

Many of Japan's Buddhist temples, as is well documented, have formal services to help women cope with their feelings after an abortion.[49] It would seem that women in Thailand who have had abortions do not go to monks for direct consolation. Acharn Passano told me that in his twelve years as an abbot, he had never been approached for advice or solace with regard to abortion. He thought that this was because in Northeastern Thailand, where his monastery is located, the traditional morality, family structure and social safety nets are relatively intact, making abortion unthinkable. Unfortunately, he seems to be wrong—the studies mentioned earlier show abortions to be very frequent in his part of the Kingdom and to be well accepted as part of traditional rural life. My hypothesis is that he has never become aware of abortions in his congregation because they would not care to trouble a monk with such low matters.

Furthermore, I suspect that Thais would be very uncomfortable with the idea of having an open service to deal with the karma and feelings resulting from an abortion. Such things are much safer and less dangerous if kept secret for oneself. In fact, there are rituals within Thai Buddhism that women use to help them deal with their abortions.[50] The very common ceremonies of making money, flower, or incense offerings to Buddha images, and releasing birds, fish or turtles at temples are frequently resorted to by women to assuage their feelings of guilt and to lessen the harm done to the aborted fetus. This would be achieved by transferring the merit of the ritual to the fetus.

Generally speaking, in cases like these, where religious theory condemns a prevalent practice, there are ritual ways to deal with the ensuing psychological pressures. So it is not at all surprising to find parallel practices in Thailand and Japan.

Notes

[1] 'Special squad to track illicit abortion clinics', *The Nation* (Bangkok, Jan. 24, 1994), A5.

[2] Much of the general ethical discussion to follow is based on some of my earlier papers: R.E. Florida, 'Buddhist Approaches to Abortion', *Asian Philosophy*, Vol.1, No. 1, 1991, 'Buddhist Approaches to Euthanasia', *Studies in Religion/Sciences Religieuses*, Vol. 22, No. 1, 1993, 'Buddhism and the Four Principles' in Gillon and Lloyd, eds, *Principles of Health Care Ethics* (Chichester: John Wiley and Sons, 1994) and 'Buddhist Ethics', *Religious Humanism*, Vol. 28, No. 3, 1994. Some of the Thai material appeared in my address entitled 'Buddhist Attitudes towards Abortion: Thailand and Japan Contrasted' in the Public Lecture Series of the National Museum Volunteers in Bangkok, delivered on 8 June 1993.

[3] Edward Conze, *Buddhist Scriptures* (Harmondsworth, Middlesex: Penguin, 1959), 70. See also Alex Kennedy (Dharmachari Subhuti), *Buddhist Vision* (London: Rider, 1985), 78.

[4] Hema Goonatilake, 'Women and Family in Buddhism', in Sulak Sivaraksa, ed., *Buddhist Perception for Desirable Societies in the Future* (Bangkok: The Inter-Religious Commission for Development, 1992), 235.

[5] Étienne Lamotte, *Histoire du Bouddhisme Indien* (Louvain-La-Neuve: Université de Louvain, 1976), 38ff.

[6] Louis de La Vallée Poussin, tr., *l'Abhidharmakośa de Vasubandhu* (Bruxelles: l'Institut belge des hautes études chinoises, 1971), 6 vols., ii. 62–3.

[7] Taniguchi, 'A study of biomedical ethics from a Buddhist perspective' (Berkeley: Graduate Theological Union and the Institute of Buddhist Studies, M.A. Thesis, 1987), 19.

[8] R. H. B. Exell, 'Science, Technology and Buddhism', in Sulak Sivaraksa, *Buddhist Perception*, 220.

[9] K. L. Moore, *The Developing Human: Clinically Oriented Embryology* (Philadelphia: Saunders, 1973), 1.

[10] Frank E. Reynolds and Mani B. Reynolds, trs. and eds., *Three Worlds According to King Ruang: A Thai Buddhist Cosmology* (Berkeley: University of California, 1982), 5–45.

[11] Ibid., 118–9.

[12] Conze, *Scriptures*, 70–1.

[13] Exell, 'Science', 220. On pp. 220–1, he has an interesting discussion of several different aspects of the morality of abortion from the Buddhist view. His paper has no scholarly citations at all, and it is not clear that he is familiar with the usual commentators. In any case, it is an open ended, sensitive consideration of the issues.

[14] I agree with Exell ('Science', 220) on this point but not in the case when there is a conflict between the life of the mother and of the fetus.

[15] The analysis that follows here is loosely based on Taniguchi, 'Study', ch. 4–5.

[16] Kennedy, *Buddhist Vision*, 96–97.

[17] Reynolds, *Three Worlds*, 98.

[18] Conze, *Scriptures*, 72–73.

[19] Conze, *Scriptures*, 72–73.

[20] Phra Nyanavorotama, *Plan*, 78.

[21] Pinit Ratnakul, *Bioethics: an introduction to the ethics of medicine and life sciences* (Bangkok: Mahidol University, 1986), 276–7.

[22] Ibid., 97.

[23] Much of the material in this section derives from conversations with my colleagues at in the Department of Humanities of Mahidol University in 1989, 1992, and 1993. Suporn Koetsawang, M.D., Siriraj Hospital, Department of Obstetrics and Gynaecology, Faculty of Medicine, and Institute for Population and Social Research, Mahidol University, who has been very active in abortion reform in Thailand, was also very generous with his time (1993). Finally,

Acharn Passano, Abbot of Wat Pah Nanachat in Issarn Province graciously discussed the issue of abortion with me in May, 1993.

[24] Bencha Yoddumnern-Attig et al, *Changing Roles and Statuses of Women in Thailand: A Documentary Assessment* (Bangkok: Mahidol University Institute for Population and Social Research, 1992), 30.

[25] Phra Nyavorotama, *Plan*.

[26] Somdech Phra Mahā Samaṇa Chao Krom Phrayā Vajira-avarorasa, *The Entrance to the Vinaya (Vinayamukha)*, (Bangkok: Mahmakuarjavidyalaya, 1969, first published in Thai in 1913), vol. 1, 45.

[27] Siralee Sirilai, 'An Analytical Study of Buddhist Ethics, Ethical Rules, and Criteria for Judgement of Ethical Problems in Medicine at the Present Time' (Bangkok: Abstract presented to the National Research Council of Thailand, 1986), 4.

[28] Taniguchi's thesis takes this line. In my opinion, it does so in a rather mechanical way and tends towards the error of eternalism.

[29] Ratnakul, *Bioethics*, for example, stresses that the first precept must be central in any Buddhist bioethical theory.

[30] The relevant sections of the Penal Code are translated in The Population Council, *Abortion in Thailand: A Review of the Literature* (Bangkok: The Population Council, Regional Office for South and East Asia, 1981), Appendix II, 101ff and Institute of Population Studies, Chulalongkorn University, *Knowledge and Attitudes Concerning Abortion Practice in Urban and Rural Areas of Thailand: Paper Number 43* (Bangkok: Institute of Population Studies, Chulalongkorn University, 1982), 2–4.

[31] This includes intercourse against the will of the woman, intercourse with any woman under thirteen years of age, intercourse with any woman under eighteen in the sex trade, or intercourse with any woman over eighteen who is in the sex trade against her will (ibid).

[32] Ruth Roemer, 'Laws of the World' in R. Hall, ed., *Abortion in a Changing World*, 2 vols., (New York: Columbia University Press, 1970), 122.

[33] The Population Council, *Abortion in Thailand: A Review of the Literature* (Bangkok: The Population Council Regional Office for South and East Asia, May 1981) in addition to considerable

original interpretive work, has useful summaries of the work done up to the date of publication, including English summaries of Thai publications. Two later studies are also important: Institute of Population Studies, Chulalongkorn University, *Knowledge and Attitudes Concerning Abortion Practice in Urban and Rural Areas of Thailand: Paper Number 43* (Bangkok: Institute of Population Studies, Chulalongkorn University, July 1982) and Amorn Koetsawang, M.D. and Suporn Koetsawang M.D., *Nationwide Study on Health Hazard of Illegally Induced Abortion* (Bangkok: Mahidol University or United Nation Fund for Population Activities, 1987).

[34] Estimated for 1981 in Christopher Tietze and Stanley K. Henshaw, *Induced Abortion: A World Review 1986*, 6th ed (New York: Allan Guttmacher Institute, 1986), 50.

[35] Adapted from ibid., table 2, 28–42.

[36] Koetsawang, *Study*, 1–4.

[37] Ibid., 7.

[38] Ibid., 6.

[39] Ibid.

[40] Ibid., 2 & 4.

[41] Population Council, *Abortion*, 90.

[42] Ibid., 81.

[43] Reviewed in ibid., 88–99.

[44] Ibid., 91.

[45] Population Council, *Abortion*, 48–51.

[46] Suporn, *Study*, tables 10 & 11, rounded to the nearest whole per cent, 11.

[47] Population Council, *Abortion*, 4.

[48] Suporn Koetsawang, personal communication.

[49] William R. LaFleur, *Liquid life: Abortion and Buddhism in Japan* (Princeton, N.J.: Princeton University Press, 1992).

[50] Personal communications.

3

Abortion and Prostitution in Bangkok

Cleo Odzer

Introduction

During the three years between 1987 and 1990, the author re-searched prostitution in Patpong, a renowned red light district in Bangkok. Of the fifty-one female prostitutes met, the lives of eleven were followed closely while contact was maintained with as many of the others as possible.

Though pregnancy and abortion were not studied directly, the overall opinion that developed was that although the women of Patpong were well versed in contraception, a surprising number did become pregnant but did not seek abortions. I speculate here that childbearing was viewed as a positive, desirable thing and that the reason was grounded in their religious beliefs—their version of Buddhism. This is not necessarily the original or 'true' religion, but a version jumbled with folklore and superstition.

What I am proposing is that the women of Patpong see them-selves as born into a low status position—female. Even worse—a poverty stricken female with no option other than to support herself and her parents by prostitution. Founded on the belief in reincarna-tion, religious doctrine explains these women's lot in the present lifetime as due to a lack of sufficient 'merit' from past lives. Hav-ing children is a way to ensure a better fate in the next incarnation.

In this chapter I give an overview of Patpong, its sex tourist in-dustry, and my research on Patpong; a look at Thai women's subordinate position in Thai society; an account of prostitution in Thailand; a description of the rural, impoverished background from which the Patpong prostitutes come; a glimpse of religion on Patpong with examples of informants' desire and need for 'merit', and how they hoped to achieve it; and I offer observations of birth control, pregnancies and abortion on Patpong, including folk ways that hinder the acceptance of biological reproductive science. I end with arguments as to why pregnancy does not seem to be staunchly avoided nor abortions sought.

Patpong and the Initial Research on Patpong

Patpong, the sex tourist district in the downtown, commercial centre of Bangkok, houses bars, massage parlours (that is, whorehouses, where dozens to hundreds of women sit behind glass walls waiting to be picked), 'sex-and-a-shave' barber shops, and short-time hotels. Contrasting the tall modern buildings surrounding it, the Patpong streets hold dumpy, two-storey structures. The women working in Patpong bars are prostitutes. Bar work is only half the job. The real money comes from selling sex.

Polygamy and prostitution have long been a privilege of Thai men, but during the Vietnam War Thailand became proficient in serving up its women to foreigners. Aside from the Americans stationed in the US bases in Thailand, American military personnel throughout southeast Asia flocked to the country for 'rest and recreation'.

Although the Vietnam War may have boosted Patpong into the entertainment industry, Thailand's reputation as a sex paradise took off on its own at the war's end. Men flew in from all over the world as Thailand encouraged 'tourism' to fill its foreign income gap. Some countries arranged organized sex tours. Now, certain areas of Bangkok specialize in specific nationalities. There is a district for Arabs, and the Japanese have an entire street of 'members-only' clubs. The most famous strip catering to Westerners is Patpong.

Forty-six go-go bars were catalogued during the initial seven months of mapping the Patpong area. During this period, a group of prostitute women and men were chosen as informants and befriended. I later visited their hometowns in the rural countryside and met their families.

On several occasions I took informants away from Bangkok for a few days to observe their behaviour in different settings. These trips were made mostly to Pattaya, a famous prostitution district, or Samet Island, a resort frequented by prostitutes and their customer-boyfriends. When possible, I conducted in-depth interviews.[1]

The Status of Women in Thai Buddhist Beliefs and Thai Culture

Typically, women in Thailand are undervalued in respect to men, a situation endorsed by the Buddhist religion[2] to which ninety-five per cent of the population adhere. A basic notion of this religion is that one's life is a link in a chain of lives, each conditioned by acts committed in previous existences. Karma is the sum of actions and thoughts of those previous lives and determines one's present status. Being born a woman in this life reveals that one had an inadequate store of 'merit' from previous lives. Hence, women believe the injustices they suffer are deserved, and a study of young Thais showed that 'female youth have greater tendency than their male counterparts to believe in Buddhist doctrines'.[3]

Hantrakul quotes Lord Buddha as calling women 'the enemies of purification efforts' and points out that in 'everyday life there are customs which attribute defilement to the female sex'.[4] Female clothes, for example, are not to be washed with male, nor hung to dry where a male might pass below. It is also forbidden for a wife to step over her husband and she must sit or sleep only on his left side. In addition, woman are generally not allowed to touch sacred Buddha images and cannot possess certain objects that are charged with protective power because they may spoil the magical value.[5] In the British documentary about prostitution in Thailand, *Foreign Bodies*, the narrator noted that according to Thai Buddhist beliefs, if women lead 'a blameless life and are very lucky, they might just make it back as a man in the next life'.[6]

Hantrakul recounts, 'a parable about the Lord Buddha mentions a lady named Ambapali who, after serving her terms in hell for having cursed a [member of the monkhood] in her previous life, was born a woman of exceptional beauty in the Indian city of

Paisali. She soon was made a [prostitute], publicly shared by all noblemen and their sons who had long been fighting over her. Ambapali gave birth to a son named Kontanya who became a disciple of the Lord Buddha. After her son attained to *arahat* (a state of enlightenment), Ambapali entered the Buddhist Order and also became *arahat*'.[7]

The ancient female order, that was similar to the order of monks but with additional precepts to follow, lapsed into obscurity after three centuries. The white robed female *chis* found in modern Thailand are not comparable to monks.

Today, fewer routes are available to women than to men for 'making merit', and especially to prostitute women whose work already breaks social taboos. A major means of acquiring merit is to spend time as a monk, which is allowed only for males. One way available for women is through having children. Children make merit in their parents' names, even after the parents have died. Therefore, having numerous children means they will have numerous people contributing to their store of merit, which hopefully will lead to a better life the next time.

Hantrakul reports that although 'Women are ... denied the most efficient way of altering their balance of merit and demerit to improve their moral and religious position because they are denied admission to the Buddhist Order [a] mother may, however, redeem her demerit should her son don the saffron robe to enter monkhood'.[8]

Beyond the religious factor, Thailand considers women to be 'the hind legs of the elephant'. Khunying Yossundara, who wrote an 'Ann Landers'-type column in a Thai magazine for twenty years, was interviewed on the characteristics of Thai men:

> I hate to say it. Thai men are usually spoiled by that belief, that value, that they are the two front legs of an elephant and that they are more or less superior. They are brought up that way. Literature says it that way, newspaper reports always say it. That's how men convince themselves.[9]

When questioned about the most frequent problem she has been asked about in her column and if the problems have changed over time, Yossundara replied, 'the problems remain the same, mainly that the men are not just, not fair toward the rest of the family'.

From their privileged positions, Thai men believe it is their right to have sexual pleasure with various partners, while Thai women must retain themselves for the one man to whom they give their sexuality. The revised Code of 1805, commonly known as the Law of the Three Seals, said that a woman should not let more than one man gain access to her body. 'This code of conduct has passed generation after generation as a cultural legacy for Thai women. The Committee for Promoting Moral Values of Thai Ladies, appointed by the government in 1979, maintained similar advice in their teachings.'[10]

While the Law of the Three Seals barred women from sexual adventure, it endorsed polygamy and spelled out three categories of wives:

1) the major wife, whose parents consented to the marriage;
2) the minor wife, who was proposed to marry a married man;
3) the slave wife.

Slavery was abolished in 1905, and though monogamy was declared the only legal marriage in 1935, men today still register marriages to different women one after another. By the law's 'recognizing all children conceived by a man, irrespective of the mother, if he chooses to register them shows that the polygamous legacy is very much alive' .[11]

A study of a Bangkok slum found that 'almost all the women in the slum were economically and socially dependent on men and on the sexual services they provided for men'[12]—this being true whether they were major wives, minor wives or prostitutes. Abused wives who considered leaving their husbands found it impossible. Mostly, the women accepted their lot in the Buddhist belief that they were born 'as a woman because of bad karma or a lack of sufficient good merit'. The men controlled the money. If there was a surplus, they used it for fun, gambling and minor wives. The women accepted this as normal.

A pamphlet on the status of Thai women[13] notes the difference between Bangkok and the rural areas, which include eighty per cent of the population and where social and economic conditions have remained practically unchanged over centuries. It is only in Bangkok and other commercialized regions that educational and economic opportunities have allowed women any freedom from being tied to the home.

Although urban and rural practices vary greatly, by today's law at least 'as far as legal status is concerned, unmarried women are put, to all intents and purposes, on an equal footing with single men'.[14] However, upon marriage women lose many rights:

> The husband becomes the head of the family. He has the right to choose the place of residence and it is the duty of his wife to reside there with him ...[15]

> A married woman cannot set up a trade or business or a profession without her husband's consent.[16]

> ... adultery is a ground for divorce on the application of the husband only ... Thus, under the law as it now stands, the husband is still allowed scope to acquire concubines who are called 'mistresses' and there will neither be bigamy charges nor action for divorce based on adultery against him.[17]

> A married woman cannot apply for a passport to go abroad without the consent of her husband.[18]

A newspaper article entitled 'Thailand Lags Behind in Women's Rights' states: 'One example where the constitution itself discriminates against women is in the instance when the children of Thai women married to foreign men are denied automatic Thai citizenship'.[19] A woman is thus proclaimed a lesser citizen than a man.

The life of a Thai married woman, despite the 'respectability' it offers, in many ways upholds the idea that females are born the cursed sex. The average Thai woman is pregnant every twenty-two months while twenty-eight months is suggested as the minimal rest period needed between pregnancies.[20]

The majority of marriages in Thailand, especially among the poorer classes, are unregistered. The Thai word *mia* is an informal term for wife, and a *mia noi* is a 'minor wife' as compared to the 'major wife' who is awarded more legal rights over her husband's estate. Sometimes just sleeping with a woman is enough for a man to call her his *mia.*

Thai Women and Opportunity

From olden times, the men in Thailand had opportunities the women did not have. Boys studied in the temples but it was not deemed necessary for females to be educated.[21] During the Ayuthaya period (from the fourteenth century) and early Rattanakosin periods, women had no rights to be independent or self-possessed. They 'could be beaten and scolded or even sold to other people without their consent'.[22] As proof that the situation has not changed that much, a contemporary study in a Bangkok slum 'found that 50% of these women are battered by their husbands regularly'.[23]

During the reign of Rama IV (1851–68), Thailand was faced with the critical situation of being a buffer state between Britain and France. The king felt compelled to adopt a policy of modernization through Westernization. Education was provided for the male and female aristocracy. Modernization was continued by Rama V who established the first formal school in 1868, for civil servants. The first school for females outside the palace was built in 1874. However, women were not admitted into universities until 1927, the year of the Compulsory Education Act. In line with this, I found that many of the Patpong women had no more than one or two years of school. The Patpong male prostitutes, on the other hand, had completed higher levels.

Today, the more valued employment is dependent upon a certain degree of education, which is restricted to the elite classes.[24] Despite the fact that Thai women in recent history have been involved in economic affairs, they are still barred from the highest ranking positions.[25] Meesook reports that women comprise close to fifty per cent of the workforce. However, 'close to one third of employed women do not earn sufficient income for their basic needs'.[26] Many work in the informal manufacturing sector where they are given manual or low management positions. Their average wage is much lower than men's. About ninety per cent of factories in Thailand are 'small scale industries employing less than 50 workers ... They have to work around ten to twelve hours per day with no overtime payment and no welfare'.[27] In this manner, even if a woman has her own income, it, her work, and even herself can be viewed as 'inferior'.

Prostitution in Thailand

The minimum wage law in Thailand is often ineffective, with ninety-seven per cent of workers in enterprises having less than ten workers earning less than the minimum wage.[28] In enterprises with more than ten workers, the percentage under minimum wage is seventy-eight per cent. Where factories do adhere to the minimum wage law, women can be hired for a sixty day probation period at below minimum wage and then fired. With these conditions in mind for the migrant women who come to Bangkok, it is easy to understand that, in terms of necessity only, 'other jobs are so poorly remunerated that prostitution represents a rational choice in order to support their rural families'.[29]

Prostitution in Bangkok enables many rural families to survive an otherwise hopeless economic situation. Daughters head to Bangkok one after another as soon as they are old enough. Due to the rural-urban financial gap, within a few years the women are able to buy houses back home for both themselves and their families as well as to amass the capital necessary to begin their own small businesses.[30]

The prostitute's income is on average twenty-five times greater than that of a non-prostitute female.[31] To many people in the countryside, prostitution is seen as the means to upgrade one's social standing. It was reported that in Northern Thailand:

> Seeing the women who became prostitutes in other parts of the country wearing expensive clothes and accessories when they visit their homes, many young girls in the villages acquire a common dream to make prostitution as a 'career'. Some young schoolgirls shocked their teachers with their remarks ... one girl's compliment to her teacher who dressed beautifully was: 'You look as pretty as a whore today'.[32]

Not only does it upgrade one's social standing but also that of one's family:

They show up in beautiful clothes, glistening jewels and gold ornaments, bringing money for their parents to build a new house, to buy a motorbike, refrigerator, furniture and even land.[33]

Isan

Much of Thailand's hinterland is living in poverty and underprivileged conditions. Isan, the northeastern sector, is cited as barely able to maintain a subsistence level standard of living.[34] A flat limestone plateau with poor soil and insufficient irrigation, Isan's natural vegetation is limited to shrub, grasses, and weeds. Isan has the lowest annual per capita income in Thailand.[35] The average peasant family survives by primitive methods that include hunting and gathering in the forests and doing odd jobs for irregular wages.

Isan is the home of many Patpong prostitutes. Patpong and other tourist areas like to hire Isan women because of their dark skin, which Thais believe Western men prefer. Thai and Chinese brothels mostly hire women from the North, where skin colour is lighter. 'Northern Thai culture ... puts great emphasis on men. Women were born to please men in general. So, Northern Thai girls are quite prevalent and preferable to Thai men in this trade.'[36] Outside of tourist areas, Isan women do not make as good a living from prostitution.

Prostitution is heavily stigmatised in Thai society. While the right of sexuality is granted to men, it is forbidden to women outside of marriage. Women who have sex with many men are considered 'bad women', 'no good' and 'dirty'. But the stigma of Patpong prostitution involves other factors as well. Since many of the women come from Isan, they are discriminated against because of their place of origin as much as because of their profession. With Isan on the economic bottom of Thai stratification, they are considered uneducated and backward. They are also discriminated against along racial and ethnic lines because the northeast is geographically and culturally related to Laos. On Thai television, household servants are typically portrayed as Lao, ignorant and objects for laughter.

Plus, there is the issue of 'class'. People from Isan are considered 'low class'. Class markers include level of education, behaviour, speech, food preferences, dress, etiquette and notions of personal space. Some slights suffered by Isan people are due to their infringing on others' concepts of good manners. They speak too loudly and are not conditioned into using the niceties of 'please', 'thank you' and the Thai particles of speech placed at ends of sentences to denote courtesy. Speech patterns can immediately brand someone as a member of a particular group deemed undesirable.[37] Relationships with foreigners often offer Patpong women an escape from Thai society's discrimination by class and race.

Religion on Patpong

The majority of the people who work on Patpong are Buddhists. However, other beliefs systems are incorporated into their religious ideology. Every Patpong bar has a shrine, usually situated high on a wall near the ceiling. Mounting the stage, go-go dancers *wai* it (steeple their hands before their faces). Sometimes they then run their fingers through their hair to spread the holy influence over their heads. This is done so fast and automatically that few in the audience notice. The *wai* connotes respect and is made to people in greeting as well as performed toward religious objects. I was told that *wai*-ing the shrine brought good luck in attracting a customer. If a customer pays the bar to take a woman out, she may *wai* the shrine in thanks or in hope that the customer turns out to be a good one and generous. Penny Van Esterik, from the Women in Development Consortium in Thailand, noted that the *wai* has the additional meaning of asking forgiveness. She suggested it may also be a way to ask forgiveness from the ancestors for sins about to be committed.

The 'Patpong Musical',[38] presented by Empower, an organization for Patpong bar girls, and performed by a group of Patpong workers, provides some clues to their world view:

> The land of Isan is harsh and dry
> With no one to turn to
> Waiting for years, yet the rain and sky have not been kind
> Neither are the powers-that-be
> The land of Isan is cracking

and our hearts are breaking
Is this our sin or karma …
Is this our sin or karma …
That Isan should suffer so … Oh
Brothers and sisters have to turn their backs
Brothers and sisters have to turn their backs
Leaving their homes and the paddy fields heading for the city
To the city to sell their labour
With little education not even Primary Four
Hopeless for a good job
Hopeless for a good job
Fighting and kicking just to be a coolie
It hurts the more you think
Of father and mother, brothers and sisters left behind
Of what have become of them, what have become of them
But we can only keep on wondering …
It's so sad to think
To be beaten by hardship and poverty
Longing for the day we can return
To the land of Isan, the legend of suffering
So we can change this grieving land
Oh oh oh … sons and daughters of Isan
We must join hands and not be buried in sorrow
We must not let our elders wait
Forever for our homecoming …

Narrator: Who is it who says that people are of equal worth? If it's so, the son of the field should not have to struggle, to take a chance, to escape from hardship and head for the city; the daughter of the land, who has not even the minimum compulsory education, has to sell her labour from a young age, risking being raped and bullied, just for so little in return. Many lost children with little education here are just like her, disappointed with love and ruined in relationship. They are also mothers who sacrifice their bodies so their children would have a better chance in this society.

Yes, this is the life that has to struggle and hang on to the hopes and dreams, that things will be better … just like everyone else.

Typically, when I would pay a bar to take a woman out of bar work and take her away from Bangkok for a few days, she would try to get me to buy things for her, the same as she did with her male customers. One thing the women tried to persuade me to buy them was a bird. These birds are sold throughout Thailand so that people can set them free, which gives them 'merit'.

In one bar, before opening each night, the manager performed a ceremony. With a symbolic piece of wood, she blessed the bar, the tables and even the chrome stage poles that the dancers use during their shows. She said she was doing it to 'make merit' as well as for good luck. Some of the bar girls held out their hands to be tapped by the wood.

Charity is also good for karma. Before one Thai New Year, a group of Patpong bars collected donations, which were then distributed by the women to a children's home. During disasters, prostitutes are often noted in the newspapers for contributing a percentage of their earnings to help victims.

> Women from five New Petchaburi Road massage parlours have raised over 200,000 baht to help southern flood victims.

> Under the half-month programme, more than four hundred service girls will donate ten baht from each of their ninety-minute 'precious' sessions to the victims of the flood.[39]

Birth Control, Pregnancy, and Abortion on Patpong

The women of Patpong are fully aware of how pregnancy occurs and how to prevent it. The bars ensure that their employees have this information. It is in the bars' interests to keep their employees from becoming pregnant. Although women have told me that pregnancy would not restrict their sexual activities—some even declared that men liked to have sex with pregnant women—time is lost from work when the woman goes through the actual birth process. So for the management, at least, pregnancy would best be avoided.

There is, though, a continuum of how much Patpong bars care about the welfare of their employees. A hierarchy of bars exists on Patpong, with high quality (no hustling, more attractive women) at the top, sleazy, sex-on-the-spot bars lower down and 'ripoff' bars at the bottom. A 'ripoff' bar is one that overcharges customers and resorts to violence to collect. They exist through bribes to police and government officials.

Because Patpong is a tourist spot, catering mostly to Westerners, it is often in the spotlight. Competition between bars is fierce, so if one bar institutes a policy of declaring its women disease-free because they go to the doctor after every encounter with a customer, other bars are pressured into following suit. The high profile bars make arrangements with venereal disease clinics to have their women checked regularly. Information from a doctor is therefore available to all who seek it.

Another source of information for the women of Patpong is Empower, an organization for bar girls. Along with a bimonthly newsletter, Empower offers free English lessons as well as Thai lessons for women unable to read or write Thai. The organization makes sure the women know about condoms and AIDS risks, and they emphasize that the organization is available for other types of information if needed.

During the time of my study, AIDS was not talked about much or known about much and condoms were spoken of little. Some of the women knew about condoms and perhaps used them on occasion, especially if initiated by the customer, but it was not a regular practice. Now, the government has instituted wide ranging AIDS awareness campaigns and condom use is declared mandatory in many bars and brothels. Women have told me, though, as recently as the summer of 1994, that some customers still refuse to wear one and offer to pay more to have sex without one. In addition, the women often have a Thai boyfriend, and sometimes the way to differentiate a boyfriend from a customer is by not using a condom with the one you love.

Most of the women who practised birth control used Depo Provera. This was the easiest method, requiring only an injection of the drug every three months. Some women did not use any contraception, for a variety of reasons. The education level of Patpong prostitutes is generally low, with some totally illiterate and others having completed only rudimentary schooling. In addition, the remote rural environment from which they come is infused with superstitions and belief in magic. Hantrakul reports that some women put a Buddha image under the pillow during sex in order to prevent pregnancy.[40]

Not being able to afford, or have access to, modern health care, many upcountry folks depend on the *maw du* (fortune teller, psychic healer) for medicinal needs. One woman told me she did not practise birth control because a *maw du* had told her she was unable to become impregnated. She later did become pregnant, twice, during the time I knew her. Other Patpong people also told me that when they were young and ill they went to the *maw du* and only later to a hospital if the condition worsened. So, while they are aware of biological reproductive theories, conflicting magical beliefs lead them to act in ways illogical to science.

All the women who spoke of abortion knew where to get one or at least knew whom to ask for the information. Despite it being illegal in Thailand, an abortionist is relatively easy to find and especially in a district like Patpong that is based on the sex industry.

A surprising number of the Patpong prostitutes I met became pregnant during the time I knew them and none had an abortion. In Muangman and Nanta's study[41] of one thousand masseuses, they reported that nineteen per cent had had an abortion. In that study, seventy-five per cent came from the North, though, not from Isan. The reason for the discrepancy between Muangman and Nanta's study and what I saw on Patpong may be due to the difference in type between typical masseuses who work for Thai customers and the women of Patpong who work for foreigners. It may also be due to the difference between working in a massage parlour versus working in a Patpong bar.

In general, these two groups can be said to have different experiences. Tourist areas pay more than the average prostitute earns from local clientele. The women who work in Patpong bars look down on prostitutes from brothels and massage parlours. On the other hand, troublemakers and drug users who originally work in high profit tourist spots end up in brothels or massage parlours after being fired repeatedly from higher level establishments.

In an article in the *Bangkok Post*,[42] two reasons were given for why Thai women seek an abortion: 1) the lack of social support for unwed pregnancies, and 2) the inability to support a child. Because abortion is illegal in Thailand, 'faced with the prospect of both social ostracism and arrest, women may resort to abandoning a newborn baby or committing suicide. Women sometimes kill their babies because they cannot find a place for them and they are scraping to survive.' Due to Thailand's double standard of sexuality, 'there is a big issue of respectability to be overcome for women who are solo and they face a big decision when they are pregnant. If the woman is a state worker, for instance, she could be expelled from her job on the grounds of immorality'.[43]

Patpong women, though, are already accustomed to social ostracism in Bangkok society and Patpong has its own community, an esoteric community with its own values and prestige systems, which offers a shield against the greater society's condemnation of 'immorality'. When they return to their hometowns bearing gifts and money, the women's freehandedness protects them from outright criticism from family and neighbours.

In addition, the women of Patpong may not be in fear of the inability to support a child. Aside from their comparatively high earnings for sexual services, they have another source of finances. The women who service foreign tourists do not live from the sale of sex alone. A big part of what they sell is love, romance and an ongoing relationship. After a customer/boyfriend returns to his country, the relationship continues by mail and phone. Some Western men send money for years after returning home, ranging from a monthly stipend to keep the woman's head financially above water, to once or twice a year for a real, or invented, emergency. Westerners often plunge to emotional depths in their encounters with Thai women, and whole systems of letter writers/translators have developed to handle this lucrative business.[44]

The Western men involved in Thailand's sex industry can be roughly divided into two categories. Some tourists and long term residents display overt sexist and racist leanings as demigods reigning over, and being serviced by, inferiors. And resident men, especially, adopt Thai men's privilege of having 'major' and 'minor' involvements with various women. But for the younger and/or newly arrived or transient Western men who get caught in intense emotional relationships with Thai prostitutes, there is another factor at work—an Eliza Doolittle syndrome. Men become obsessed with 'saving' a woman, turning her into a lady, protecting her from the vagaries of life, trying to implant in her the values of their own culture, such as the work ethic and the quest for knowledge, helping her in her seemingly self-sacrificing commitment to help her family. Western storybooks and video games emphasize the hero saving a maiden in distress. Patpong and Thailand present Western men with the prime ingredients to play out this scenario. Beyond feelings of love, and long after romance has no longer been an issue, men feel compelled to prove, and live out, cultural ideals they may or may not have practised back home. Notions of Christian charity guarantee that men continue to send money and support for long periods of time. They play out the role of hero.

It was not unusual for me to find a woman who had five or six men in different countries sending her money. The Patpong women may, therefore, feel more secure that they can support a child. If they must stop working to give birth, they know they will still have a source of money coming in.

In Bangkok and Pattaya, Thai female/Western male marriages are commonplace. Many Patpong women told me it is easy to get a Western husband—some advise their friends to marry a Westerner and then divorce him. In an English language newspaper in Bangkok, one columnist noted that it is a bar girl's practice to marry a Westerner and get him to buy a bar, which he puts in her name. She then divorces him.[45] Whether or not the women want to marry a Westerner (and most do not) they believe the opportunity to do so exists. If nothing else, it can be viewed as a failsafe option.

Bars allow their employees time out in order to return home for a few days every now and then. The babies the women give birth to are usually left at home in the care of their mothers. Families are closeknit in Thailand and links are further solidified through remittances. Typically, the women and men of Patpong send home a portion of their monthly earnings. Family members grow completely dependent on the person living in the city. Once the standard of upcountry living is elevated, it needs to be maintained—electricity bills, gas for the motorcycle, keeping siblings in school and so on.

Conclusion

My conclusion is that the women of Patpong believe pregnancy is desirable for the end result it would have on their next incarnation. And, because financial security is not as tenuous as it would be for a similarly poor woman working elsewhere, they opt to have the child if pregnancy occurs.

An informant of mine named Chai was a male go-go dancer who earned his living through prostitution. Many of the male prostitutes were not gay—like the women, they had no other way to support themselves and their parents. Chai, though, was gay. During the year and a half I followed his life circumstances, I interviewed him at length about his desire to find a male partner with whom to have a love relationship. I was surprised, one day, when he told me that his plans for the future included marriage to a woman. Despite his sexual orientation towards men he planned to marry a woman when he had saved enough money or when he turned twenty-five, whichever came first. He said he had to do this in order to have children. To go through life without offspring was inconceivable for him. At another time, a heterosexual male prostitute working in a gay bar said he pitied the gays because having no children meant they had 'no future'. Children are also mandatory for one's old age for practical reasons. Without any form of social security, old folks rely on children to care for them. Thais have a concept of 'gratitude' toward their parents for giving them life. In many areas, children are expected to support their parents as soon as they are able and to continue to do so for their parents' entire lives.

Of the women who did practise contraception, many already had children, often more than one, and perhaps this influenced their decision to hold off having more, for the moment at least.

Only once did I hear someone say she was planning to have an abortion. She thought she was pregnant (she wasn't). Knowing the background of her situation I was convinced she would not go through with it if she could avoid it. She was living with a Western man, a twenty-one year old, good looking Belgian. I was sure it was his idea for her to have the abortion, but that she would want to have his baby, if only for the reason of reinforcing the relationship to him.

There is a stigma attached to a mixed Western-Thai child. These children are at a disadvantage with respect to Thai law and Thai societal acceptance. Though I saw examples of society's rejection of them in Bangkok, this didn't seem to hold true in Isan, to where the women of Patpong returned as superstars. So, a mixed

child, especially a lighter skinned child in a colour conscious country, may have increased status there.

The anticipated future of most of my informants involved living
with their parents. They envisioned a family life that included both
their parents and their own offspring. For the most part, the women
of Patpong saw themselves in a familial perspective tied to generations above and below, and to incarnations behind and before them.
As women in the here and now, they still considered themselves
the hind legs of the elephant.

Notes

[1]   Cleo Odzer, *Patpong Sisters: An American Woman's View of
the Bangkok Sex World* (New York: Blue Moon Books—Arcade
Publishing, 1994).
[2]   Penny Van Esterik, *Women of South East Asia* (Detroit: Cellar
Book Shop, 1982). Isaline Horner, *Women Under Primitive Buddhism* (Amsterdam: Philo Press, 1979 (orig. 1930)).
[3]   Wilawan Kanjanapan, *Youth Profile: Thailand* (Bangkok:
UNESCO, 1986), 79.
[4]   Sukanya Hantrakul, 'Prostitution in Thailand' Paper presented
to the Women in Asia Workshop (Melbourne: Monash University,
July 22–4, 1983), 1–2.
[5]   Khin Thitsa, *Providence and Prostitution—Image and Reality
for Women in Buddhist Thailand*, (London: Change, 1980), 17.
[6]   Tim Cooper and Alison Porteous, *Foreign Bodies*, a documentary film, (Britain: 1988).
[7]   Sukanya Hantrakul, 'Prostitution in Thailand' in *Development
and Displacement: Women in Southeast Asia*, Glen Chandler,
Norma Sullivan, and Jan Branson, eds (Australia: Monash papers
on SEA 18, date not available), 115.
[8]   Martin Schalbruch, 'The Hind Legs of the Elephant' *Bangkok
Post*, newspaper, (Bangkok: August 14, 1988), 25.
[9]   Hantrakul, see note 4 above, 3.
[10]   Ibid, 4.
[11]   Susanne Thorbek, *Voices From the City: Women of Bangkok*
(London: Zed Books Ltd., 1987), 79–84.

[12]   Sanya Dharmasakti and Wimolsiri Jamnarnwej, 'The Status of Women in Thailand: a Working Paper for the United Nations Seminar on The Status of Women in Family Law' (Tokyo: May 8–21, 1962).

[13]   Ibid, 25.

[14]   Ibid, 10.

[15]   Ibid, 11.

[16]   Ibid, 17.

[17]   Ibid, 17.

[18]   *The Nation* newspaper, 'Thailand Lags Behind in Women's Rights' (Bangkok: March 10, 1989), 25.

[19]   Malinee Wongpanich, 'Health Development of Women in Thailand' Aspects of Thai Women Today presented for The World Conference of the UN Decade for Women by the Thailand National Commission on Women's Affairs, (Copenhagen: 1980).

[20]   Vipa Chulachart, Introduction to *Aspects of Thai Women Today* presented for the World Conference of the UN Decade for Women by the Thailand National Commission on Women's Affairs (Copenhagen: 1980).

[21]   *Thai Development Newsletter, Fourth Quarter Vol 2, No. 3 (Issue 4) 2: 1984, 11.*

[22]   *Thai Development Newsletter, Second Quarter Vol 4, No. 1: 1986, 26.*

[23]   Barbara Ward, ed. *Women in the New Asia: The Changing Social Roles of Men and Women in South and South-East Asia* (Amsterdam: Unesco, 1963).

[24]   Fred Springer and Richard Gable 'Modernization and Sex Roles: The Status of Women in the Thai Bureaucracy' *Sex Roles* 7, July 1981, 723–37.

[25]   Kanitha Meesook, 'The Economic Role of Thai Women' Aspects of Thai Women Today presented for the World Conference of the UN Decade for Women by the Thailand National Commission of Women's Affairs, (Copenhagen: 1980).

[26]   *Thai Development Newsletter, Second Quarter Vol 4, No. 1: 1986, 5.*

[27]   Tongudai, Pawadee, 'Women Migrants in Bangkok: An Economic Analysis of Their Employment and Earnings' in *Women in*

the Urban and Industrial Workforce Southeast and East Asia. Gavin W. Jones, ed. (The Australian National University: 1984).

[28] Aihwa Ong, 'Industrialization and Prostitution in Southeast Asia' *Southeast Asia Chronicle*, 96 Jan. 1985, 5.

[29] Pasuk Phongpaichit, *From Peasant Girls to Bangkok Masseuses* (Geneva: International Labour Office, 1982).

[30] Debhanom Muangman and Somsak Nanta *Report on AKAP Study of 1,000 Thai Masseuses Concerning Family Planning, Pregnancy and Abortion, Venereal Disease Infections, and Narcotics Addiction* (UNFPA Project No. THA/76/PO5/E22–011) (Bangkok: Mahidol University, 1980).

[31] Mayuree Rattanawannatip, 'Prostitution Plays on Rural Ignorance' *The Nation*, newspaper, (Bangkok: February 18, 1988), 16.

[32] Supapohn Kanwerayotin, 'More New Faces in the World's Oldest Profession' *Bangkok Post*, newspaper, (Bangkok: October 28, 1988), 31.

[33] Charles Keyes, 'Isan', Regionalism in Northeastern Thailand Data Paper No. 65 (Cornell University: 1967).

[34] Sonny Inbaraj, 'Great Expectations That End in Misery' *The Nation*, newspaper, (Bangkok: June 21, 1988), 31.

[35] Muangman and Nanta, see note 31 above, 11.

[36] William Labov, *Sociolinguistic Patterns* (Philadelphia: University of Pennsylvania, 1984).

[37] EMPOWER, an organization for bar workers, *The Patpong Musical*, Bangkok: 1987.

[38] *Bangkok Post*, newspaper, 'Masseuses Raise Cash for the South' (Bangkok: December 16, 1988), 1.

[39] Hantrakul, see note 4 above, 5.

[40] Muangman and Nanta, see note 31 above, 57.

[41] *Bangkok Post*, newspaper 'The Abortion Issue—A Plight Condemned by Society' (Bangkok: June 3, 1994).

[42] Etain McDonnell, 'Abortion: Damned if You Don't' in the *Bangkok Post*, newspaper, (Bangkok: June 5, 1994).

[43] Eric Cohen, 'Lovelorn Farangs: The Correspondence Between Foreign Men and Thai Girls' *Anthropological Quarterly*, 59 (3): 1986, 114–127. 'Sensuality and Venality in Bangkok: The Dynamics of Cross Cultural Mapping of Prostitution' *Deviant Behavior* 8: 1987, 223–34. Dave Walker and Richard S. Ehrlich 'Hello My Big

Big Honey' *Love Letters to Bangkok Bar Girls and Their Reveal-ing Interviews*, (Bangkok: Dragon Dance Publications, 1992).
[44] Bernard Trink, 'The Trink Page' a weekly column in the *Bang-kok Post* newspaper.

4

Socio-Medical Aspects of Abortion in Thailand

Pinit Ratanakul

Introduction

It is an established fact in present-day Thailand that most hospitals, both government and privately owned, have, for years, been performing therapeutic abortions on women for health reasons, and, lately, on women infected with the AIDS virus. Apart from these abortions, there are also illegal abortions performed at private clinics, particularly on teenage mothers who were pregnant out of wedlock, to get rid of their unwanted babies. Though the exact number of such illegal abortions is not known to the public, it was estimated by the Ministry of Public Health that in 1993 there were as many as 80,000 cases.[1]

Under existing Thai law, illegal abortion is a crime punishable by imprisonment and/or fine for both the women and the medical personnel who perform it. The law makes all abortions criminal, except those done in case of rape or threats to the mother's health. Morally speaking, abortion is tantamount to killing, which is against the teachings of Buddhism. The high rate of illegal abortion is a matter of urgent concern for the Buddhists who form the majority of the Thai population. Most, if not all, women who have abortions—legal or illegal—are Buddhist. This reality is a pressing challenge to Buddhist concepts and principles, as it raises the question of the applicability of Buddhist perspectives and precepts to new realities faced by members of modern Thai society.

The further complication of contemporary Thai society is the increasing number of babies born from HIV positive mothers. The Ministry of Public Health estimates some 750,000 Thais are infected with the AIDS virus, with nearly 20,000 having developed full-blown AIDS. This poses complex ethical and practical problems for the mothers, and for the medical professionals who are also Buddhists. It is a dilemma for both parties. The seriousness of these problems is aggravated by the forecast of social analysts that in the process of modernization, which the country has been pursuing energetically, illegal abortion will increase rather than decrease in the future, particularly among teenagers who are caught up in the modernizing process without proper preparation.

The main purpose of this article is to discuss the current issues raised by abortion among Thai Buddhists, and their struggle to resolve them. The paper is based mostly on the data gathered from field research done from 1992 to 1994.[2] The research includes intensive interviews with Buddhist monks and lay people, consisting of obstetricians, nurses, students and women who have gone through abortion experiences. Some of these women were treated at government hospitals for the adverse effects of illegal abortion.

Saṃsāra, Karma and Nirvana

Theravāda Buddhism, also known under the name of Hīnayāna, has been a dominant cultural force in Thailand since the establishment of the first Thai Kingdom in the thirteenth century. Though the present constitution does not make it compulsory for every Thai to follow the Buddhist beliefs and practices, it requires the king to be a Buddhist. For the majority of the Thai population, one cannot be a true Thai without being a Buddhist. Since early times, the monarchy, the *sangha* (the order of Buddhist monks), and the nation have been considered the basic triad of social solidarity and identity in Thailand. They have been so intermingled in the course of history and are so deeply meaningful to the hearts of the people as to form the core of what may be called the civic Thai culture.[3]

The basic teachings of Theravāda Buddhism, which provide the basis of Thai cultural orientation, are the concepts of *saṃsāra*, karma and nirvana. *Saṃsāra* refers to the perpetual cycle of re-births. It comprises three realms (*loka*): the realm of desire (*kāmaloka*), the realm of forms (*rūpaloka*) and the formless realm (*arūpaloka*). The realm of desire consists of the higher spheres of gods, the middle spheres of sentient beings, humans (*manussa*) and animals (*tiracchāna*), and the lower spheres of ghosts (*peta*), spirits (*bhūta*) and hell-beings (*niraya*). The celestial realm of forms and the formless realm are the abodes of the refined and subtle beings (*deva*) at very high levels. Despite differences in life-span, dwellers in all realms are subject to death and rebirth, and revolve in *saṃsāric* existence according to their karma. Karma means inten-tional, mental, verbal, or physical action and its result (*vipāka*). The sequence of actions and their effects, known as the retributive law of karma, acts as the moral law regulating the movement of be-ings between rebirths. The rebirth of beings is the natural result of their own deeds, good or bad, and not the 'reward' or 'punishment' imposed by a supernatural, omniscient ruling power. All beings reap what they have sown in the past. When a being dies, the kar-mic result acting as the individual life-force passes to other forms of existence, in a series of higher or lower rebirths. This life-force will become completely inactive only with the cessation of all forms of craving (*taṇhā*), the inherent force of karmic action. Such cessation is referred to as nirvana, or absolute emancipation.

The Preciousness of Human Rebirth

Saṃsāric existence is always in a state of flux, with constant mi-gration of beings from one realm to the other regulated by the law of karma. Human rebirth is considered incomparably precious be-cause the human sphere in the realm of desire is the only place where there is enough suffering to motivate humans to seek ways to be liberated from misery and enough freedom to act on that aspi-ration. In the higher realms, the gods are too absorbed in the bliss-ful state to find the way out of *saṃsāric* existence, while animals, ghosts, spirits and hell-beings are in irremediable misery and have little freedom to do either good or evil. These suffering beings will gain a precious human rebirth only when the result of the bad karma that led them to their lower rebirths is exhausted. When this happens, the results of their previous good actions, performed when they were human, will lead them to better rebirths, and, sooner or later, to the human sphere again.

Karma, Abortion, and Merit-Making

With such a cultural orientation, Thai Buddhist monks and lay people alike believe in the uniqueness and preciousness of human life irrespective of its stages of development. For them, human life begins at the very moment of fertilization with the infusion of the *gandhabba*, the individual karmic life-force, into the womb.[4] Even though human life manifests itself in a minute form, called *kalala* in Buddhist terminology, it is still precious, and its destruction is a transgression of the Buddhist precept against killing. The whole question of the personhood of the fetus at a particular stage of development does not enter into consideration by Thai Buddhists. For them the stages when personhood is or is not present cannot be distinguished, since the physical and the mental are interdependent. Life is life at any given moment, no matter whether it is in the simple form of the fertilized egg (zygote) or in the complexity of the fetus. To destroy any form of human life will yield bad karmic results: brevity of life, ill-health and constant grief and fear in this life and after, as well as rebirth in states of suffering as animals, ghosts or hell-beings.

The gravity of these results depends on many factors, such as the intensity of the doer's intention and effort, as well as the size and quality of the being that was killed. The killing of a virtuous man or a large animal, for example, is regarded by Thai Buddhists as more evil than the killing of a vicious man or a small animal, because a stronger intention to kill (ill will) and a sustained effort are needed to kill them, and the loss involved is considerably greater. In the case of induced abortion, the stages of the development of the fetus aborted influence the degree of the karmic consequences for those who perpetrate abortion. These different stages also imply different degrees of the potential of the fetus which itself influences the weight of the karmic consequences.

It is such a line of thinking mentioned above, I believe, that influences the timing of abortion for Thai women who, when it is unavoidable, prefer to have abortion at the early stages of pregnancy to minimize the bad karmic results they have to suffer. Before having an abortion, these women usually suffer from anxiety over their unwanted pregnancies and from the fear of pain and death. After the abortion experience, they are filled with remorse and sorrow for the aborted fetuses and try to relieve their psychological pain, as well as to improve the condition of the dead fetuses in their next rebirths, by performing meritorious deeds. This attempt to reverse the full karmic effects is a common practice among Thai Buddhists, who are more concerned with the accumulation of merit than absolute emancipation. In the practice of Buddhism, they tend to confine themselves to merit-making to ensure good rebirth in *saṃsāric* existence. For them, merit-making is an important way to produce fresh good karma and to mitigate the due effects of the previous bad karma.

Thai Buddhism emphasizes both teachings and rituals to help its adherents on the path to spiritual progress. Thai people like to use the teachings to guide them toward conduct most favourable to the production of good karma and away from conduct that generates bad karma. At the same time, they depend on rituals to strengthen their morale and ability to deal with the strains and stresses of modern life. There are prescribed rituals for the important events of life such as birth, death, marriage, etc. There is, however, no specific memorial rite for the aborted fetus, and women who have an induced abortion usually follow the way Thai Buddhists ordinarily make merit for a dead person.[5] These activities include alms-giving to the community of monks, installing statues of the Buddha in temples, offering money for the ordination of monks or novices and getting themselves ordained as temporary monks or nuns. All these activities are regarded as 'auspicious actions' (*kusala karma*) that yield benefit to the doer. After the performance of these meritorious acts, it is customary for Thai Buddhists to transfer the merit acquired to the dead person by pouring water as a libation while uttering words such as: 'This merit is dedicated to (name of the deceased). May he (she) rejoice in it.' The merit is transferred in the sense that the one to whom it is dedicated benefits from the good deeds, such as alms-giving, performed by the person concerned. Dedication is a way of sharing, spreading the benefit of good deeds to the other. By rejoicing in the merit so transferred, the other can generate good karma.[6]

This act of transfer does not take away any part of the merit from the perpetrator. It is like the lighting of candles from one candle. The light of the original is not diminished even though its light is transferred to the others. On the contrary, the sharing even increases merit for the one who does it because the action itself is meritorious.

Genetic Abnormalities, AIDS and Abortion

Economic hardship, unreadiness for childbearing and contraceptive failure are the main causes of abortion among Thai women. In all these cases it is women who make the decision to have an abortion—some alone and some, in the case of married women, in consultation with their husbands and/or close relatives. The use of modern diagnostic techniques, such as amniocentesis to detect chromosomal abnormalities in the fetus, has placed Thai physicians in a more important position in the morality of abortion. When chromosome analysis indicates mild or severe abnormalities in the fetus, they will, for the patient's best interests, have to decide whether to inform or not to inform the pregnant woman about the defective condition of the fetus. The information that she is carrying even a mildly handicapped fetus may make the would-be mother suffer from fear and anxiety. Such information may also be used by her to seek an illegal abortion. Faced with this ethical dilemma, some Thai physicians have decided to inform the patient about the chromosome analysis to help her to prepare herself psychologically to accept and care for a handicapped child. This is in line with the Buddhist teaching that advocates truth-telling as our social and moral duty, and makes no exception for lying in any circumstance. In the Buddhist view, lying is an abuse of trust, as well as an act of cowardice and selfishness. The practice of deception, of withholding the truth supposedly to benefit others, is too often only self-serving. It relieves us from facing up to emotionally trying situations, relationships and responsibilities for others.[7]

In the case of a defective fetus, the usual response from Thai women is the decision to continue pregnancies to full term because of the fear of the karmic effects of abortion.[8] After delivery, however, they act differently. Due to economic hardship and their unwillingness to rear handicapped babies some abandon them at the hospitals with the hope that these handicapped babies will be taken care of by government agencies. Some decide to bring these babies up themselves, believing that this act of nurture, as well as the different meritorious deeds they will perform, will contribute to the improvement of their own karma and that they will not have to repeat such an experience. They also anticipate that these meritorious deeds will benefit their offspring as well, i.e. the effects of the previous bad karma of the handicapped will be mitigated by the meritorious deeds of the parents, while the circumstances of love and care in which the handicapped is brought up will also prevent the full fruition of that bad karma. These actions, together with great effort on the part of the handicapped person, will probably enable him or her to have a better prospect. In the case of a severely defective fetus, such as one afflicted by Down's Syndrome, Thai women will rarely abort it, for they believe that, for the benefit of the fetus, it is better to let its bad karmic effect exhaust itself in the present even if a still-born child is the result. But should the life of the mother be threatened by a continued pregnancy they will face the difficult decision about the priority choice. Though Thai law clearly opts for a mother in such a case, Thai women as Buddhists still face the dilemma.

The number of defective babies abandoned in the hospitals is estimated as 70,000 for the years 1992-1994.[9] Among them are found those born of HIV positive mothers. The increased number of women inflicted with the HIV virus puts both these women and their physicians in a great dilemma, for they have to decide whether the afflicted fetuses should be aborted. Some physicians advised their patients to abort the fetuses out of compassion i.e. to alleviate the suffering of these women and their families, though it is against the law. Some even performed abortions with the consent of their patients. By so doing, the physicians believed that they were performing a noble task for the women and society as well as for the unborn babies who, if allowed to be born, were more likely to die an agonizing death.[10] Despite their noble intention, the ethical question still cannot be avoided regarding the right of anyone to play the role of an arbiter of life and death. The problem is serious for physicians whose vocation is to save rather than destroy life, even if the advice is given out of compassion.

Reproductive Rights and the Principle of Interdependence

While abortion is a pressing problem in Thailand and a challenge to Buddhist morality, the realities of modern life—with the small family as the ideal and the need for sensitivity to demographic pressures—are among the factors which pose many questions to Thai Buddhists. In this age of globalization, there is a constant interchange of ideas from different parts of the world.

One of the predominant ideas which Thai society readily promotes, as it progresses towards democracy, is the concept of human rights. In the West, the abortion debate usually involves this concept. In this debate, the right of choice in reproduction is claimed to be one of the basic rights of women with regard to their own lives and bodies.[11] Thai women in a modern society see the importance of family planning and the need to provide their children with the best conditions whether in health, education or environment. Limiting the number of children is looked upon as a responsible approach to marriage and family life, which is also in conformity with Buddhist teachings. As Thai women widely practise birth control, they are also coming under the influence of feminism from the West. Some are beginning to discuss the abortion issue in the language of rights and want to demand the revision of the restrictive abortion law to give room for the right of women to decide whether a pregnancy should be terminated, as they are the party directly affected. [12]

For the Buddhist majority, such a demand is not in conformity with the tenet of Buddhism centring on the mutuality and interdependence of human beings. One does not exist in isolation, but in social relations and inter-relationship—for example, as a member of a family, a society or a religious group.[13] Adhering to this teaching, Thai Buddhists see human actions in the totality of their circumstances, and human responsibility in the inter-webbing of relationships of self to self, others and society. They thus do not view a woman and a fetus as an isolated moral unit and abortion as an isolated act. Everything and everyone exists only in mutuality—even the fetus. Abortion thus involves many people and not just the pregnant woman alone. Therefore one cannot dwell exclusively on the abortion right of the woman. This right cannot be claimed in isolation from the rights of the fetus, the father, and society. This makes the decision for abortion a more complex issue, involving the individual emotions of concerned persons and its impact on society. Undoubtedly, it is the pregnant woman herself who has to make the final decision on what is best for her, but with consideration for the feelings, duties and responsibilities of others, including the physician who may be asked to violate his code of conduct and even break the law.

For the majority of Thai Buddhists, the pressures of modern life place difficulties in the way of their desire to observe the primary precept against killing. Even in the face of the increase in illegal abortion, however, they oppose the call for a liberal law which would, in effect, completely decriminalize all abortions. Such liberalization, they believe, can only lead to an increase in abortions overall. It is only when the causes of unwanted pregnancy are directly addressed that the number of abortions will be diminished. What is needed is more systematic sex and moral education of the young, and family planning assistance on a larger and more effective scale. Counselling and adoption facilities should also be expanded. Since poverty is one of the major motives in the decision to abort, efforts must be increased to diminish its influence through the expansion of educational opportunities for women and economic support and opportunities for families. Without these measures, there will be little chance to stem the tide of illegal abortions in Thailand.

Conclusions

For Thai Buddhists, abortion is a complex issue that cannot be dealt with in isolation from other aspects of life, such as family and societal well-being, economic pressures, educational practices, medical ethics and religious teachings and the wants and emotions of individual women and men. Too often, the attempt is made to treat abortion as only a matter concerning women, or to deal with the abortion issue in isolation from issues of the status, education, employment and economic well-being of women and men, and from issues of societal resources for the health care and prosperity of children and families. The Thai view of abortion, based on the Buddhist notions of mutuality and interdependence, is a more holistic approach to the questions surrounding the abortion issue.

Pregnancies resulting from rape and incest, pregnancies involving severely defective and HIV afflicted fetuses, and those of women living in situations of dire poverty, are the hard facts of life that Thai Buddhists have to grapple with as they try to be faithful to Buddhist teachings in their daily lives. The majority follow the 'middle way' in lay Buddhist ethics—a way that avoids the two extremes of laxity and rigidity in the observance of the precepts. This ethics recognizes that 'to err is human' and that the average lay person is not a saint, nor aspires to perfect righteousness. He or she is a being of mixed motivations, a combination of strengths and weaknesses, such that the transgression of the precepts is always possible.

While Buddhism does not make any exceptions to its precepts, it deals realistically with human wrong. In its awareness of the complexity of the human condition it takes into consideration mitigating factors. The motivation behind the deed is of primary significance: there are hard choices to be made between greater and lesser harms, greater and lesser good, and the nature of the suffering of all involved. Buddhism, therefore, does not want those who violate the precepts to brood over past deeds or to develop a sense of guilt. Rather, it encourages them to look forward to future prospects. Regretting a past bad action and resolving not to do it again, however, can lessen the bad karmic result of that deed, as it is conductive to spiritual development.

In this understanding of lay Buddhist ethics, all precepts are believed to be ideals to live up to and not 'commandments' to be obeyed. It is up to each individual to follow them in the life situation in which he or she finds himself. In the case of abortion, whatever decision has to be made must be done assuming full personal responsibility and in consciousness of the consequences of that decision for oneself, other concerned people, and society at large. When an abortion seems unavoidable to save oneself and others from greater harms, the course to be adopted is to minimize as much as possible the karmic effect of this inauspicious action (*akusala karma*) which violates the precept against killing. The emphasis on individual human effort to overcome past bad karma encourages ethical development by relieving the individual from the paralysis of guilt which often follows wrong doing, and inhibits future moral development. This is an optimistic perspective, and realistic in terms of moral psychology. Combined with belief in rebirth, it holds out the possibility of eventual human advancement to freedom from all ills and failings and from *saṃsāric* existence itself.

This 'middle way' ethics perhaps influences the Thai approach to abortion. In present-day Thailand there are restrictions on abortion which only legally permit it in cases of rape or threats to a mother's health, but abortions are also practised in hospitals in cases of HIV positive fetuses. There is an insistence on the Buddhist teaching that makes every stage of human life precious, yet Thai Buddhists do not condemn those women whose life situations make the decision to abort seem unavoidable. There is a concern for the dilemmas women face with unwanted pregnancies, the result of poverty, immaturity, contraceptive failure or severely defective fetuses and maternal health threats, yet there is a refusal to isolate abortion simply as a matter of a woman's reproductive choice. This approach is the Thai 'middle way' in the abortion issues between the extreme positions found in different Western views.

As evident in our field work, the majority of ordinary lay Thai Buddhists are not conservatives who rigidly prohibit all abortions even in case of rape or threats to a mother's health. Neither do they adopt the other extreme view, which advocates abortion as a personal choice of a woman alone, a right to control her own reproduction in isolation from the relations and responsibilities to concerned others, society and religious teachings. Even the members of this group who say they would personally not choose to abort, believing in the sanctity of life, do not demand a legal prohibition on abortion. Almost all would permit abortions on moral grounds in cases of rape, incest, or threats to a mother's health. Most want to leave the decision to abort in case of severely defective fetuses in the hands of women and their families who are most directly affected by the decision. Many are concerned about pregnancies involving teenagers and women afflicted with the HIV virus, and are aware that future child abuse is a factor in unwanted pregnancy among those suffering poverty and deprivation.

One might say that these ordinary Buddhists recognize the complexity of the abortion issue which mirrors the complexity of life circumstances, and thus finds that in some situations where women, children, families and society are all involved, abortion cannot be perceived as an either/or option. They also find that abortion as such is never a positive good but it can sometimes be the lesser of evils in the grey light of human reality.

This inclination to make a stand on the middle ground—avoiding the extremes of laxity or rigidity—based on a common awareness of the complexity and frailty of the human conditions may be more difficult for Westerners to justify in light of the tendency toward the polar positions which receive the most publicity. But such a 'middle way' approach is both more realistic and compassionate than the extreme stances, and more in keeping with Buddhist teachings. It speaks not in the language of rights—the right to reproductive choice of a woman versus the right to life of the fetus, which sets them in an adversarial position. It speaks more in the language of benefit and harm, with the intent of relieving as much human suffering in all its states, stages and situations as circumstances allow. It neither glosses over the potential for harm in possible tragic circumstances involving human sexuality, nor does it ignore the wonder and value of human reproductive creativity. It does not deny the highest human aspiration for the good which is contained in the ideal of the sanctity of life.

Abortion is a serious transgression of our deepest moral conviction of the sanctity of life. This human failure is a part of life in *saṃsāric* existence fraught with the potentiality and actuality of human suffering. In this life-cycle with the frailty of the human condition, compassion towards those who suffer and the relief of human suffering is the primary moral virtue. Abortion is a hard fact of life in our contemporary society, and our concern with it is an act of compassion. Genuine compassion, however, should not so much be concerned with the abortion issue as only a matter of 'pro' and 'con', but rather with the causes of abortion, the physical, psychological, economic and educational life-circumstances which make many pregnancies unwanted, and the birth of a child a matter of fear and regret, rather than wonder and joy. We have already devoted too much time, energy and resources to the debate between the pro-life and pro-choice positions without coming to a satisfactory conclusion. Our thoughts, time and effort should rather be expended on finding the means to reduce the need for abortion. This

intention and action, perhaps, is a way of following our moral in-
tuition regarding the sanctity of life more fully and responsibly.

Notes

[1]   Ministry of Public Health, *Public Health Statistics* (Bangkok:
Thirawong Press, 1993), 211.

[2]   The field research was conducted from February to December
1994 in metropolitan Bangkok with the assistance of Miss Mali
Lerdmaleewong and Mrs Chanutra Ittishumwinit of Mahidol University. The research involves interviews with 10 monk-scholars,
30 obstetricians, and 40 women who were treated at government
hospitals for adverse effects from illegal abortion, and questionnaire distributed to 200 nurses, 100 medical students and 500 high
school teachers, of which 650 were returned.

[3]   See also Frank E. Reynolds, 'Civic Religion and National Community in Thailand,' *Journal of Asian Studies* Vol. xxxvi No. 2,
1977: 267-82.

[4]   Here, *gandhabba* refers to a suitable individual life-force ready
to manifest itself in that particular womb. This term is used only
with this particular meaning, and must not be mistaken for a permanent soul.

[5]   In Japanese Buddhism, there is a special memorial rite for the
aborted fetus. See Bardwell Smith, 'Buddhism and Abortion in
Contemporary Japan: Mizuko Kuyo and the Confrontation with
Death', in *Buddhism, Sexuality and Gender*, ed. Jose Ignacio Cabezon. (N.Y.: State University of New York, Press, 1992), 65-90.

[6]   From the Buddhist perspective, the mental act of rejoicing produces merit. A person with nothing to give can act auspiciously by
simply rejoicing in another person's giving. In Thailand, this is expressed by uttering the ritualized word *sādhu*, meaning 'It is
good!', when someone is making merit, for example by giving
alms to monks.

[7]   See Pinit Ratanakul, 'Bioethics in Thailand: The Struggle for
Buddhist Solutions,' *The Journal of Medicine and Philosophy* No.
13, 1988: 301-312.

[8]   From the author's interviews with 40 women who had abortion
experience.

[9]   This statistic was given by an official of the Department of Public Welfare which is in charge of government nursing homes for handicapped babies. The statistic has not yet been published.

[10]   *Bangkok Post*, Thursday, January 9, 1992, p. 4.

[11]   See Michael Tooley, *Abortion and Infanticide* (Oxford: Clarendon Press, 1985).

[12]   These so-called 'Thai feminists' have not put any pressure on the government for the liberalization of abortion law because of the lack of public support.

[13]   See Pinit Ratanakul, 'Community and Compassion: A Theravada Buddhist Look at Principlism,' in *A Matter of Principles: Ferment in U.S. Bioethics* ed. by Edwine R. Du-Bose et al. (Pennsylvania: Trinity Press International, 1994), 21-129.

5

Abortion in Japan: Towards a 'Middle Way' for the West?[1]

William R. LaFleur

Dogma or Pragmatism?

Nakatani Kinko is an expert on criminal law. In 1970, she writes, she attended a legal-issues conference in West Germany. It became the catalyst for her deepened interest in abortion law. This was because she was shocked to hear Western scholars debating at great length about the exact day of the soul's entry into the fetus according to Christian doctrine—and how pinpointing that event seemed somehow crucial to the whole matter. She writes, 'For me as a Japanese involved in the study of criminal law the debate conducted within this framework of thought seemed beyond belief. I fully realized at that point that when it comes to abortion the history and way of thinking of us Japanese and the people of the West is very, very different'.[2]

There are also persons in the West, it is worth noting, to whom the focus of that particular conference would have seemed just about as absurd as it did to Nakatani. Yet even if we ourselves might have trouble entering into such a debate with seriousness, we are able to recognize the mentality that assumed the abortion question might be somehow solved by answering a technical question and then fashioning law to fit that answer.

In this basic approach there is, as Nakatani intuited, something very Western. Even if we cannot share the theology and metaphysics of the debate she observed in Germany, we continue to conduct our debates as if there were simple and 'right' answers to issues as complex as this. We also, like the conferees, tend to believe that with such answers we will be able to fashion good law. We will then, we tend to think, be able to decide whether abortion is 'right' or 'wrong'.

Or, when the struggle becomes pitched, we define our positions in stark terms. This means avoiding ambiguity and disapproving of ambivalence in those we count as our allies. Thus the battle over abortion turns into one between the 'rights of a woman over her own body' and the 'right of a fetus to live'. Large and complicated positions are reduced to single points of focus, points that make legalized abortion 'right' to one side and 'wrong' to another.

Neither side can or will recognize even a modicum of truth in the other's position. If this, in fact, tends to be a characteristic of the Western—or at least American—way of approaching this issue, it does contrast quite sharply with one found in Japan. With her characteristic ability to get to the core of such matters, Takie Sugiyama Lebra writes:

> The Japanese are used to sayings like: 'Even a thief may be 30 percent right' and 'To hold a grudge against others is not good, but to do something that arouses a grudge in others is just as bad'. The Japanese tend to hold everyone involved in a conflict responsible for it. The Anglo-American compulsion for a court trial that determines one person guilty and the other innocent is in remarkable contrast to the Japanese ideal that mutual apology and compromise be attained between the parties before the conflict attracts public attention.[3]

It is not by accident that the complex body of differences that separate one side from the other in the American debate over abortion have settled into rival claims over interpretation of the law. Appeal to the Constitution and its interpretation become the place where everything lies. The focus of one side is on the right to life while that of the other is the right to choice and privacy. Both sides hope—or fear—that the entire 'abortion war' will be won or lost by past or future legislation. But, aware only of how pitched their battle must be, both sides seem oblivious to the commonality in their rhetoric.

To say this is not to minimize the awesome power of laws to impact on our lives, even on the most private aspects of them. The point to be noticed, simply, is that we may have built ourselves into a very tight box. We have become a people who cannot think beyond legal solutions to our societal problems or apart from public actions and reactions designed to effect law. Our range of cultural, societal options thereby becomes impoverished. Flexibility is lost.

This loss of flexibility also means we have moved farther away from the American tradition of pragmatism—pragmatism that is increasingly difficult to find when the rhetoric is as heated and heavily ideological as it has become. The point here is that although the West's tradition includes a heavy dependence on legal frameworks for addressing problems there is, at least in the American context, also a tradition of pragmatism.[4] And pragmatism, especially as a social philosophy, will make us wary of ideologies both of the left and of the right. The pragmatist is concerned about what may be happening to community and social solidarity when opposing participants in public debate are insisting on total victory. That is, although he or she is intensely interested in finding solutions to specific social problems, if social solidarity has been sacrificed, it has not been a real solution at all.

In American life the protracted struggle over abortion has rapidly become a face-off between two heavily ideologized agendas in pursuit of clear-cut victory. There is little sense that an entire nation's need for solidarity should also be factored in.

The gain to us in looking hard at how the Japanese have dealt with this problem could come, perhaps, in the form of a stimulus to us to reappreciate the importance of pragmatism. In some sense it is the Buddhist position that articulates a kind of societal pragmatism.[5] It forefronts the need for a solution but, importantly, one that does not tear the social fabric apart. Community matters.[6]

Japanese Perspectives

In 1975 I was in Japan for studies that had nothing directly to do with abortion. But since the Roe v. Wade decision was already beginning to kick up a storm back home in the United States and since during that year I was already spending a lot of time talking with Japanese Buddhist monks and scholars, I sometimes casually dropped the question, 'What, by the way, do you Buddhists think

of abortion? Have the Buddhist denominations in Japan taken up
this problem and made any kind of pronouncement on it?'

My second question was, I will admit, a bit disingenuous, since
I already knew it is not the practice of Buddhist organizations, at
least in Japan, to state public 'positions' on social issues. In response to my first question, a certain pattern emerged in the answers:

> Oh, of course, Buddhism teaches that we are not to take the
> lives of others! The scriptures are very clear about that—as well
> as that babies in wombs are life. But, yes, if it is the question of
> abortion in today's society we are really in a dilemma. It's
> really a problem, isn't it? We cannot say it is absolutely wrong.
> Women who have to get abortions go through a tremendous
> amount of pain and stress. We have to show compassion for
> them in that, don't we? Still, we also need to feel sorry for the
> aborted infants, too.

This struck me as a waffling kind of answer, an uneasy forcing
together of the orthodox proscription against the taking of life and
sympathy for the plight of women who are pregnant although they
do not wish to be. Japan's abortion rate had been soaring. I noted
discussions of that fact in the major Japanese papers. Then, on rec-
reational walks through the cemeteries on the hills around Kyoto, I
began to observe what I learned—through questions about the matter—were the 'parents' of aborted fetuses going to the cemeteries
for simple rituals. Wondering about that, I inquired into what it
meant. I talked to people, took notes, found things in scattered
books, and bit by bit tried to work out an approach to this study.

I found that in Japan, although some aspects of the religion and
abortion problem are similar to what they are in the West, in other
important ways they are also very different. It is those differences,
I believe, that help explain why in today's Japan, in spite of problems, the abortion issue does not polarize the society into two opposing camps as it does in ours. Over time one of my questions had
become, 'How have the Japanese managed to deal with abortion so
that it has now become a matter over which the society does not
tear itself apart?' The answer fascinates me. It is my core concern
here.

This chapter examines the whole abortion and religion problem from an eccentric angle. It is about abortion in a culture that, while strikingly modern, is also decidedly not Western. Japan is a civilization that is in many ways inextricably intertwined with our own—in business, the arts, scientific exchanges, and world philanthropy—but its intellectual and religious traditions have made it significantly different from the West.

Books on basic Buddhist teaching and guides to meditation are now fairly accessible. Yet we in the West know next to nothing about what might go into decisions about ethical questions in communities informed by Buddhism. This chapter deals with only one example, and there are Buddhists who may object very much to the way in which the Japanese seem to have handled the question of abortion. The Japanese, to be sure, do not represent all Buddhists. Yet they stand within that tradition, and how they happen to think about sexuality, reproductivity, the family and abortion are therefore things we do well to know.

Clearly I could not write about this topic without reference to the nature of the debates that are raging within our own society. I make no apologies for doing that, since I have on a number of occasions found it necessary to make explicit and implicit comparisons. Moreover, if some of the ideas presented here could be used as a heuristic tool for looking at—and trying to solve—our own abortion dilemma, I would be doubly pleased. At the same time I will not be surprised if some readers object strongly to parts of this chapter—or prejudge it as belonging to an inappropriate 'learning from Japan' genre. But perhaps that kind of prejudgment is part of our problem today or, at least, an index to it.

Behind the Great Buddha

Tourists in Kamakura, both Japanese and foreign, are virtually certain to stop to see what is commonly referred to as the 'Great Buddha' at Kotokuin, a 37.7-foot high cast-iron image of Amida Buddha seated outdoors in a pose of tranquil contemplation. Only two blocks away, however, is a Buddhist site that relatively few non-Japanese will include on their guided tours. Having once seen the Great Buddha, you must follow a back street to find it, a temple named Hase-dera. Like much in Kamakura, it has a history reaching back to the medieval period.

If you are not Japanese, you will probably never get beyond the Great Buddha, and in the event you do go down the side street to see Hase-dera, you will more than likely return after a quick view of its Kannon. But that is unfortunate because, as a matter of fact, one of the most interesting and revealing scenes in today's Japan consists of what is taking place in the cemetery that is 'out back', behind the Kannon of Hase-dera. The Buddhist cemetery there stretches in tiers up the slope of the hill behind the temple. And the careful observer will note that it is to that cemetery, not the Kannon image, that the majority of Japanese visitors to Hase-dera now throng. Many of them will spend more time there than anywhere else in Kamakura—in spite of the fact that tour books and guides make only a passing reference to the cemetery.

Recently one could obtain a small leaflet of information about the Hase-dera in English. It reads:

> *Mizuko Jizō*
> The Kannon is a Buddhist deity whose special task is to help raise healthy children. Many people come and set up small statues, representing their children, so that he can watch over them. More recently, parents have set up statues for miscarried, aborted or dead-born babies, for the Kannon to protect. These are called Mizuko-jizō and in the Hase-dera there are about 50,000 such Jizōs. Mothers and fathers often visit the Mizuko-jizō to pray for the souls of the children they have lost.

It is this casual, almost passing, reference to 'aborted babies' that tells why there is a constant stream of people to the cemetery tucked behind a temple that is itself much less well-known than the nearby Great Buddha.

At one time, what was remembered here were mostly miscarried or stillborn infants; now, however, it is certain that the vast majority are the results of intentionally terminated pregnancies. At Hase-dera in 1983 the tally of the miscarried, stillborn and aborted was already about fifty thousand; since then it has risen much higher.

Hase-dera, however, is only one of a growing number of Buddhist temples in Japan that offer such services. Many of these temples began by offering other kinds of services to their parish-ioners. In recent years, with the rise in the number of abortions, their priests found that more and more people were looking for some kind of religious service specifically attuned to the needs of parents who had had abortions, such religious service being a rite through which such people obviously seek to assuage the guilt or alleviate the distress they are feeling about abortion. These temples have responded with the provision of *mizuko kuyō*, the now-common name for such rituals, which have recently shown phe-nomenal numerical growth. For temples such as Hase-dera, it ap-pears that the provision of rites for aborted fetuses was an additional service that was at least initially subordinate to the more traditional rituals of the temple. In recent years, however, this aug-mentation has progressively become a major service of the temple, and people come from all over the greater Tokyo metropolitan area to Hase-dera because they feel somehow compelled, rightly or wrongly, to 'do something' about the abortions they have had. The *mizuko kuyō* of Hase-dera meet a certain public demand.

Purple Cloud Temple

There is another kind of temple, however, for which the *mizuko kuyō* is the original and only reason for the temple's existence. Such temples are relative newcomers to the scene and have been the object of most of the public criticism of *mizuko kuyō* in Japan. There are some striking differences. Unlike Hase-dera, the place described below began its existence as a memorial park to provide rites almost exclusively for deliberately aborted fetuses. It occupies ground dedicated for that purpose, has advertised itself as such in the public media, and provides no other observable public service.

A good example of this kind of institution is a place named Shiun-zan Jizō-ji, on the outskirts of the city of Chichibu in Sai-tama Prefecture, approximately two hours from Tokyo by train. Its name rendered into English is 'The Temple of Jizō on the Moun-tain of the Purple Cloud'. This institution also has a branch office in the city of Tokyo. The main temple in the Chichibu mountains (here abbreviated to 'Purple Cloud Temple') can best be under-stood if I describe what I saw on my own visit there.

There is no mistaking the place once it has been reached. It occupies a sequence of adjacent hillsides, all of which are carefully tiered and set with narrow walking paths and row upon row of nearly identical, small, stone images—statues of Jizō. These are very similar to the ones seen in the cemetery at Hase-dera, except that virtually all those at Purple Cloud Temple are newly chiselled and carefully installed. Their grey granite is still precise in outline and shiny on the surface, not worn down by the elements—that is, they do not have the Buddhist image's famed reputation for showing the attractive signs of great age or antiquity.

There is something very striking about the scene—but also perplexing, perhaps even disturbing, to someone who does not know exactly what is going on there. Unlike most Buddhist institutions which have a prominent, architecturally impressive temple building as the centre of focus, the 'temple' on this site is a diminutive, modern building and almost insignificant in the midst of the carefully honed hills with their multitude of Jizō images. Inasmuch as the images constitute a 'cemetery', it is clear that here the ordinary pattern for temples has been reversed. That is, although in most Buddhist institutions—Hase-dera, for instance—the temple building itself stands forth prominently and has a cemetery 'out back', Purple Cloud Temple immediately presents itself as in fact a cemetery, and its 'temple', by contrast, serves much more as a kind of business and promotion office. Although it calls itself a 'temple', in layout and architecture it is really what the Japanese call a mountain *bochi*—a cemetery or memorial park.

Also striking to the first-time visitor is the uniformity of the stone Jizō images on this site. Row upon row upon row—they are the same in basic shape. They differ only very slightly in size; most are approximately two feet in height. The stone is cut so as to suggest that each image wears the foot-length robes of a Buddhist monk, who is also tonsured. There is no cut in the stone to suggest even a hint of a hairline or hair; these figures are perfectly bald. Their eyes are almost completely shut, in the manner found in most Buddhist images, a manner that denotes the meditation and tranquillity into which the figure has become absorbed. To anyone able to recognize the signs, there can be no doubt that these figures are, at least in some sense, monks who are aspirants to the highest goals of Buddhism.

The robes, the tonsure, and the eyes closed in meditation all combine to make this clear. At the same time, however, something else comes quickly to mind. These are diminutive figures, child-sized. The visage they present, while that of tranquillity, could also be seen as one of perfect innocence. And even their lack of hair connotes something of childhood, if not infancy. The statue, which on first sight may have suggested a monk, now prompts something of a double-take; the monk is really a child. More precisely, it's also a child.[7]

The figure's accoutrements make this certain. Virtually every one of the stone Jizō images wears a large red bib—of the type usually worn by an infant or a young child. Then, as if to push the identification with childhood beyond doubt, Jizō images are frequently provided with toys. Whole rows of them at Purple Cloud Temple are provided with pinwheels, whose brightly coloured spokes spin audibly in the wind. But individual statues are given individual toys as well—for instance, the kind of miniature piano a child might play with. For some of the images, sweaters or even more elaborately knitted garments and hats are provided. And, of course, flowers are placed by each one.

The double-take effect—seeing in the figures both monk and child simultaneously—is important, because the image is meant to represent two realities at the same time. For the visitor to Purple Cloud Temple who does not understand such things, there is a readily available guide sheet, which says:

> A Jizō image can do double service. On the one hand it can represent the soul of the mizuko (deceased child or fetus) for parents who are doing rites of apology to it. At the same time, however, the Jizō is also the one to whom can be made an appeal or prayer to guide the child or fetus through the realm of departed souls.[8]

Jizō is quite remarkable in that it is a stand-in for both the dead infant and the saviour figure who supposedly takes care of it in its otherworld journey. The double-take effect—one moment a child and the next a Buddhist saviour in monkish robes—is intentional.

Visits to such places as the temple at Purple Cloud are in no way limited to adults. In fact, one finds there a surprisingly large number of children. They join their mothers—and sometimes fathers or grandmothers in putting flowers in front of the Jizō images, in washing down the granite stone with water carried over from a nearby faucet, and in saying simple prayers before the sculptured stones. At Purple Cloud Temple there is even a small playground in the middle of the cemetery where children can be seen enjoying themselves.

To note the presence and play of these children is also to call attention to the relatively 'happy' mood in this kind of place. The atmosphere is far from lugubrious. The red-bibbed images on the hills, the gentle whirring sound and bright appearance of the thousands of upright pinwheels, the presence and play of well-dressed children—all these combine to provide a lightness of feeling that would probably be totally unknown, even incongruous, in the cemeteries of Europe and America. In the garb provided for some of the images, in the toys they are given, and in the pins and medallions attached to them there is a playfulness—even a gentle levity. In fact, the notion that Jizō is a saviour who very much enjoys playing with children goes back some centuries in Japan's religious history.[9]

The non-Japanese who might chance to visit such a place would probably at first have their perplexity compounded with the feeling that all of this is a type of religious kitsch or, at least, is rather 'inappropriate' for a place dedicated to memorializing the departed dead. An hour spent walking around the stones and carefully observing the Japanese and their activities might, however, bring the visitor to quite different conclusions—especially if the intent of the activities were explained.

The sense of kitsch arises because two things are conflated here that we in the West usually want to separate as much as possible—that is, the cemetery and the nursery. But such temples are, after all, cemeteries not for adults but for children—children who, even though dead, are assumed to be, in ways explained below, still 'alive' and related to this place. Consequently, a sense of play is deemed entirely appropriate, as are the toys that make that possible. These cemeteries are the concrete embodiment of human imagination directing its attention to beings who, while no longer in the same world with us as they once were, still are present in our memories and projections. In the minds of most Japanese, the cemetery is the place par excellence that links this world with the 'other' world; it is the node of contact between the metaphysical and the physical. And when it is the departed children or aborted fetuses that are being remembered, it is the Jizō image and cemeteries such as these that provide such a tangible, empirical contact point with the 'other' world in which they are thought to reside.

Levity, it is worth noting, is not altogether absent from the cemeteries of the West. The inscriptions on occasional tombstones and even the designs of some memorial architecture show that clearly. However, what reinforces the tendency of the Japanese to make their Jizō cemeteries places of lightness and play is the sense that the deceased children 'on the other side' are, if anything eager to enjoy a few happy moments with the family members who come out from their otherwise busy lives to visit them. The promotional literature provided by Purple Cloud Temple makes it clear that most of the time spent by such children in the 'other world' is far from happy; since they are quite miserable there, the visit from their families is especially appreciated. Thus, the whole experience is modelled after that of reunion rather than separation and, as such, the proper thing is to demonstrate the joy rather than the sorrow of the occasion. Loving attention to the dead is shown by washing down the memorial image—an ancient Buddhist practice—providing fresh flowers, and bringing the occasional new toy or garment. These activities and the recitation of simple prayers are expected. But beyond these there is the sense of an active communication, emotional if not verbal, between the living family and the departed child.

'Child' is the term used, but there can be no doubt that the overwhelming majority of children memorialized at Purple Cloud Temple are fetuses whose progress in the womb was terminated. The assumption throughout, however, is that in the other world such fetuses are fully formed; they are not so much infants as children and are able to react as a child of at least a year or two might to the attention they receive from parents and siblings in this world.

Liquid Life

Mizuko is, in fact, a very subtle word and, because understanding it is crucial for grasping how even Japanese of today view abortion, it deserves a close look. Although there is a rare usage of the term to refer to a live newborn, the predominant usage is to refer to a dead infant, a still-born, or a fetus that has been aborted.[10] In his important studies of Japan's demographic history, Takahashi Bonsen sees the term—and the concept it suggests—as traceable to the accounts of what is called the 'leech-child' in the *Kojiki* and the *Nihonshoki*, early Japanese cosmogonic myths written down in the eighth century.[11] The *Kojiki*, for instance, narrates that Izanagi and Izanami, the primal couple, while in a progency-producing phase, happened to make a ritual mistake: 'Nevertheless, they commenced procreation and gave birth to a leech-child. They placed this child into a boat made of reeds and floated it away'.[12] Although the emphasis on ritual propriety in early Japan is itself fascinating, the item of compelling importance here is 'hiru no ko', the term translated as 'leech-child'.

Takahashi Bonsen points out that the *Shiojiri*, a work written around 1697 by Amano Sadakage, notes that the way in which sericulturalists in the countryside discarded unusable silkworms, by putting them into the river in straw vessels, and the way people reduced the number of their children were both interpreted as being like the way the mythical primal couple disposed of their leech-child.[13] We cannot know whether this was new or old usage, but it at least suggests an attempt to relate the reduction of children to the actions of a primal couple in the national myths.

In a sense, then, the leech-child became the prototype for all children sent either literally or figuratively back into 'the waters' —all *mizuko*. Although the term 'liquidate' in our language has rather horrible connotations, in Japanese the phrase 'to make into liquid' is philosophically and ethically much more acceptable. In an interesting essay on the role of water in Japanese psychology and philosophy, Iwai Hiroshi stresses that the Japanese tend to have very positive, relatively fear-free attitudes *vis-à-vis* water, rivers, oceans and the like. He also believes that in the Japanese psyche water tends to connote things maternal and is powerfully linked to the watery but comfortable environment of the womb.[14]

If Iwai is right, we can see the structure of meanings embraced by the term *mizuko* and also why as a piece of language it connotes something approachable and comfort-bringing rather than awful and frightening. The child who has become a *mizuko* has gone quickly from the warm waters of the womb to another state of liquidity. Life that has remained liquid simply has never become solidified. The term suggests that a new-born, something just in the process of taking on 'form', can also rather quickly revert to a relatively formless state.

In that sense the term tells of a death. But simultaneously it appeals to the *fons et origo* function of the waters and the sea; it suggests with great power that the child or fetus in question will come to life again. That is, it straddles and embraces both truths. Of course, to the eye of strict reason only one of these truths is allowed: the child or fetus that has become 'liquid' has become dead. But to the eye that allows the symbol to be ambivalent, the second truth is also a reality: the water-child has reverted to a former state but only as preparation for later rebirth in this world. And in Japan the acceptance of both truths was wide, having deep roots in cultural history. There both the most archaic stratum of religious belief and Buddhism, something introduced later from abroad, maintained that in some sense the dead 'return' to this world.

To regard the water-child as in some way suspended in water is to say that willy-nilly a fetus is a still-unformed child, a child still in the 'becoming' stage rather than emphatically existing as a discrete entity or 'being'. A water-child is a child who has only just begun to emerge from the great watery unknown; it could just as easily be said to be water that has only just begun to take shape as a human-being-to-be.

Flexible Return

Although the physical facts of abortion may be startling and crude, the language humans use to describe them is clearly meant to soften and humanize them. This is exactly what is shown by the terminology used by Japanese who have, either by natural death or human agency had a *mizuko*. Two Japanese researchers, Chiba Tokuji and Ōtsu Tadao, have examined the language used in rural areas from one end of Japan to the other—language that probably relates to usage over many centuries—and discovered that it is replete with references to 'returning' the unborn and to the 'return' of the *mizuko*.[15]

These references could be dismissed as nothing other than euphemisms—the making pretty through language of that which is, if the truth were told, simply horrifying and abominable. To do so would be to miss the impact of the curious wedding here between archaic belief systems, Buddhist teachings, and the language of common folk. Language about 'return', first of all, implies that what has appeared in our world—a newborn or, in this case, a nearly-born infant—has not appeared entirely *de novo*. Although many Japanese, especially in modern times, prefer to be somewhat imprecise about the 'preexistence' of the fetus or newborn, there is, in keeping with Buddhism, a vague sense that a life that appears in our world or in a woman's uterus is the re-formation of a being that was before either in this world in other incarnations or in the world of the *kami*, or gods.

It is important here to note that the very notion of 'return' makes for a rough sketch—in fact a conveniently rough sketch—of a reality that no one seems to want to specify with any greater precision. There is just enough detail to keep the concept rich and open to variant interpretations. The point is to avoid so much specificity that the notion gets hardened into a rigid—or refutable—doctrine. Adumbration is of the essence.

The practical result seems clear. For the parent who wants to imagine its deceased or aborted *mizuko* as potentially coming back to be reborn into the same family at a time more convenient for all concerned, referring to its 'return' can imply that although it is being sent back to another world for a period of waiting, it is fully expected to be reincarnated into this world—and perhaps even this family!—at some later date. In that sense the aborted fetus is not so much being 'terminated' as it is being put on 'hold', asked to bide its time in some other world.

In such cases the *mizuko* is imagined as going to a kind of limbo, a place of clear deprivation, until the time comes for its release to a better place. And traditionally, at least, the parent could do things to make sure that the *mizuko* would go only to a place of temporary repose. Lest the unseen 'powers' that control such things mistake the intention of such parents, rural folk, we are told by Chiba and Ōtsu, sometimes bury their infant with fish in its mouth. This conveys a subtle meaning. Since Buddhism teaches—at least officially—that it is wrong to eat flesh, a dead child appearing in the world of the Buddhas with a fish in its mouth would, such parents surmise, surely be rejected for passage into final Buddhahood. In other words, its re-entry into this world, and preferably into their own home, could thus be guaranteed![16] Rural people often prove to be imaginative and clever manipulators, even of events in metaphysical realms.

It appears also that to some people in traditional Japan the very simplicity of a disposal method for such fetuses and newborns would, ironically, facilitate their rebirth into this world. By contrast, to make much to-do about a grave site and especially to provide such a child with a *kaimyō*, a posthumously applied Buddhist name for honoured ancestors expected to progress far beyond this world, would be to urge the infant too far out of reach and out of mind. Until very recently, at least, simplicity was of the essence for those who wanted a *mizuko* to come back again.[17] Too much ritual could be as dangerous as too little.

But what if a parent were content to have the *mizuko* progress onward and never return—at least not into his or her own family? That is, what if the parent or parents in question happened to be, either because of advanced age or an already full complement of children, not especially eager to have the *mizuko* be reborn to them at some later time? For such people the very flexibility of the 're-turn' notion provided another option. They could 'return' the child to the abode of the gods and the Buddhas. Prayers could be said that would ritually facilitate the progress of the *mizuko* to a place far better than either a family that does not want it or the 'limbo of infants' in which it might be temporarily housed. In that sense it was imagined that the child, after the time in limbo has passed, would make a more final return to a positively pictured location in the 'beyond'—a place alternately thought of as that where ancestors and *kami* abide, as a heaven or Pure Land, as the realm of the Buddhas, as nirvana. The exact ways of picturing such a place could differ, but the sense that it was a fundamentally good place was always clear. Either way the notion of 'return' was full of positive possibilities. Either way there was a real consolation for people experiencing great loss.

Mizuko Kuyō

Today the *mizuko kuyō* ritual can be performed in many different ways. It comes in a wide variety of sizes, types and costs. And monetary cost, of course, is usually directly correlated to the elaborateness of the ceremony and whether religious experts—priests and the like—are to officiate.

The simplest rite of all is probably the one with the oldest pedigree—that is, the one carried out by local women who have organized themselves into a confraternity to take care of the local Jizō shrine or shrines. This involves a kind of perpetual care for a simple sculpture or sculpture at a junction of streets—or at a roadside. The care involves putting out flowers in front of the icon, washing it down from time to time, and lighting a few sticks of incense once in a while. These Jizō shrines, whose otherworldly protection extends both to deceased children and aborted fetuses, are as close as possible to whole communities. It takes very little effort for anyone with concerns about such departed children to stop and bow at such sites. In the Japanese countryside and even in the residential sections of a metropolis such as Tokyo, such shrines can be found in abundance; from time to time people of the neighbourhood, most likely women, will be seen stopping for a momentary act of *kuyō*.

Also very simple will be the rite at the household shrine. Fairly often today the *mizuko* will be remembered as if it were merely another 'ancestor'—although technically it is not. When fine distinctions are not made, the fetus, which did not precede the living, is treated as an ancestor and will be remembered along with them at the Buddhist altar in households that have them. In homes a small icon of Jizō can be placed on the altar and reverential bows can be made to it. If a bit more pious and concerned for such things, members of the family may also recite the words of the *Heart Sūtra*[18] or a prayer addressed simultaneously to Jizō and the invisible dead fetus.

The next level of complexity involves paying for a stone image of Jizō and having it properly enshrined at one of the many cemeteries specializing in this. Such cemeteries can, as noted above, increasingly be found connected to temples of the established Buddhist denominations. During the past couple of decades, however, there has—in connection with the '*mizuko* boom'—been a large growth in the number of independent temples like Purple Cloud that deal exclusively in *mizuko* memorializing; often such institutions have little or no antiquity and may even be regarded as semi-private business ventures. Their commercial aspects are patent. Persons who initially visit such places are often presented with stories of others who experienced tragedy when they 'neglected' their *mizuko*, and such stories are soon followed by an outline of the temple's services and the fees charged. For a price, a concerned parent can have what in these cemeteries is tantamount to the 'perpetual care' in American mortuary contexts. Periodic rites for the *mizuko* can be purchased—and it is not strictly necessary for the parent to be personally present on such occasions. The requiem then is vicariously performed.

Within the context of many established Buddhist temples, there is often a large Jizō icon or a set of six or more smaller ones bedecked with red bibs. There a parent can perform simple rites—largely bowing, observing reverential silence, lighting a candle and maybe saying prayers or chanting. Some temples have an alcove filled with dolls and other items that in their own way relate to the departed child or fetus. Others have Jizō cemeteries or, in special instances, a collection of look-alike and rough-hewn stones that are designated as the Riverbank of Sai.[19] Candles can be lit and coins deposited in such places. More and more, however, the *mizuko kuyō* is moving inside the temple as well. Many temples now have special days set aside for *mizuko* remembrance rites. Robed priests will then officiate, and the concerned parents will join a larger congregation of persons, the 'parents' of *mizuko* like themselves.

In fact, the *mizuko* rite now has an important role even outside of Buddhism; some of the 'new religions' have made them a part of the panoply of services offered. Helen Hardacre vividly describes such a rite in the Oi church of Kurozumikyo, on the outskirts of Okayama City. In this case it is one offered to nonmembers:

> The woman making the request, invariably the one who would have been the mother of the child, comes to the church, and a minister prepares an ancestral tablet [*mitama bashira*] for each aborted or miscarried child, writing a name and approximate

date on each slip of white wood. Initially this is placed on a small movable altar adjacent to the ancestral altar of the church. The church's ancestral altar is decorated with particularly colorful flowers and food offerings and with a large red and white paper streamer, representing a symbolic offering of clothes for the child. Before the ancestral altar, the ministers recite the Great Purification Prayer and read a *norito* to console the child's spirit, directing it to enter the ancestral tablet previously prepared. The officiating minister, who has donned a paper mask covering the mouth, and an assistant then move to a temporary altar on which the tablet rests. The officiating minister directs the spirit of the child to enter the tablet as the assistant intones a long 'Ooooo' indicating the spirit's passage into the tablet. Then the tablet is removed to the ancestral altar, and all assembled offer *tamagushi* before it while music is played.[20]

Here, as in many of the new religions of Japan, there is a mix of Buddhist, Shinto and even Christian elements. Much of the terminology of the rite just described is Shinto; moreover in that context, according to Hardacre, the soul of the unborn has to be purified, because in abortion or miscarriage it has been polluted by contact with blood—a distinctively Shinto theme. The institution performing this kind of *mizuko kuyō* is, significantly, a 'church' and its officiant a 'minister'.

This confirms the fact that the impulse to deal with abortion through a ritual such as this comes from deep roots in Japanese culture. Although the practice has historically centred around the figure of Jizō and the largely Buddhist *kuyō* rituals, it can with apparently little difficulty now enter into the religious context of the new religions. There is, it seems, a deeply sensed need for such rituals and, when abortion is practised across denominational and religious lines, so too, it seems, will rituals emerge.

Perhaps one of the most fascinating questions is whether the *mizuko* ritual will enter into Japanese Christianity—or whether it has already begun to do so. Japanese researchers have already noted what seems an undue interest in the *mizuko* ritual by Western Catholics residing in Japan.[21] It is not unreasonable to expect that in Japan what begins as the Christians' effort to understand phenomena within Japanese culture eventually may, with great caution, be accepted into the Christian context itself. Many Protestants have done just that with respect to rites for ancestors: although since the Meiji period, many Protestants in Japan scorned the *kuyō* for ancestors as compromises with false religion, in recent years even foreign missionaries in Japan have, according to reports in Japanese newspapers, been exploring the importance of ancestor rituals for family coherence. That is, once the Japanese family is understood to be—in its basic structure—even stronger than that of the Christian cultures of the West, it seems to some wasteful not to make an accommodation to the practices that make it so.

Mizuko Kuyō may, in time, prove to be a context wherein the Catholic Church's adamant opposition to abortion comes at least in Japan—face to face with what some perceive to be the emotional and ritual needs of persons who, rightly or wrongly, have had abortions. If this happens in Japan, even non-Catholics will have reason to watch with great interest. And perhaps the underlying question will then become: Is such a rite merely something that arose to fit the peculiar and idiosyncratic needs of one culture, that of Japan, or does it accord with more generally human needs?

Controversy

It should not be thought from the above that *mizuko kuyō* is free of controversy. Purple Cloud Temple, for example, has been the object of considerable public suspicion.

It is first necessary, however, to pay attention to more general criticisms of Japanese Buddhists for what some see as their failure to level a stern condemnation of the abortion practices now widely accepted in their society. Not only observers from the West but also a good number of non-Japanese Asians—Buddhists among them—tend, at least at first sight, to find something terribly odd and incongruous in the Japanese Buddhist temples' practice of providing guilt-relieving rituals for persons who have had abortions.

Isn't it, such observers will ask, the responsibility of a religious body to bring abortion itself under control? What possible justification could there be for lending abortion what is all but a religious seal of approval? Isn't there something fundamentally unscrupulous about a religious organization that collects monies from people for providing a mass, Buddhist in this case, for an aborted fetus?

Some Buddhists, especially if they are not Japanese or have no acquaintance with the cultural factors involved in this way of handling abortion, are likely to find a flat contradiction between abortion and what is universally called the 'First Precept' of Buddhism—a vow of moral behaviour that states, 'I will not willingly take the life of a living thing'. This commitment to not killing is not found somewhere at the end of the Buddhist equivalent of the Ten Commandments but at the very top of the list. Its priority in the Buddhist moral code is certain—Buddhist teaching includes a very strong statement against the taking of life. In the rules of the early Buddhists, this proscription had clear implications: 'As far as the human being is concerned, even the abortion of an embryo which was just conceived is regarded as a crime'.[22]

One way around this, at least in theory, would be to define the unborn fetus as 'nonlife', as some kind of mere stuff or relatively inert matter. If that were so, we can imagine how the Japanese Buddhist might conceivably find a way out of his or her dilemma. As a matter of fact, however, Japanese are for the most part much less ready than persons in the West to refer to an unborn fetus in terms that suggest it is something less than human or even less than sentient. The Japanese tend to avoid terms like 'unwanted pregnancy' or 'fetal tissue'. That which develops in the uterus is often referred to as a 'child'—even when there are plans to abort it. Many Japanese Buddhists, committed by their religion to refrain from taking life, will nonetheless have an abortion and in doing so refer to the aborted fetus as a child, one that clearly has been alive.

Perplexed as to how this could possibly be, we rightly wonder what prevents such persons from feeling they have been split in two by the gap between their religious principles and their real practice? How are the two reconciled? One answer to these questions, of course, would be to claim that these Japanese—or at least those morally compromised in the above fashion—are not, in fact, Buddhists at all. This would be to judge that they carry the name without a real right to do so; it would be to see the conflict between principle and reality as simply too great. This judgment that Japanese Buddhism is inauthentic, we should note, is quite often made both inside and outside of Japan, by both non-Buddhists and Buddhists alike. It is tantamount to saying that Japanese 'Buddhism' is really a thin veneer over a mind-set or religious view that is, in fact, non-Buddhist, perhaps even anti-Buddhist.[23]

Clearly, to move to that judgment closes the whole discussion from the outset. As a matter of fact, however, most of the religions of the world would fare miserably if measured against the emphatic demands and commands of their founders. Few are the Christians who take the command of Jesus literally when he requires that they sell all their possessions in order to follow him. Likewise, both Jews and Christians have felt the necessity of 'interpreting' the command in the Decalogue that they not kill; everything from allowances made for capital punishment to theories of the 'just war' have turned up as ways, for better or worse, in which religious persons and communities in the West have accommodated the proscription against killing to what they see as clear, realistic needs. Lay Buddhists in Southeast Asia as well have found their way clear to serve in armies. Likewise Buddhist kings and presidents have dispatched armed troops into battle. The 'interpretation' of seemingly unambiguous commands and precepts goes on all the time in religion.

There are, in fact, a lot of adjustments between the strict ethical axioms that are laid down at the base of a tradition and the moral realities of everyday life in the present. There have to be. And these adjustments that take place 'in between' are, in fact, the tradition. It is from within this tradition that today's person takes what is needed to put together for himself or herself a script for making moral decisions.

Our moral lives and our moral reasoning are, in fact, very much as Jeffrey Stout describes in his *Ethics after Babel*; that is, in finding our way through moral dilemmas—especially relatively new ones—we have no alternative but to 'draw on a collection of assorted odds and ends available for use and kept on hand on the chance that they might someday prove useful'. Stout's important study takes Claude Lévi-Strauss's notion of the *bricoleur*, an odd-job expert who can create something impressive and eminently useful out of leftover bits and pieces, and goes on to show how what we call 'ethical thought' is almost invariably just that—namely, moral *bricolage*.[24]

Stout's claim, one that seems clearly right, is that 'great works of ethical thought' are often brought into being when people 'start off by taking stock of problems that need solving and available conceptual resources for solving them [and] proceed by taking apart, putting together, reordering, weighting, weeding out, and filling in'.[25]

With respect to how most Japanese Buddhists today think about abortion, I suggest that Stout's notion of doing ethics by putting together bits and pieces into an acceptable—and useful—assemblage describes the process exactly. In much of their history, the Japanese have, it seems almost as if by a clear preference, carried out moral reasoning in this fashion. In ethics they have long been *bricoleurs*, very skilled ones in fact. This is the reason why many Japanese today regard their solution to the abortion dilemma as 'traditional'. The result is a compromise which finds space for both early Buddhism's precept against killing and the conscience of the contemporary Japanese woman who has an abortion and still wishes, in spite of that, to think of herself as a 'good' Buddhist.

Conclusion

Although by this point the reasons should be fairly clear, it is significant that what we here call the 'Buddhist' position on these matters has no easily identifiable functional equivalent in Western societies. Although certain liberal Protestant denominations and groups and some Jewish ones may have views that approximate these, there remain rather striking differences.

The Japanese Buddhist orientation is rather distinctive on a couple of points that are worthy of note. For instance, the Buddhist posture permits—and even encourages—language about the fetus as human life in some sense but refuses to draw the conclusion that, therefore, abortion is disallowed. It avoids the dualizing dilemma often found in the American and European abortion polemics: namely, that of feeling compelled either to think of the fetus as life equivalent to that of a fully formed young child or, alternatively, as so much inert matter or 'tissue'. On the one hand it is not 'LIFE!' and on the other it is not just 'AN UNWANTED PREGNANCY!'

This is an extremely important point and one obscured by the polemics of the current debate in the West. The practical benefits of this position are likely to be very real. The natural feelings of a woman—or even a man—toward a developing fetus need not be denied or repressed. If a woman has an impulse to regard what is inside her uterus as a 'child', that need not be negated. At the same time, precisely as her condition is taken to be one involving pain, she is permitted to see her way clear to a relative release from that pain by way of abortion. The presence of a 'child' in the womb does not forbid that.

Some advantages in this should be clear. This view makes abortion permissible but, at the same time, makes unnecessary any denial of strong emotions a woman might have about her fetus as life and even as a child. In short, there is no need to reduce the options to 'inviolable life' or 'an unwanted pregnancy'. A third option—perhaps a middle way between the others—is opened. That is, a woman is free to acknowledge any feelings of bonding that have developed within herself. Such feelings need not bar her from deciding to have an abortion.

In addition, of course, this high degree of pragmatism allows for close attention to the education and welfare of children. It prioritizies the well-being of real children in this world over putative children in other worlds. It contributes directly and substantially to what the Catholic observers in sixteenth-century Japan noted about good life conditions and behaviour of such children. And it contributes as well to what Robert Nisbet has pinpointed as the Japanese possession of what may be the strongest family system in the world.[26]

Notes

[1]   This chapter has been adapted from the author's book *Liquid Life: Abortion and Buddhism in Japan.* (Princeton: Princeton University Press, 1992). The book deals not only with present practice but with a large amount of historical material which has shaped contemporary attitudes and practice. The historical material has been omitted here for reasons of space.

[2]   Nakatani Kinko, 'Chūzetsu dataizai no toraekata' in Nihon kazoku keikaku renmei, ed., *Onna no jinken to sei: watakushitachi no sentaku* (Komichi Shobō, 1984), 29.

[3] Takie Sugiyama Lebra, *Japanese Patterns of Behavior* (Honolulu: University of Hawaii Press, 1976), 11.

[4] Richard Rorty in recent years has been the most articulate advocate of a reappropriation of the American pragmatists, especially in his *Consequences of Pragmatism* (Essays: 1972-1980) (Minneapolis: University of Minnesota Press, 1982) and *Contingency, Irony, and Solidarity* (Cambridge: Cambridge University Press, 1989). But see also Jeffrey Stout's definitions of a 'modest pragmatism', questions about some of Rorty's statements, and strong defence of this position as being not relativist in ethics. Jeffrey Stout, *Ethics after Babel: The Languages of Morals and their Discontents* (Boston: Beacon Press, 1988).

[5] For a similar assessment of Buddhism and Pragmatism, see Kenneth K. Inada and Nolan P. Jacobson, *Buddhism and American Thinkers* (Albany: State University of New York Press, 1984), esp. 76.

[6] William Safire, perhaps in this instance more 'Japanese' than he realized, advocated the pragmatics of compromise in his 'Option 3: "Pro-Comp"', *New York Times*, July 6, 1989.

[7] The child-monk was common in medieval and early-modern Japan, especially because orphaned children were often sent into monasteries for care. Artistic and iconographic representations of them were prized. Innocence, holiness, and charm were seen combined in such figures.

[8] A translation of the entire document is available as as appendix to *Liquid Life*.

[9] See essays in Sakurai Tokutarō, ed., *Jizō Shinkō* (Yūzankaku Shuppan, 1983); Ishida Mizumaro, *Jigoku* (Kyoto: Hōzōkan, 1985), 236-54; and Ogura Yasushi, 'Ojizōsan to kodomo: hitotsu no bunka henyō', *Hikaku bungaku kenkyū*, no. 48, 74-94.

[10] *Nihon-kokugo daijiten* (Shogakkan, 1975), 18:553.

[11] Takahashi Bonsen, *Nihon jinkō-shi no kenkyū*, Sanyūsha, 1941-1962, 348.

[12] Donald A. Philippi, trans., *Kojiki* (Tokyo: University of Tokyo Press, 1968), 51. Philippi holds to the eighth-century pronunciation of *piru-go* for leech-child. Original text is Aoki Kazuo et al. eds., the *Nihon shisō taikei: Kojiki* (Iwanami Shoten, 1982), 23.

[13] Takahashi Bonsen, *Nihon jinkō-shi no kenkyū*, 348.

[14] Iwai Hiroshi, 'Nihonjin to mizu no shinsō-shinri', *Risō* 614 (July 1984): 89-99, and esp. 93.

[15] Chiba Tokuji and Ōtsu Tadao, *Mabiki to mizuko: kosodate no fuōkuroa* (Nōsangyōson Bunka Kyōkai, 1983), esp. 31-38. The common words are *kaeru/kaeus*, *modoru/modosu*, and combinations thereof.

[16] Chiba and Ōtsu, *Mabiki to mizuko*, 24.

[17] Terauchi Daikichi, a writer who is also a Buddhist priest, notes that the records of his temple show that until recently there was ritual simplicity and no use of *kaimyō* for such infants. See his 'Gendai no mizuko jizō', in *Jizōsama nyūmon*, Daihōrin-Henshūbu, ed. (Daihōrinkaku, 1984), 92-93. On *Kaimyō* and ancestral rites as a way of putting distance between deceased ancestors and the living, see Robert J. Smith, *Ancestor Worship in Contemporary Japan* (Stanford: Stanford University Press, 1974).

[18] Known as the *Hannya Shing* in Japanese. An English translation is given in my *Buddhism: A Cultural Perspective* (Englewood Cliffs, N.J.: Prentice-Hall, 1988).

[19] In medieval Japan it was imagined there was a special place that constituted a limbo for children. Its name was Sai-no-kawara or 'the riverbank in the land of Sai'. The dead children gathered there were thought to be miserable because, on the one hand, they could no longer be with their beloved parents in the land of the living and, on the other, they could not cross the river, which is taken to be the boundary between them and a good rebirth.

[20] Helen Hardacre, *Kurozumikyō and the New Religions of Japan* (Princeton: Princeton University Press, 1986), 151.

[21] See Hashimoto Mitsuru, 'Fuan no shakai ni motomeru shūkyō: mizuko kuyō', *Gendai shakai-gaku* 13:1 (1987): 42.

[22] Shundo Tachibana, *The Ethics of Buddhism* (London: Curzon Press, 1926), 81. Texts refer to *brunahatiya*, 'killing a fetus'.

[23] In the years immediately after World War II, the self-criticism of many of Japan's Buddhists often led to such a conclusion. An especially strong censure from within was Watanabe Shōkō, in his *Nihon no bukkyō* (Iwanami Shoten, 1958).

[24] Jeffrey Stout, *Ethics after Babel*, 74. Stout, objecting to Lévi-Strauss's attribution of this only to so-called primitive peoples,

writes, 'We are all *bricoleurs* insofar as we are capable of creative thought at all' (p.74).

[25] Jeffrey Stout, *Ethics after Babel*, 75.

[26] Robert Nisbet, entry on 'Abortion', in his *Prejudices: A Philosophical Dictionary* (Cambridge, Mass.: Harvard University Press, 1982), 1.

6

'I can only move my feet towards *mizuko kuyō*' Memorial Services for Dead Children in Japan

Elizabeth G. Harrison

Mizuko, literally 'water-child', is the name now given in Japan to children who have died 'out of order', that is, before their parents. This includes children who have died as a result of spontaneous or induced abortion as well as stillborn infants and those who have died from any manner of illness or accident after they were born.[1] The Japanese practice of *mizuko kuyō*, often identified as Buddhist memorial services for these dead children, centres around the performance of some variation of a memorial service for ancestral spirits (*senzo kuyō*). As such, the *mizuko* service usually includes elements which are standard to Buddhist memorial services in Japan: the chanting of special texts and presentation of offerings by clergy and audience, manipulation of religious implements and supervision of the audience by the clergy, and acts of purification performed by the audience.

The object of such services is to appeal to an appropriate deity to provide for the well-being of the dead, to transfer merit to the karmic account of the dead child so that he or she may proceed more quickly to a felicitous rebirth, and to appease the dead so that they might become a benevolent influence in the lives of their living family.

93

Visitors to Japan today can hardly miss seeing the rows of child-like figurines, as large as three or four feet or as small as two or three inches, that line pathways, shelves, and racks, both indoors and out, at temples and shrines across the country. They are visible evidence that tens of thousands of people, mostly women, have commissioned or participated in *mizuko kuyō* services for their children each year since the early 1970s.[2] Despite the negative press which depicts them as passive dolls being manipulated by money-hungry priests, Japanese people, especially women, continue to participate, and *mizuko kuyō* has now become a routine practice at religious sites—primarily Buddhist temples—all around Japan. The connection of this practice with Buddhism is a created one, however, and until quite recently their relationship has not been an especially happy one.

Arising in the early postwar period as a reaction to the 1948 Eugenics Protection Law which made abortion legal in certain specified circumstances,[3] *mizuko kuyō* was easily associated with Buddhism in the minds of the lay public. Historically, especially in medieval and pre-modern times, Buddhism in Japan had demonstrated a strong focus on death and the welfare of the dead. This interest was institutionalized in the early seventeenth century by the Tokugawa shogunate pronouncement that Buddhist temples would thenceforth be the site for funeral and ancestral rites for parishioners, thereby removing the locus of such formal observances from the home. The relocation was so successful that today, even though most funerals are not now done in temples, Buddhism in Japan is commonly known as 'funeral Buddhism' (*sōshiki bukkyō*), and anything having to do with death is first assumed to take place in a Buddhist context.[4]

One interesting aspect of this Japanese Buddhist involvement in rituals associated with death is its focus on dead adults and the resulting lack of any widely recognized, formal public rites for very young children who had died. In pre-modern Japan, it was thought that a child did not become a real 'person' until some time after birth; the evidence for this lies in the many customs which distinguished a newborn baby from other 'people', such as not giving it a name and not putting its arms through sleeves for a certain number of days after birth. The pre-modern saying 'Until the age of seven, a child is of the *kami*' (*nanasai made wa kami no uchi*) suggests that a child's existence in this world remains unsettled until it reaches seven years of age. If it died before age seven, it was usually not given a proper funeral or burial in the manner of those who died at an older age; if it died before it was named, it most likely did not receive a funeral at all, and its birth would not have been registered. Such would have been the case for infants killed by infanticide, for example, as well as fetuses from pregnancies terminated by either spontaneous or induced abortion.[5]

In the post-World War II context of the huge number of war dead and the new abortion law, when the number of reported abortions in Japan rose steadily to a peak of 1,170,143 in 1955, I would argue that children, including unborn aborted children, became recognized by some as a new type of war dead.[6] Religious sites (most of them Buddhist) for performing memorial services for those children began to proliferate around the country in the 1970s. Several pseudo-Buddhist sites appeared as well, sites which made use of the identification of Buddhist forms with rituals for the dead to lend them legitimacy.[7] By 1978, Buddhist priests and others who regularly performed services for *mizuko* were appearing on daytime television shows, further spreading word of the practice while the commentators sensationalized it. In 1984, when I began studying *mizuko kuyō*, it had become perhaps the most controversial practice in modern Japanese religious history: publicized by the mass media as a fad and a scam, denounced by many Buddhist clergy and some Buddhist institutions as un-Buddhist, yet nevertheless perpetuated by both clergy and lay participants all around Japan.

This paper will focus on the disjunction between the various images of the practice of *mizuko kuyō*. An overview of the images constructed in promotional literature and those presented by the media will give us a context for examining the arguments of several Buddhist priests both for and against the appropriateness of this practice at Buddhist sites. Some of these reactions were delivered publicly, in print, while others were obtained privately in taped interviews. What has tended to go unnoticed in this debate over *mizuko kuyō* are the attitudes of the lay people who participate in or request *mizuko kuyō* services. We will consider the practice as it has been constructed by lay participants and how they see it informing their lives, particularly their feelings about and relationship to their dead (aborted) children in order to demonstrate the complexity of the practice that is lost in the more public images.

Promotional and Media Images

By the mid-1980s, references to *mizuko kuyō* could be seen almost daily throughout Japan on billboards and posters, in advertisements in the public media, in newspaper and magazine articles, in publications available at religious sites and sold at bookstores, and even in comic books (*manga*). Much of this was promotional material meant to bring people to particular sites to participate in the practice as it was performed there. Many reasons were given for the need for such practice. In some cases, mothers were blamed for the death of their children, no matter how that death might have occurred, and told they must make amends through performance of *kuyō*.[8] In others, the practice was put forth as a way for women who were grieving the loss of a child, whether before or after birth, to recover by establishing a relationship with the spirit of that child. Another approach was to promote the performance of *mizuko kuyō* as a way to help solve major, unforeseen problems occurring in a woman's life, such as the unexplained, grave illness of a living child, or a sudden, disastrous turn in the family's fortunes; in the mid-1980s such problems were often interpreted first as the result of the intervention of a forgotten *mizuko* into the family's affairs. As an extension of this, the practice was also portrayed as a way to encourage a family's *mizuko* to play the role of protector of its living family and to provide for the future of its siblings. Spiritualists went even further, often warning readers that forgotten, untended *mizuko* were angry and could be dangerous to the health and livelihood of their living relatives. In short, from the mid-1980s on, promotional literature, including television interviews, sought to establish the necessity of the practice of *mizuko kuyō* for all dead children, although the special focus of the practice remained on dead unborn children, for they were most often forgotten.

In response to the obvious success of the new practice, the media began to publicize it in a different light, as a fad (*būmu*, lit. 'boom', implying great but short-lived popularity) and a money-making scheme. For example, a three-page photographic essay in a

1980 issue of *Shūkan Bunshun*, a popular weekly literary magazine, suggested several reasons for the 'Mizuko Jizō Boom'. According to the article, elderly women who had lost children due to the war, wives whose pregnancies had ended in miscarriage, and women who had aborted pregnancies resulting from 'free sex' were becoming religious (*busshin ga dekite*) and buying statues of Jizō to offer for their dead children. In addition, temple priests, whom the article describes as 'very good at business', were making the most of this opportunity to make money by encouraging such sales. The article ends with the statement that 'no amount of this kind of *kuyō* will help dead children rest more easily'.[9]

A 1983 TBS television special report on the '*Mizuko* Boom' echoes this presentation. After examining the amount of money represented by the rows of memorial tablets for *mizuko* at one temple, the lines of people paying entrance fees to enter another temple for *mizuko kuyō*, and the number of orders for *Mizuko* Jizō statues being received by a foundry, the show's reporter interviews a religion critic who criticizes religious establishments for using people's suffering to create a 'boom' for themselves. The studio commentator remarks later, 'If someone does *mizuko kuyō* and is helped by it, then there is a reason for doing it. But I can't help feeling that this is [primarily] a business'.[10] Although both of the reports described above at least acknowledge that participants may obtain some benefit or help from the practice, later pieces tend to focus on the negative business and manipulative aspects alone. A 1985 article entitled 'Temples in Japan Capitalize on Abortion' in the English-language Mainichi Daily News explains that 'guilt and dark superstition still nag at many Japanese who turn to abortion. In the past decade, Buddhist temples around the country have exploited that fact to build what one Japanese magazine has called a multimillion dollar "business of terror"'.[11] The terror mentioned here is the fear of *tatari*, actual physical reprisal from forgotten and uncared-for *mizuko*, which might take the form of illness or accident, birth defects or other problems with later children, or similar changes in circumstance that would disturb the harmony of the family and thus the rhythm of a woman's life. Such media images were simply built onto an already existing critique of religion in contemporary Japan as worldly and outdated.

It was in this context that I began studying *mizuko kuyō* in 1984. At that time I found Buddhist clergy and institutions around the country struggling to define their positions with respect to the new practice in light of the negative reputation it had acquired from the media. As we shall see in the next section, those who performed *mizuko kuyō* services were searching for Buddhist justifications for doing so, while those who rejected the practice also did so for ostensibly Buddhist reasons.

Buddhist Clergy and *Mizuko Kuyō*

Perhaps the strongest reaction against *mizuko kuyō* as a Buddhist practice came from Nishi Honganji, one of the major subsects of Shin (Jōdo Shinshū or True Pure Land) Buddhism in Japan. After many years of posting messages condemning the practice on their roadside billboard in downtown Kyoto, an official sectarian study group finally published the rationale for this stance in 1988 in a small book about rebirth for women. The carefully constructed argument turns on the assertion that *mizuko kuyō* is not consistent with the original Buddhist meaning of *kuyō*: the new practice focuses on angry spirits of the dead, while originally, in the *sūtras*, *kuyō* meant to take care of the Buddha, the Dharma, and the *Sangha* with respect and offerings.[12] The present practice is depicted as based on belief in evil spirits and the desire to appease them in order to avert disaster and bring good fortune, and for this reason it is dismissed as derived from folk customs and the intentional planning of certain individuals who sought to create a market. In Shin Buddhist terms, the practice misses the point in two ways. It defines the central problem to be the need for *kuyō* rather than the practice of abortion, which in Buddhism is seen as the taking of a life. And it draws a karmic connection between the spirits of dead children and real life problems, a belief that fourteenth-century Shin founder Shinran called 'imitation religion' (*nise no shūkyō*). Since that purported karmic connection is mistaken, *mizuko kuyō* might make the performer feel better, but it won't change the basic situation. In fact, according to this argument, the performer's real life problems will only get worse, since their true cause is not being addressed.[13]

Most denials that *mizuko kuyō* is Buddhist have not been so well-articulated, however. As I interviewed clergy around the country in the mid- and late 1980s, I was told many times that *mizuko kuyō* was not Buddhist. The reasons given were usually very general: it is not in the *sūtras*; it's new (We've never talked about it before, have we?); it's based on *tatari*, which is not Buddhist; it was started by new religions, not Buddhist sects; it's only about making money, not about religion; it is simply a public way of con-doning abortion and giving a quick moral fix.[14] While the clergy who offered these reasons for refusing to perform the practice seemed sincere in their opposition to it, my sense was that some were as concerned with avoiding negative publicity as with the question of whether it was genuinely Buddhist or not.

On the other hand, many Buddhist clergy found *mizuko kuyō* completely within the sphere of normal and acceptable Buddhist practice. Arguments for this stance tended to be historical: it's in the *sūtras* (though no one would give a specific citation); it's just another form of ancestor worship; we've always done it, but under different names. The head priest of a Nichiren temple in Miyazu, Kyoto Prefecture, for example, explained that what is known as *mizuko kuyō* today began in medieval times as the performance of *segaki-e*, memorial services for unattended spirits of the dead wandering the lower realms of existence. Another head priest, of a Pure Land (Jōdo) temple in the city of Kyoto, claims that his temple was the birthplace of the practice of *mizuko kuyō* roughly a thousand years ago. It began with the priest Saichō's mother, according to the legend of the temple which was published as a children's story in 1982.[15] When Saichō ascended Mt. Hiei to the northeast of Kyoto to open a monastic centre in the tenth century, his mother, unable to accompany him because she was a woman (and thus not allowed to ascend the sacred mountain), remained with her hus-band's family at the eastern foot of the mountain. On the death of her husband, her ties to his family were cut, and having nowhere else to go she moved to the western outskirts of Kyoto to an area controlled by her brother. There she took up residence in a Bud-dhist chapel built on the remains of an older temple and spent her days as a Buddhist nun, praying, taking care of the chapel and chil-dren in the area. She became recognized throughout the area for her great compassion and love of children. One day, the story continues, someone left a newborn baby on her doorstep, knowing that she would care for it. She walked far and wide to beg milk for it, and that experience opened her heart to the plight of unwanted babies and babies who had died before, during or after birth. Particularly concerned for those who had died before and during birth, she had a stone monument in the shape of the Buddhist bodhisattva Jizō erected near her chapel and performed memorial services for them, praying that Jizō protect their spirits in the other world and that they achieve a good rebirth. This concern for the welfare of dead children, articulated as it was in a Buddhist ritual vocabulary, is claimed by the author of the story and by the priest at this particular temple to be the origin of *mizuko kuyō*.

While this story would seem to solve the problem of the relationship of *mizuko kuyō* to Buddhism, I hasten to add a postscript. Not long after I made the acquaintance of this priest and heard his story, I had the opportunity to interview the author he had commissioned to write it in publishable form. I asked to see the historical sources concerning *mizuko kuyō* that he had used for the book, but he replied that there were none. The temple priest had simply told him the story and asked that he, a Buddhist priest and celebrated author of Buddhist children's stories, turn it into a children's book. As far as he could tell, this story of the origin of *mizuko kuyō* was completely made up.[16]

The conclusions to be drawn here are perhaps not so obvious as the reader might expect. In their collection of essays entitled *The Invention of Tradition*, Hobsbawm and Ranger have demonstrated both the ordinariness and the ideological power of invented traditions; no small part of that power is the ability to re-configure the collective memory, to efface any memory of a time when the invented tradition was not common practice.[17] In the case of *mizuko kuyō*, this was accomplished by situating the practice within the Buddhist cultural space in which matters of death and what comes after are generally articulated in Japan. From its beginnings in the 1950s and 1960s, *mizuko kuyō* has borrowed much of its ritual vocabulary from the contemporary Buddhist repertoire, as described above. But without a more substantial link between the two, such borrowing could only lend a surface legitimacy to the new practice;

simple borrowing, or adaptation, of received elements into a new form would not, in such a short span of time, engender the kind of symbolic, even ideological power and concomitant public attempts at denial that we see in *mizuko kuyō* or the kind of effacement of memory that has resulted.

In creating the story of a contemporary practice originating a thousand years ago, the head priest of the Kyoto temple has given the practice a history, and that history is demonstrably Buddhist: the mother of a great Buddhist priest living a religious life and performing rituals for the dead in a Buddhist context cannot easily be construed in other than Buddhist terms. The Nichiren priest has done the same thing, though through a different set of associations. Since medieval times in Japan, the performance of *segaki-e* services for the wandering dead has been associated with the Buddhist vision of six realms of existence and has become an unremarked part of the annual celebration, performed in a Buddhist context, of ancestral spirits that takes place during mid- and late summer in Japan. The invention of these histories, as well as the claim that the practice can be found in the *sūtras*, thus serves to make it incontrovertibly Buddhist, and as such, an observance properly performed by priests at Buddhist sites around Japan.[18]

The invention of a Buddhist history for *mizuko kuyō* does something more, however. It situates this new concern for the welfare of dead children and for their continuing tie to their living families within the symbolic system of Japanese Buddhism. On the one hand, this means that the power of that symbolic system can be mobilized and experienced through the new practice, giving it a depth usually not found in something so new. In giving offerings both to a deity and to the dead child, in saying prayers, in chanting Buddhist texts as part of a formal service, one is not simply taking part in a newly invented practice but in a(n invented) tradition which is tied to nearly fifteen hundred years of Buddhist presence in Japan. On the other hand, by establishing the practice as old rather than new, these priests have made it a part of everyday life—not simply because it is available at more and more sites, but because it is a part of the arguably Buddhist fabric of life in Japan.

Inventing history is not the only tactic that has been used to bring the new practice of *mizuko kuyō* into the grammar of Buddhist practice in Japan, however. I have interviewed a number of local parish priests around the country who were originally strongly opposed to the practice, for many of the reasons given above, but who eventually decided to make it available to their parishioners. Their reasons for this change were similar: in the face of regular requests from temple parishioners for *mizuko* services or for a *mizuko* statue to be placed in the temple precincts as a locus for practice, they began to feel that their personal opposition to *mizuko kuyō* was leading them to avoid their duty to address the needs of their parishioners. In swallowing their misgivings and beginning to perform services for those who requested them or allowing parishioners to establish a temple site for their own *mizuko* observances, many of these priests saw themselves using a questionable practice as a means to bring lay people closer to the Buddhist path rather than as espousing or condoning the practice itself. Several described their versions of *mizuko* services not as *mizuko kuyō*, but as 'chanting the *sūtras*' (*okyō o yomu*) which, together with the homily or counselling given to the person who commissioned the service, was designed to shift the person's focus away from their dead child toward how they might lead a more Buddhist life. Even Nishi Honganji, in the same publication (cited above) in which it argues that the practice is not Buddhist and therefore should not be done, suggests that Shin priests can address followers' concerns related to *mizuko* in more generic Shin ways.[19]

Together with the increasing repetition of *mizuko kuyō* observances at religious sites around the country since the late 1970s, these two tactics—of inventing history and of redirecting a practice toward an aim different from the one it is purported to address—have contributed in large part to the success of the invented tradition of *mizuko kuyō*. Whereas in the mid-1980s the practice was being questioned publicly in nearly every corner, today it goes largely unremarked and seems to have taken its place alongside ancestral services in the standard repertoire performed by most Buddhist clergy throughout Japan. Questions of whether it is Buddhist or not have largely disappeared, as well they should: woven into the fabric of Buddhism in Japan by the redefinition of its history and by common performance, when performed at Buddhist temples *mizuko kuyō* is now effectively a Buddhist practice.

It is important to understand that the intentionality behind these tactics becomes irrelevant once they enter the public sphere; in public such constructions easily lose their determinacy, becoming available for appropriation by anyone sharing in the cultural soup. For example, we have seen how Buddhist clergy who originally objected to performing *mizuko kuyō* began to do so in an attempt to move lay people interested in the practice away from it. While it may have helped the clergy justify to themselves their involvement in a practice they objected to, in the public view this tactic nevertheless served to spread the practice as well as to make it more identifiable with Buddhist sites. It is this public view, that is, lay people's constructions of the practice of *mizuko kuyō*, that we will turn to in the rest of the paper in order to understand how individual practitioners have appropriated public elements of the practice to make sense of their own experiences.

Lay People's *Mizuko Kuyō*

The promotional and media images of *mizuko kuyō* that we have examined above present a stereotypical image of the Japanese women who participate in the practice as passive and easily manipulated. Male participants—and there are more and more—are never mentioned. Told by money-hungry clergy and spiritualists that they must make amends to their dead children by taking part in *mizuko kuyō* services, which may mean paying substantial amounts of money, women are assumed to do so dutifully. Blamed for the death of their children, whether they were lost by abortion or otherwise, the mothers of *mizuko* are assumed to be motivated to participate in the practice by strong feelings of guilt and naive belief in the 'dark superstition' of *tatari*, which threatens that the spirits of their dead children can come back to harm them or their families. What is left out, along with recognition of men who participate in the practice, is any examination of the variety of motivations that bring people to *mizuko kuyō* and any acknowledgment of participants' actions as considered and knowing, as active attempts to deal with the strong feelings that are tied up with the loss of a child.[20]

The Buddhist clergy we have heard from, on the other hand, appear more concerned with the doctrinal implications of the new practice than with the people who take part in it. Only in the Kyoto priest's story of Saichō's mother do we find recognition of someone trying to address her feelings for dead children, but as a historical archetype, this story, too, keeps us safely distanced from the feelings and experiences of those who find personal reason to participate in *mizuko kuyō*. As we have seen above, clergy strategy has been to establish the practice within the universalized structure of Buddhism, where it would become routine and repeatable, and thus controllable. Here, too, we find the stereotype of Japanese women as passive and unknowing, guilt-ridden and in need of the help of the professional clergy to lead them onto the proper path.

In contemporary Japanese society, the loss of a child, whether through abortion, miscarriage, or any other means, is such a personal and private experience that it is difficult for anyone outside those immediately involved to obtain personal accounts of that experience; perhaps this is one reason the media and clergy constructions of *mizuko kuyō* have gone virtually unchallenged in the public forum. Especially in the case of miscarriage, when in Japan there may be some question of the mother's responsibility for the loss, and of abortion, which always raises the issue of responsibility, few if any of those involved are willing to discuss their thoughts openly. Yet it is precisely the thoughts of lay practitioners of *mizuko kuyō* that we need in order to uncover the complexity of the practice that has been flattened in the public constructions we have examined so far.

The material in this section is based primarily on written responses to a questionnaire composed by my collaborator and myself and made available to *mizuko kuyō* participants at a wide array of religious sites in Japan during 1987. The aim of the questionnaire was not to collect statistical data, but to elicit individual statements regarding *mizuko kuyō* and respondents' personal experience of it that would help us to understand the practice from the participants' point of view.[21] I do not present this material here with any claim of its being a more valid view than those we have examined above, however, for we must recognize lay people's *mizuko kuyō* as the same order of construction as those others. Rather, we will use these individual glimpses to interrogate the public images and to explore the tactical uses made of them by lay practitioners.

Respondents to the questionnaire described their feelings about their loss of a child in many different ways. They found that loss regrettable (*nasakenai* and *kuyashii*), unavoidable (*yamu naku*), and the result of selfishness on their part (*watashi no mikatte*), all terms from ordinary language which they might have used about any unfortunate event in their lives for which they felt some responsibility. While some specified that they were speaking of either an abortion or a miscarriage and a few sought to distinguish a different moral responsibility in the case of abortion, others did not. Most wrote of the relief they experienced after doing *mizuko kuyō* and of their intention of continuing it as long as they live. Indeed, one of the interesting aspects of the practice as it has become formalized in Japan over the last twenty years is the lack of any distinction in the ritual itself in relation to how the children being offered *kuyō* were lost: all *mizuko* are treated the same. For the most part, participants are aware of the circumstances which led to the death of the child they are commissioning the service for, but most clergy who perform the service and offer individual counselling do not ask and say they do not want to know those circumstances. Thus although the media has continued to sensationalize the practice as aimed specifically at women who have had abortions and some Buddhist clergy have rejected it for the same reason, it is clear from participants as well as from the structure of the practice that it is construed to be appropriate for anyone who has lost a child in any manner.

It is the sense of responsibility for having done something regrettable, I think, that is simplified and stereotyped as guilt in the public image of the practice. This is not to deny that guilt is a part of what many participants feel concerning the fact that they 'have' a *mizuko*. Indeed, a number of respondents expressed this feeling of guilt quite strongly: 'As I look at it now, I am tormented by the crime of having killed an individual life'. Yet the very naturalness of this feeling is brought into question by other statements on the questionnaire. 'These children, while they had tiny lives, were consigned from darkness into darkness by the selfishness of adults when in reality they should have been growing up vigorously ...' This common image from both the promotional and the media constructions of the practice appears verbatim in a number of responses. While it serves to define the basis for feelings of guilt (mainly in the case of abortion), it is also an effective way of eliciting those feelings.

Despite the successful deployment of this image of guilt by those interested in expanding the *mizuko kuyō* market and by elements of the media interested in sensationalizing it (which amounts to the same thing), the sense of responsibility that participants acknowledge extends beyond the single event of the loss of the child to the circumstances which brought that event about. Many respondents expressed the grief they felt at the unavoidability of aborting a child:

> We conceived a child, and as a result of talking it over with my boyfriend, I understood the difficulties in the future if I gave birth. Swallowing my tears, I aborted the child ... (age 20)

> I got pregnant right after the birth of my first child. Since I had no way to manage and had not yet recovered from the birth, I had no choice but to abort ... (age 57)

The source of the strong emotion in these and many other statements like them is the authors' perception that they were in a situation where there was no choice other than abortion. If there was a choice, it was earlier, when something could have been done to prevent the conception of a child:

> I had one abortion before I was married. After I married, I got pregnant right after my second child was born and had an abortion for economic reasons. I wanted to have both of those children, but in each case it was a situation in which I absolutely had to get an abortion ... I am a nurse, and I berate myself now wondering how this could have happened. Knowing very well what to do [to prevent it], I have created two *mizuko*...

Yet in Japan reproductive control is in the hands of men on almost every level—sexually, as women are socialized to accept the wishes of their male partners; socially, in that women are brought up to see mothering as their main role; medically, in the overwhelmingly male control over all means of contraception (the condom is widely publicized as the most effective means of birth control, which literally puts the decision to use it in the hands of the man); legally, in the male-controlled medical and governmental worlds which legislate (both publicly and in private) the conditions for abortion. In this context, it is not difficult to understand a woman's feeling of being caught in a situation in which the only seeming solution is the often anguishing one to have an abortion. Very few of our respondents suggested that, given the chance to re-live their decision to have an abortion, they would give birth to the child instead. Rather, they expressed regret that they had conceived a child in the first place, hoped never to repeat that irresponsibility again (several wrote that the experience was a call for self-reflection, *hansei*), and thought it only right that they do something for the absent child.

Miscarriage, stillbirth, and child loss by more 'natural' causes are depicted by some in a similar way:

> I lost three children by miscarriage and gave birth to one still-born child. I have been doing *kuyō* in my own way for the still-born child, but I felt somewhere in my heart that the three miscarriages were not my fault (*tsumi*)[22] because they left be-fore coming into this world. But I came to think that that wasn't so. Since each [miscarried] child came into my belly with a life that was supposed to enter into this world, after all I think they are my fault (*tsumi*), too. Now I'm simply filled with feelings of repentance for the sad thing I did [in not giving birth to them]. (age 59)

Here the sense of responsibility is more diffuse than in the case of abortion. The woman isn't sure whether to think of her miscarried children as her responsibility or not, but perhaps influenced by pro-motional literature or advertising for *mizuko kuyō*, she comes to think that they are no different from her stillborn child in their rela-tionship to her. Other women who had had miscarriages stated they were always concerned to do something for the welfare of those children. In 1987 I interviewed an elderly woman who was attend-ing the formal dedication of four small gilded *Mizuko* Jizō statues for her miscarried children at a rural Zen temple in Shiga Prefec-ture. Her miscarriages had come as she worked in the fields during the years after World War II. She saw the formal repertoire of *mi-zuko kuyō* as a way of 'doing something' for her dead children at long last—even though she had offered a cup of water for them every day at her family's home altar (*butsudan*), to her mind that informal, personal gesture was not sufficient.

Herein, I think, lies the heart of *mizuko kuyō*. It provides a formal, public, ritualized way to acknowledge the existence of a child—both its potential existence in this world as a result of its conception and its continuing existence somewhere else after death, to (re)establish a relationship with it, and to care for it wherever it may be. In this construction, although the child might be absent from this world, it nevertheless remains a child to its parents and a sibling to its living brothers and sisters. This acknowledgment of the child's existence is implicit in the way many respondents expressed their reason for doing *mizuko kuyō*: I want to apologize to it (*ayamaritai*); I feel sorry for it (*kawaisō*); I'd like it to forgive me (*yurushite moraitai*); I want it to be reborn a Buddha (*jōbutsu shite moraitai*); I'm sorry (*sumanai* and *mōshiwake nai*, both expressions commonly used as a direct form of apology as well as to describe something inexcusable); the situation calls for recompense (*tsugunai*) or amends *(wabi)* to be made.

In the Japanese religious context of which Buddhism makes up one element, those who have died are believed to be reborn into another realm after a period of time for determining which of the six Buddhist realms of existence they will proceed to next; standard funeral practice defines this period to be forty-nine days. But because young and unborn children who had died were not included in standard funeral practice historically, their movement after death is only now, with the emergence of *mizuko kuyō*, being charted.

The most ubiquitous image of their situation depicts them stranded on the barren, rocky shore of the Sai River, which serves as the boundary between the Buddhist hells and other realms of existence. There they have nothing to do but pile stones into small towers (a common practice in Japan for earning karmic merit) and bemoan their separation from their parents. When demons cross the river from the hells and begin to harass them, the bodhisattva Jizō appears as protector.[23] It is not clear how long this displacement out of the standard route to rebirth lasts for *mizuko*, but the implication is that they are stuck in this in-between existence on the river bank. The image suggests that they are unhappy and uncomfortable, perhaps even in danger, in this place, and that they have no substantive way to help themselves. Here, once again, is an image that invites people to feel that they should do something for their *mizuko*.

Now, through the practice of *mizuko kuyō*, parents are able to do something constructive to help their *mizuko*. Attendance at or commissioning of a *mizuko* service is an opportunity for parents to accrue karmic merit on behalf of their dead children. Offerings of religious images, food, clothing and toys can be made to both the child and a deity, to bring comfort to the former and to enlist the protective aid of the latter.[24] And money may be paid to the religious site to ensure continuing ritual care. Parents or other relatives of the *mizuko* do this with feelings of repentance (*zange*) and responsibility or guilt (*tsumi no ishiki* and *zaiakkan*) which, when coupled with the new relationship the practice enables them to establish with their absent child, has led many respondents to declare that they would not forget their absent child or children. Thus although we might view lay people's continuing participation in *mizuko kuyō* as the result of coercion or manipulation, I think we must also see that participation as an act of silent resistance and subversion which turns the practice toward their own lives and motives: we will take part in this practice, as you suggest we should, but we will do so for the sake of our dead children, whom we will not forget, for we have made them a part of our lives once again.

For many women who have lost children through abortion or other means, the practice seems to resonate deeply with their feelings of loss and of responsibility. The elderly woman with three miscarriages and a stillborn child whom we met earlier wrote:

> I went on the Saikoku pilgrimage of 33 temples. *Mizuko* Jizō was being worshipped at every one of the temples. Until then, in my heart I had never forgotten those children, and I had always felt deeply that I should do *kuyō* in some form for them. (age 59)

A twenty-five-year-old woman expressed similar feelings about her aborted child in poetic form:

There was someone I loved I believed.
Forgive me ... we were too young.
I've lost something important, seen a destiny I should have
known.
I can't forgive myself
What, in the end, can I do?
Lots of crying, tired, thinking
To give form to *kuyō* for that lost life
all I can do
is move my feet toward *mizuko kuyō*.

We cannot, of course, separate these women's own feelings from
whatever outside influence they may have felt in an atmosphere in
1987 which encouraged women to admit their responsibility for not
giving birth to and raising all their children. We can, however, acknowledge their participation in *mizuko kuyō* as a choice that made
sense to them at the centre of contradictory messages from society.
Socialized to believe that to be a woman is to be a mother and that
as mothers they are responsible for their children's well-being, they
have at the same time been socialized to accept the sexual advances
of their men without real resistance and encouraged to assume responsibility for resulting pregnancies after the fact. For some, this
tension between the need to mother and the need to make hard
choices for the benefit of their own lives and the lives of their family is at least partially addressed by *mizuko kuyō*: it provides a way
for women to mother their *mizuko* that is conceptually similar to
the way they care for their living children.

In the case of a woman who has lost a child, her participation
in *mizuko kuyō* acts as an acknowledgment that there was (by virtue of its conception), would have been (in that a child conceived is
the seed of a child born), and still is a child, even though that child
is not now present in the mundane sense of the word. Indeed, one
of the most common explanations given for the failure, until now,
of women to care for that absent child, wherever it may be, is its
lack of a tangible form in this world; 'out of sight, out of mind' is
the ruling paradigm here. To address this problem, the giving of a
name (either a Buddhist 'dharma name' or, less commonly, a regular 'Keiko' or 'Tarō' name) or a form (such as Jizō or the bodhisattva Kannon) to the child is an almost universal element of *mizuko*

kuyō. With this concrete artifact, the child's existence becomes visible and real.

And yet, for whom is the child's existence now made real? I think we must question the assumption that a woman's relationship with her child is based on its visible presence. While this may be the case for those around the woman-mother, whose swelling belly or newborn baby provide visual cues for our construction of her motherhood, for the woman herself the relationship begins much earlier, and without visual aid. The physiological fact of pregnancy together with the social construction of motherhood within which the woman was raised combine to place her into an imaginary (in the psychoanalytical sense) relationship with her child from the moment she knows she is pregnant, as this woman describes:

> I had a miscarriage when I was two months pregnant. I was in the hospital for a week before, but it was no use. The doctor said, 'There's no special cause for a miscarriage this early. The fetus probably wasn't strong enough'. But that fetus was my child from the day it was conceived in my body ... So even though it was never born into this world, even though it has no form, it is still a member of my family. I did *kuyō* because that fetus's life was lost. I have the feeling that through my doing *kuyō*, that fetus will receive life sometime and give its first cry after birth somewhere ... (age 27)

For some Japanese women, that relationship is not sustained beyond the fact of the pregnancy, and the lure of *mizuko kuyō* holds no allure at all, despite the strength of the social linking of womanhood with motherhood in Japan:

> In my case, I became very depressed emotionally [after my abortion], but it was not a simple feeling of having done something wrong *(zaiakkan)*. I just felt strongly that I wanted to say, 'I'm sorry' to my child. But with the passing of time (about a week?), I recovered completely and was back on my feet.[25] (age 40)

Indeed, it is undoubtedly the case that the majority of Japanese women who have had abortions do not participate in *mizuko kuyō*. There are no statistics available on the number of people who do *mizuko kuyō* in Japan each year, and because of the personal nature of the issue it will probably be impossible to obtain anything more than a loose estimate based on those who identify themselves at particular sites. But I believe it is safe to say that the number of living Japanese women who have lost children through abortion or other means far exceeds the admittedly large number who participate in the practice. But that does not change the fact that many women do participate and that the practice takes on a variety of meanings for them.

For some women, the practice is simply something to do because it should be done, as in these two responses from the questionnaire:

> Just before my first son's wedding, his bride came down with a high fever, and other inconvenient things happened. Because of this, I asked someone to look into the situation and was told that I had better do *mizuko kuyō*. I was surprised, but I went to [a temple] and had it done. Since then, everything has been going well. (age 62)

> Nothing in particular happened [to induce me to do *mizuko kuyō*]. I do it simply because everyone else does. Nothing bad has happened, and neither has anything good. I do it because I'm afraid I'll be talked about if I don't ... (age 63)

It appears that the public *mizuko* rhetoric has been successful in convincing these women to take part in the practice, although their ambivalence is clear. Each does *mizuko kuyō* for her own sake, not for the sake of her absent child, and neither thinks in terms of an ongoing relationship with that child. In addition, neither sees herself becoming a better Buddhist through her participation. Then why do it? For both women, *mizuko kuyō* seems to provide a way of controlling their lives, in the face of unforeseen and unfortunate occurrences on the one hand and of social gossip on the other. The second woman almost certainly feels manipulated into performing *mizuko kuyō*; indeed, she writes later that she suspects that *mizuko kuyō* is done at temples according to 'mood' rather than from the heart. The first woman is more accepting of the practice, presumably because she feels it has helped make her situation (in this case, the situation of her son) more stable. Yet she, too, does not seem to be terribly invested in the practice. Her statement at the end of the questionnaire that 'I will continue doing *kuyō* for as long as I live' has the same unengaged ring to it as her statement that she began *kuyō* because someone told her to do it.

Many respondents wrote very differently of their involvement in *mizuko kuyō*, however. Some simply said they did *mizuko kuyō* because they could not forget, leaving the subject of their memory unspoken: there are bad feelings in my heart (*kokoro ni wadaka-mari ga aru*); it remains in my heart (*kokoro ni nokoru*); there's something that always pulls at my heart (*itsumo kokoro ni hik-kakaru mono ga ari*). Others were more explicit:

> When my children were all grown and on their own, I was re-lieved, but the child I miscarried when I was young appeared before my eyes, and I wanted to do *kuyō* for it ... (age 62)

> It was about four months after the abortion [that I first did *kuyō*]. I had really wanted to do *kuyō* as soon as I could, so now I feel somewhat relieved. Everyday I feel that I did something terrible to my child, and I've never forgotten my child once. The only thing I can do for it now is *kuyō* ... (age 20)

> I'll continue to do *kuyō* because I'm always wondering what it would be like if that child were alive. (age 45)

These are people who cannot forget their lost children or the expe-rience that led to their loss, and for whom *mizuko kuyō* provides the only way they can see to constructively address both the child's perceived situation and their own feelings. For these lay people the practice is a way to 'do something' for their dead children that could not be accomplished simply by remembering them infor-mally at home. For them, the prayers, images, incense and other of-ferings made as part of the formalized practice become powerful through the relationship that is established between lay participant, child and deity as mediated by the Buddhist clergy and symbolic system. Many, perhaps most, participants are aware of the negative images of *mizuko kuyō* that we have reviewed above, but they do not seem to connect that criticism with their own practice; the intent of the clergy, whether it be greed or sectarian interest, is not central to the *mizuko* relationship, as one woman observes:

> Recently one hears talk of temples that do *mizuko kuyō* for purposes of making money, but setting that aside, I think the feeling that one wants to do *kuyō* is a good thing.   (age 30)

What is important is that the formal practice of *mizuko kuyō* gives lay people a way to care for absent children, although it is not only parents who take part for the sake of their own children. Mothers do *kuyō* for their grown children's *mizuko*; women participate for the sake of their mothers' or sisters' or grandmothers' unmemorialized *mizuko*; individuals like the following thirty-year-old man do *kuyō* for their *mizuko* siblings:

> I've just turned thirty recently, and the other day I heard for the first time that I have siblings who did not receive life in this world and became *mizuko*. I think that if they had been born, I probably wouldn't have had my life, and in this, my thirtieth year, I did *mizuko kuyō* for them for the first time.

And most say they will continue doing *kuyō* at least once a year (on the anniversary of the death; on a Buddhist festival day) for the rest of their lives. That so many would say this demonstrates the weight of the responsibility they feel, although we cannot know whether these intentions will be carried out. Many responses shared the sense of relief (*hotto shita kimochi*) or peace of mind (*anshin shita* and *kimochi ga ochitsukimashita*) that people felt after doing *mizuko kuyō*. But others show clearly that their authors do not consider the practice to fix anything other than their own need to do something:

> I don't in the least think that everything will be forgiven by my doing *mizuko kuyō* now, but that's all there is to do. At least it's a start.   (age 44)

> I don't think I'll be forgiven for what I've done, but I do think I've been able to express my prayer for the baby to 'Please be at

peace' and my hope that it will 'Please be reborn soon'.   (age 22)

Participants and the dead children they are remembering through *mizuko kuyō* are not the only ones to benefit from the practice, however. Many respondents wrote that they were doing *kuyō* for the sake of their living children:

> Having done *kuyō* will not take the obstruction from my heart, but I will continue in order to protect the growth of my two older sons.   (age 35)

> If I left things as they were, I wondered if my child would be wandering around in that world, and I wondered if things wouldn't begin to go badly for those in this world. That's why I did *mizuko kuyō*.

> That kind of *kuyō* is for my sake and for my family's sake. I think it's necessary and very important so that life everyday will be fun and everyone will stay healthy and happy.   (age 23)

These responses, and others like them, reflect several related understandings of the relationship between the world after death and this one. On the one hand, *mizuko* in 'that world' may have some kind of malevolent influence on those related to them who are still living in this world. *Mizuko* may cause things to go badly in general (several respondents wrote that they had led very unlucky lives), or they may cause specific problems such as illness for specific individuals. A particular target for such interventions from 'that world' are the living siblings of *mizuko*. These children receive the constant attention of their parents and relatives, while *mizuko* have tended to be left out of the circle of family attention. This is the belief in *tatari*, reprisal from the spirit world, that spiritualists teach, the media hawks, and Buddhist clergy deplore. Several respondents gave very specific examples of ways in which they saw their *mizuko* asking for attention by intruding on their lives. In this context, the practice of *mizuko kuyō* becomes a redressive action by means of which practitioners can placate their *mizuko* and thereby alleviate the problems they have caused.

The quotations above suggest another construction of this relationship, however. If *mizuko* are taken to be members of the family, then they may be expected to take part in the family in a useful way, just as any living child would. From their vantage point in 'that world', they can influence the lives of their family for the better, becoming, in effect, private protective deities, and several respondents wrote of *mizuko kuyō* as a way to enlist the protective services of their *mizuko* in assuring the health and success of other family members. In particular, the practice offers mothers new aid in raising their living children, and thus it becomes multivalent: it helps women mother all their children, both living and dead.

It should be clear from our treatment of lay people's constructions of *mizuko kuyō* above that this new Japanese practice is much more complex than either the promotional and media or the Buddhist clergy images allow. For the women we have heard, *mizuko kuyō* serves several functions. It provides a formalized public mechanism for acknowledging the existence of a child that may never have been formally recognized and for establishing a continuing relationship with that child in 'that world' after death. The *mizuko*, in effect, is reclaimed as part of the family and as such is given much the same kind of attention that those other absent members of the family, the ancestors, are given in Japan. This reclamation of absent children in turn helps some women reclaim their place as mothers and provides a means for them to both care for and mourn the absence of their children—an absence which, although seen to be unavoidable in many cases (miscarriage, accident or abortion under social or family pressure, for example), was not necessarily a felicitous event for the woman involved.

Constructed in this way, the practice of *mizuko kuyō* becomes a silent way of bringing to the foreground of public awareness some of the underlying tensions in women's lives in Japan: the loneliness of being held responsible for almost single-handedly producing and raising children properly; the frustration of being in the middle of a sexual politics in which their sexuality is held ransom to the needs of their men and the state; the anguish of losing a child and of having few, if any, public ways of dealing with that loss. Integral as they are to the fabric of Japanese women's lives, such issues remain largely unspeakable as personal issues in Japan today despite (or perhaps because of) the beginnings of some academic discussion by Japanese feminists in recent years. Indeed, I would suggest that it is the unspeakable nature of these issues which lies behind the flattened, over-simplified images of the practice that we have seen coming from media and clergy. To give credence to the lay constructions we have explored above would be to open a space for discourse; instead, we have loud, dismissive public images constructed almost with the force of Freudian denial.

I think we must see *mizuko kuyō* as a way for women to speak on those issues—not in so many words, but physically, to act out their personal sense of loss and responsibility and frustration from where they are, without threat of disruption to their lives. Buddhism provides the means for doing this, a powerful symbolic system, a rich repertoire of ritual, both of which are mediated by a cadre of experts, and a space (the physical space of its sites around Japan; the conceptual space opened by its symbols and ritual) in which to speak safely yet with effect.

Notes

[1]   In the Japanese Buddhist context, life is believed to begin at conception. The word *mizuko* is used in Japan today to refer to any life that was or would have been a child, regardless of how or at what stage that life was attenuated. For this reason I translate *mizuko* as child or children.

[2]   Although men do participate in *mizuko kuyō*, often with their female partner, the overwhelming majority of participants is female. This paper focuses primarily on women in relation to the practice for that reason and because little work has yet been done on participant men's place in the phenomenon of *mizuko kuyō*.

[3]   The conditions for legal performance of abortion appear in Article 14 of the Eugenics Protection Law and include pregnancies which threaten the life of the mother, which result from rape or incest, in families with hereditary mental illness or leprosy, and in cases where the birth of the child would threaten the well-being of the mother or the child itself. This last stipulation has been nicknamed the 'economic clause'. For the entire text of the Eugenics Protection Law, see the appendix to Nihon Kazoku Keikaku

Renmei, ed., *Kanashimi o sabakemasuka—chūzetsu kinshi e no hanmon* (Tokyo: Ningen no Kagakusha, 1983).

⁴   On government regulation of religion in Tokugawa, see Kashiwahara Yūsen, *Kinsei shomin bukkyō no kenkyū* (Kyoto: Hōzōkan, 1971), 189; *hatto* 42 (1613) in Idachi Akiyoshi, *Nihon shūkyō seido shiryō ruijukō* (Kyoto: Rinsen Shoten, 1974). On funerals in Tokugawa, see Haga Noboru, *Sōshiki no rekishi* (Tokyo: Yūzankaku Shuppan, 1991), pp. 131-133. On contemporary funerals, see Nakamaki Hirochika, 'Continuity and Change: Funeral Customs in Modern Japan' in *Japanese Journal of Religious Studies* 13/2-3 (1986): 180 and 188. On 'funeral Buddhism', see Reader, *Religion in Contemporary Japan* (Honolulu: University of Hawaii Press, 1994).

⁵   'Pre-modern' designates a historical period, from the beginning of the seventeenth to the middle of the nineteenth centuries. Ochiai Emiko, 'Taiji wa dare no mono na no ka', in *Gendai shisō* 18:6 (1990), 81-2 and 84-85.

⁶   Abortion figures, including a word about unreported abortions, are from *Onna: Ninshin chūzetsu*, Volume 9 of *Shirīzu: Ima o Ikiru* (Tokyo: Yukkusō, 1984), p.34. On the connection between *mizuko* and war dead, see this author's 'Mizuko kuyō: the reproduction of the dead in contemporary Japan' in *Religion in Japan: Arrows to heaven and earth*, edited by P.F. Kornicki and I. J. McMullen (Cambridge: Cambridge University Press, 1996), pp. 250-266. For a Japanese example of including children 'lost in the war' in *mizuko* practice, see 'Mizuko Jizō būmu' in *Shūkan Bunshun* (June 26, 1980).

⁷   The most-often publicized site is Shiunzan Jizōji, located in Chichibu, to the west of Tokyo. This independent temple was opened in 1972 for the sole purpose of performing *mizuko kuyō* for dead—mainly aborted—children. Although almost all of Jizōji's ritual elements and decorative trappings are borrowed from Buddhism, it is not affiliated with Buddhist institutions in any way. *Mizuko kuyō* is also performed by many new religious groups and at a few Shinto shrines. Christian clergy in Japan are sometimes asked to perform a *mizuko* service by Japanese Christians.

⁸   The obvious focus here is on children 'killed' by induced abortion. Yet even spontaneous abortion tends to be blamed on the

mother in Japan: she should have taken better care of herself and her pregnancy. The death of an older child by accident or illness is also easily construed as the mother's fault, for it is her job to successfully raise her children to adulthood.

[9]   'Kiga demo nai no ni naze ka ima: Mizuko Jizō būmu', in *Shūkan Bunshun* (June 26, 1980): n.p.

[10]   'Hodō tokushū: Mizuko būmu' *TBS* (March 20, 1983).

[11]   'Temples in Japan Capitalize on Abortion' in *Mainichi Daily News* (July 4, 1985).

[12]   'Shinshū no tachiba kara mita "mizuko" mondai' in Nyonin Ōjō, ed. *Kyōgaku Honbu* (Kyoto: Honganji Shuppanbu, 1988), pp. 71-3. The Dharma is the teachings of the Buddha; the *Sangha* is the community of clergy.

[13]   'Shinshū no tachiba', pp. 77-82.

[14]   This author conducted interviews with clergy in Japan in 1986-88 as part of a major research project on *mizuko kuyō*. Follow-up interviews were done in 1992-93.

[15]   Takahashi Ryōwa, *Myōkō-sama* (Kyoto: Tankyūsha, 1982).

[16]   Personal interview with Takahashi Ryōwa, March 16, 1984, Kyoto, Japan.

[17]   Hobsbawm, Eric and Terence Ranger, eds., *The Invention of Tradition* (Cambridge: Cambridge University Press, 1984). See especially the Introduction.

[18]   We should note here that new religious groups that do *mizuko kuyō* invent its history within their own framework.

[19]   'Shinshū no tachiba', 88.

[20]   For further discussion of the issue of women's agency and *mizuko kuyō*, see this author's article 'Women's Responses to Child Loss in Japan: The Case of Mizuko Kuyō' in *Journal for Feminist Studies in Religion* 11:2 (Fall 1995): 67-93.

[21]   The questionnaire consisted of four write-in questions: 1) Regardless of whether you have any personal experience or not, what do you think about *mizuko kuyō*? 2) Please tell us, in as much detail as possible, what led you to do *mizuko kuyō*. 3) What did you do for *mizuko kuyō*? Please be specific (for example: went to a temple and had a service done; offered a candle; purchased a paper amulet). 4) Please tell us your feelings after doing *kuyō*. Will you continue to do it? Although the responses were anonymous, the

questionnaires were coded so we could identify the site from which each originated. For this paper, I am using only responses received from Buddhist temples. I have included the age of the respondent where it is known.

[22]   The Japanese word *tsumi* is commonly translated as crime or sin, and thus also as guilt. While those renderings are apt in certain contexts (legal or theological), I think that the broader sense of 'responsibility' is more correct here.

[23]   This image comes from a genre of (probably) seventeenth-century hymn known as 'Sai no Kawahara Jizō Wasan'. No English translation exists as far as I know. For several early versions in Japanese, see Manabe Kosai, *Jizō bosatsu no kenkyū* (Kyoto: Sanmitsudō Shoten, 1975), 198-228.

[24]   Jizō (Skr: Kṣitagarbha) is the most common, but by no means the only, Buddhist figure associated with protecting *mizuko*. The bodhisattva Kannon (Skr: Avalokiteśvara) and the more minor figure of Kishibōjin (Skr: Hariti) also appear in this role. More local figures, such as Saichō's mother, may also be used.

[25]   A slightly different set of questionnaires was mailed with a monthly newsletter to members of a large feminist organization based in Kyoto. This quotation is from one of the feminist replies.

7

Abortion in Korea

Frank Tedesco

Introduction

This study is a first exploration of the subject of abortion and Buddhism in contemporary South Korea.[1] Abortion in Korea has been studied as a factor in family planning policy and population control,[2] as a legal matter[3] and as an issue of sexuality and gender,[4] but minimal attention has been given to the religious perspective and almost none to Buddhism, despite the fact that Buddhists form the majority of the religious population in the country.[5]

Buddhists themselves may be partially responsible for this lack of attention regarding the abortion issue in Korea. They have not been vocal in the sporadic public debates about the issue. No Buddhist figure has become nationally prominent for a stance on abortion. The great majority of the population, Buddhist and non-Buddhist alike, does not associate Buddhism with any clear view or sentiment on the issue. There is, however, growing concern about the prevalence of abortion in the Korean media,[6] and a few Buddhist clergy and lay leaders have responded to this complex issue in books, periodicals and the Buddhist press. These publications have a rather limited readership, but the appearance of this material nevertheless reflects the Buddhist community's turn to social engagement in Korean public life in recent years, however minimal, in proportion to its size in Korea. Buddhist social welfare activities,[7] a Buddhist environmental movement,[8] the promotion of cremation of the dead as opposed to traditional Confucian burial

practice,[9] and concern for foreign workers' rights,[10] are among the
issues which demonstrate the changing character of Korean Buddhism in the nineties. The 1994 reform movement within the
Chogye Order administration has brought in a progressive, elected
sangha leadership which has spearheaded the order's influence in
the public domain.[11]

'Socially engaged' activities are not unanimously endorsed by
all members of the clergy, however. There are still many who as-
sert that the pursuit of enlightenment through austere spiritual practice (mainly meditation and study) is job enough for the ordained
clergy. These conservatives warn that celibate renunciates should
not lose sight of their purpose by diluting their energies in the cha-
otic affairs of the day before they have realized their goal of
Buddhahood. 'First attain Buddhahood, then save all sentient beings', is often heard. The issue of abortion, too, pertains to sex and
physical desire, an area of life celibates have sworn to forgo (and
perhaps ought not be reminded of!). They bolster their argument
with references to the lives of exemplary monks of the past. Many
lay people, too, believe that the only place for monks is in the
mountains. They are irked to see grey-robed clergy driving expensive sedans and living in the lap of luxury, fully compromised by
their lay constituency and feeding off them. For the purists, all
worldly involvements, even helping others in social service,
amount to the same thing: distraction from the path. They resist
calls to social action.[12] In response, some younger educated Buddhists and activists initiated a *minjung pulgyo* or 'peoples' Buddhism' movement in the 1980s—in some ways similar to the
liberation theology movement of Latin America—in order to deal
with the problems of Korea's modernization from a Buddhist value
system.[13] While only a very small movement, its ideas have been
influential among leaders of reform in the mid-90s.

Missionary dharma teaching centres (*p'ogyodang*) have multi-
plied rapidly in tandem with the rural population's mass migration
to urban centres in the last ten years. Many cities, too, like Seoul
have expanded into the surrounding countryside and have encom-
passed the Buddhist temples long sequestered within its hills. Keep
in mind that the urban population of Korea jumped from 28 percent
in 1960 to nearly 75 percent in 1990! More frequent contact with
lay people has inevitably brought their concerns to the fore, and

since the majority of regular visitors and supporters of the temples
are women, it is inevitable that women's issues and family concerns become paramount. Memorial services for family ancestors,
prayers for children's success in highly-competitive university entrance exams, funeral ceremonies,[14] healing rites,[15] lay group guidance and other activities now occupy the days of urban clergy who
once kept a strenuous monastic routine much of the year.[16] In recent years, too, personal concern for aborted babies and the performance of ceremonies for them has begun to be mentioned
publicly as women reflect more openly on the vicissitudes of their
lives. While many women in Korea allege indifference to the lives
of aborted fetuses, it is still a subject of deep consideration and
shame for many religious women in the country. Korean women
are nowhere nearly as outspoken about their bodies and reproductive functions as women in other countries, however. While married women with children have ample opportunities to express their
private concerns and reservations among their peers in many formal and informal social gatherings and organizations, single
women are especially isolated and fearful of tarnishing their vir-
ginal image prior to, and even after, marriage.[17] The rate of abortion has been accelerating steeply among single women in the last
five years however, and so, we may presume, their questions and
anxieties about their decision and possible religious resolutions.

Buddhism in Korean Studies

Although Buddhism is the largest religion in contemporary Korea[18]
and has been an integral part of Korean history and culture for over
1,600 years, it has been rather neglected by scholars of religion and
the social sciences. Specialists in Buddhism within Korean studies
are very few, and their work tends to focus on the elite monastic
tradition and its scriptures. The general literature on Korea in English provides little space for modern Buddhism and almost nothing
on contemporary popular practices, except for Buddha's birthday
lantern parade and tourist information.[19] The daily life of Buddhists
in lay society has gone unrecorded. That temple attendance on a
regular basis has been rising continuously; that Buddhist youth
groups and activities including social action organizations are becoming more prominent; that many urban temples and mountain

monasteries have been recently renovated or are being practically
rebuilt;[20] that the outcome of recent nationwide elections for local
officials seems to have been swayed by Buddhist voters' displeas-
ure with the ruling party's heavy handed tactics with an internal
Chogye Order matter;[21] that a picture of the chief executive of the
Chogye Order, Ven. Song Wolju, is now frequently found among
those leaders of social reform movements and other national events
in the major newspapers and news magazines, are obvious indica-
tions that Buddhism is alive and well, and a real force in the lives
of contemporary Koreans. These factors suggest it should be moni-
tored seriously by scholars and social commentators both inside
and outside of Asia.

Why, then, has the social phenomenon of Buddhism been over-
looked by the majority of scholars of Korea? This neglect seems to
reflect the peninsula's tumultuous past caught between major political powers, the tensions of national division and geopolitical
strategy, the South's embrace of aggressive capitalist values and
affluent Western lifestyles, and the government's breakneck course
of accelerated, economic development. Few can deny that the great
social and material benefits of Christian affiliation associated with
the very generous assistance of Western missionary organizations
have been distractions which have deflected attention from Korea's
Buddhist heritage.

A Brief Outline of Buddhism in Korea

Let us very briefly outline the history of Buddhism in Korea to
help place it in the life of contemporary Korean culture for the average reader unfamiliar with the subject. The Chogye Order alone
controls over 1,700 temples throughout the Korean mountains and
cities, and there are many smaller temples and some large monasteries possessed by other orders. It is generally accepted that Buddhism entered Korea in the late fourth century CE when monk
Sundo arrived under orders from the king of Former Chin of
China. He brought gifts of Buddha statues and Mahāyāna scriptures to the king of Koguryŏ and can be said to be one among
many Buddhist missionaries from China to introduce Sinitic culture and thought to the Korean elite. Buddhism was soon adopted

by the aristocracy, and Chinese style temple structures and monastic organizations were established throughout the country under royal patronage. The religion was promoted from above rather than arising from the lower classes of the population, but accommodations were made to indigenous beliefs and practices as Buddhism has done in other areas where it has spread. Native Korean shamanism, in fact, borrowed much from Buddhism to add to its prestige and acceptability. Many temples, too, have small shrine buildings off to the side and out of the way of the main dharma halls which are dedicated to the Korean Mountain God (Sanshin) and a Chinese Taoist Hermit figure (Toksŏng) who remain popular with women believers.

Buddhism became the dominant cultural force and social authority on the peninsula during the Unified Shilla (668-935) and Koryŏ (937-1392) periods. Most of the largest temples which still exist in Korea were originally erected in these periods, and most of the finest works of Korean Buddhist art were produced in these times. The landholdings of the temples were enormous and their influence permeated all levels of society. Buddhism was the state religion and it was believed that the powers of the Buddhas and bodhisattvas protected the people from incursions from enemies and natural catastrophes. Temple reserves and armies of serfs were utilized in public works projects and also came to the assistance of the masses in periods of misfortune and emergency. It is claimed that 'the financial power of the monasteries was so immense that it severely strained the fabric of the Koryŏ economy, contributing to the demise of that kingdom and the rise of the Chosŏn.'[22]

Buddhism lost its pre-eminent authority at the beginning of the Chosŏn (Yi dynasty) (1392-1910) and all social and political influence by its end. The pervasive 'Confucianization' of Korea from the middle of the Yi did much to undermine the Buddhist heritage of Shilla and Koryŏ in the social and institutional lives of the Korean people, but it could not eradicate its impact on the religious worldview of the majority—the women and the illiterate commoners.[23] These people helped support a small and more or less elite *sangha* of monks and nuns who practised and studied in mountain temples far from the urban centres from which they were banished. Centuries of ostracism and persecution by Confucian scholars and administrators during the Yi reduced the once influential Korean

sangha to total ineffectiveness in worldly affairs, and have left it
with a negative image which persists in the minds of many Koreans
today. Confucian ideals, too, infiltrated the minds and culture of
the Buddhist population to the extent that women lost many of the
rights and privileges they enjoyed in the Shilla and Koryŏ periods
and the Confucian patriarchal, son-preferential family (patrilineal
descent group) pattern, became the norm.[24] This remains so today.

With permission to enter the cities for the first time in three
hundred years and open temples there again during Japanese colonial rule (1910-1945), monks and nuns began to reconstitute their
position in Korean society. The *sangha* was put in turmoil, however, by Japanese colonial (Meiji) regulations which favoured a
married Buddhist clergy and subordination to Japanese state ideology. Bitter discord between the celibate and married clergy upset
the *sangha* for years after the Korean War (1950-1953) and did little to prevent a disillusioned lay following from experimenting
with new and different religions offering immediate relief from
their daily sufferings. Recovery from the civil war which levelled
the entire country and caused massive dislocation of refugees was
closely associated with very generous foreign aid from 'Christian'
countries (especially the United States) which presented an extremely favourable image of Christianity in the eyes of the Korean
population. Missionary charitable organizations from both Catholic and Protestant agencies dispensed food for the hungry, medical
care and all sorts of rehabilitation and social support services. Most
importantly, foreign Christian groups set up educational institutions which trained many subsequent national leaders who were
very much awed by, and indebted to, their patrons. These pioneer-
ing missionaries were generally quite critical of traditional Korean
religious beliefs. It is no wonder so many 'modern' Korean citizens know very little about their country's religious roots. These
circumstances may also explain why they so rarely look to Buddhism for guidance or perspective on compelling social and moral
issues.

Abortion Practice in Korea: A Brief Background Review

We know little about abortion practice in early Korean history. We may assume that in Korea, as in traditional, sedentary agricultural economies throughout the world, large families were highly valued as a labour force to share the toil of the fields and paddies. At present, this observer is unaware of any demographic research in Korea which suggests that abortion and/or infanticide was ever practised systematically or widely by any sector of Korean society during any historical period (except the present) in order to selectively limit family size, as is being debated now in Japan regarding the Edo period.[25] Anthropologists, however, have noted that female infanticide was not unknown in the recent past.[26] Out of wedlock conceptions or unwanted pregnancies in marriage would be dispatched with Chinese herbal medications,[27] physical assault and home remedies.[28]

The indigenous folk beliefs of Korea and geomancy are closely associated with fertility. Visits to Buddhist temples to pray for children have long been resorted to by Korean women who have been barren.[29] The birth of sons became especially important in later Yi dynasty times when the society became decidedly more neo-Confucian and male-oriented.[30] Females were subordinated in all areas of life except within the family. A wife had to bear a son to fulfil her most important purpose of providing a first-born male to continue the family line and honour her husband's ancestors. It was her duty; her position was secure only if her first child was a boy. The large patrilineal family was the domestic ideal in the Yi dynasty, the Japanese colonial period (1910-1945) and the baby boom after the Korean War (1950-1953).

Abortion was strictly prohibited during the Japanese occupation of Korea as it was in Japan. Prosecution of induced abortion was sporadic during this period, with penalties inflicted on both women who had the surgery as well as on those who performed the induced abortions illegally.[31] Japanese law, however, did allow the termination of pregnancy if it was due to rape or 'error.'[32]

Korea was the third nation in the world, after Pakistan (1953) and India (1958), to adopt an explicit population control policy in 1961. A national family planning program was established in 1962 as a component of the Park Chung-Hee (Pak Chŏng-hŭi)

government's first Five-Year Economic Development Plan and it
has been an integral part of population control policy in successive
plans to the present. The government was convinced that without a
proper population control policy it could not achieve economic development (per capita income increase and the elimination of poverty) within a short period of time. The general population's
aspiration for a smaller family size emerged along with the government's campaign for family planning.[33]

The government's programme, and the population's compli-
ance, very speedily reduced the average number of children per
family in South Korea. It dropped from nearly six in 1960 to less
than two in 1990. This equates to an average reduction of two persons per family per one generation. The crude birth rate was over
40 per 1,000 in the population in 1960 but fell steadily in the last
thirty years to 16.2 in 1990 and it has reached below replacement
level in the last decade. Besides an increase in the average age of
marriage due to the extension of longer education to women and
more young female participation in the labour market, contraceptive devices were widely diffused and cheaply or freely available in
this period. Incentives for vasectomy and sterilization were announced as well. Women were especially cooperative in the family
planning movement and almost invariably resorted to abortion
when contraception failed. Induced abortion rapidly increased with
the active participation of physicians and their staff and the at-
tenuation of judicial surveillance of the prohibitive Korean Penal
Code.

According to the Korean Penal Code, articles 269 and 270, induced abortion is illegal. The government did not immediately legislate more liberal laws regarding abortion when it began its family
planning campaign. Two attempts were made to legalize induced
abortion with the pressure of Protestant religious groups and politicians in 1966 and 1970 but they were defeated. A Maternal and
Child Health Law, however, was passed in 1973 by the Extraordi-
nary State Council (martial law authority) which set out conditions
in which abortions could be performed. According to the law, a
physician is permitted to perform an abortion, with the consent of
the woman and her spouse, in case of hereditary defect of the fetus
and certain infectious diseases, when the pregnancy results from
rape or incest and when from a medical point of view, the

continuation of pregnancy will be detrimental to the health of the mother. It did not permit abortion on socioeconomic grounds although the government had intended to do so in the earliest preparation phase of the law. It did not do so because of religious protest from Catholics and a few politicians.[34]

The Catholic Korean Bishops' Association protested against the Maternal and Child Health Law of 1973 without success, but the Korean Association of Protestant Churches convened and officially accepted it in 1974. We do not know what Buddhists were thinking at that time as we have not found any record of their position in the literature available. Informants say there was no organized voice, neither from the *sangha* nor from lay groups. The Roman Catholic Church has continued to oppose any further liberalization of regulations pertaining to abortion throughout the past decades. The Protestant churches, which represent a spectrum of opinion on abortion, support legislation cautiously.

Even though the problem of abortion is mainly a women's issue, the majority of Korean women's organizations have remained unresponsive to it according to Sung-bong Hong, a researcher into abortion in Korea in the period.[35] There is really no strong reason for Korean women to protest against the restrictive Penal Code or the stipulations of the Maternal and Child Health Law because lack of enforcement has rendered them meaningless. So permissive is the prevailing public attitude to abortion that more than half of those who responded to a professional abortion survey in Seoul in 1991 did not know anything about laws regulating abortion and less than a quarter who had an abortion knew it was illegal at the time of surgery. And many of those who experienced an abortion in the past did not 'feel sorry or regret.' 49 percent 'felt good to have it done' while 26 percent 'did not have any special feeling about it.'[36]

Unlike the strident and wrenching issue it is in the West, abortion in Korea is uneventful and is usually performed as a matter of course without second thought (except among the very religious) despite its illegality. The operation can be obtained very easily anywhere in the country at most private gynaecological clinics (small hospitals) or at larger institutions. A few personal questions are asked very perfunctorily. When pregnancy is positively determined surgery can be performed hygienically and efficiently at relatively low cost even on the first visit. Since the great majority of abortions do not fall within the legally prescribed categories which qualify the procedure for national health insurance coverage, physicians need not be burdened with much record keeping for taxation purposes—transactions are in cash, tax-free and sought after by thankful clients. This business is very lucrative for ob-gyn specialists, some of whom are quite reliant on abortion clients for a large proportion of their income. Knowledgeable informants opine that private ob-gyn clinics depend on abortions for up to 30 to 80 percent of their income. One commented that his own clinic performed two abortions for every one live birth on average. Would it behove Korean ob-gyn physicians to advocate greater statutory legalization?[37]

Korea has been called an 'abortion paradise' by some social commentators, for reasons set out above. Accurate statistics for induced abortion in the nation are unavailable because of its illegality. A common estimate cited in the press and by social commentators is that as many as a million to a million and a half abortions are performed annually in Korea; those who cite more (2-3 million!) are accused of irresponsible sensationalism based on improper extrapolation from limited facts. We can, however, refer to professionally gathered sampling data compiled by government research institutes to get a clearer picture of abortion behaviour:

> In spite of legal and social constraints, as well as extensive contraceptive services offered by the government program, the proportion of women who have had at least one induced abortion among married women aged 15-44 increased from 7 per cent in 1963 to 53 per cent in 1991 ... The total abortion rate of married women increased more than four times from 0.7 in 1963 to 2.9 in 1979, but it fell to 1.6 in 1988. However, the total abortion rate shows an increasing trend in recent years, particularly for women in their 20s.[38]
>
> The legal and social attitude toward abortion has been exceptionally generous and abortion has been a commonly used method to control fertility. Increasing premarital and teen pregnancies are likely to worsen the situation in the future. Though the abortion rate fell after its peak in 1979, the rate keeps on increasing for married women aged 20 to 24 and the rate for those aged 25 to 29 remains high. The recent situation that the younger

age group (20-29) were practicing less contraception but using more induced abortions, needs serious attention in the near future.[39]

More than half of Korean wives have experienced an abortion and about one third have had two or more according to surveys.[40] It is noteworthy that the abortion rate among young married and unmarried women[41] is accelerating sharply in very recent years as well. Regular abortion seems to have become part of the accepted cultural pattern of modern Korea.[42]

Another characteristic of the abortion phenomenon of Korea must be mentioned—son preference. The frequency of sex selective abortion has become an important factor in the distorted sex ratio (number of males per 100 females) in the last decade, specifically since 1985. The current ratio is about 116 males to 100 females, far higher than the normal ratio of 106. Complex statistical procedures aside, 'the annual number of female fetuses aborted appears to range between 10,000 to 18,000, amounting to nearly 80,000 during the five years 1986-90. These "missing" girls represent about 5 per cent of actual female births'.[43] The implications of this sexual imbalance for future generations are manifold, not the least of which is finding mates. Already in Korea, the marriage market for males aged 5-9 in 1990 will be extremely tight; nearly 50 per cent of them will not be able to find spouses in the traditionally appropriate age range![44] On this matter affecting the lives of males, the Korean government took quick action.

> On 31 January 1990 Korea's Ministry of Health and Social Affairs suspended the medical licenses of eight physicians who had performed sex-determination tests on fetuses, an action that was widely reported in the media. In May the same year the ministry amended the regulations on medical care so that licenses could be revoked for performing sex-determination procedures ... some observers, however, believe that the harsh regulations would only raise the clandestine service of sex determination.[45]

In response to this widespread, underground service, and the ever-deepening imbalance of the sexes in Korea, the Korean Medical Association (membership 40,000) launched a self-reform campaign in February 1995 to stamp out medical tests that identify the sex of embryos. The association declared that 'it would take the lead in seeking out fellow medical practitioners who practice prenatal sex testing for sexual identification and report them to the authorities ... doctors have to go all out to bring this practice to a halt.' It noted: 'In this issue, the biggest obstacle has been the doctors' perception that the punishment of doctors is unfair because the tests are done at the request of the pregnant women.'[46] Nevertheless, the collusion of physicians and their son-seeking clients has led the number of selective female fetal abortions to climb to about 30,000 a year.

The KMA action received widespread news coverage on TV, the radio and the press. It is yet too early determine whether this public information will affect long ingrained patterns of sex discrimination in Korea, however. Interesting, though, is a rare expression of anti-abortion sentiment which was expressed in a major Korean newspaper editorial in response to the doctors' action:

> Prenatal sex identification for the purpose of abortion has been widespread under Confucian family norms preferring sons to daughters. A 1987 law authorized fetal tests only for the detection of genetic problems, including deformities, and the monitoring of fetal growth. But the tests have been widely used to identify the gender of embryos ... Pregnancy or birth is pure and sacrosanct. Life is more precious than any other thing. An individual's desire for convenience or pursuit of self-interest should not be left to control birth. As for doctors under any circumstances, killing a fetus for money can never be condoned.[47]

The new goals of the national family planning program (including the Planned Parenthood Federation of Korea) are very much concerned with improving the quality of family life and levelling the numerical distortion of the sexes for future generations of Koreans. Korea has made remarkable progress in limiting population growth. It is now time to concentrate on 'the quality and use effectiveness of contraception, maintenance of a balanced sex ratio and the reduction of induced abortions ... the practice of selective abortions which is triggered by parental sex preference.'[48]

Contemporary Korean Buddhism and the Abortion Issue

As stated earlier at the beginning of this chapter, Buddhists have been mute regarding the issue of abortion in Korea, at least until the last few years. The Buddhist populace in general seems to have unresistingly embraced government family planning directives and the ethos of rapid national economic development through small family size which arose in the sixties. Koreans wanted desperately to catch up with more advanced nations like Japan, and the post-war population boom was an impediment. Trevor Ling's 1969 remark that in Mahāyāna Buddhist Korea 'abortion is illegal, but widely practised and socially accepted' [49] is supported by results of the Korean National Abortion Survey of 1971 which indicated that Buddhists were, in fact, slightly more likely to have abortions than other segments of the population.[50] A later abortion survey conducted by the Korean Institute of Criminology in 1990 also found that Buddhists had as high or higher an abortion rate as the rest of the population (in the Seoul sample survey) and that the highest number of repetitive abortions (3 or more) were among Buddhists.[51]

While Korea's high abortion rate and the unquestioning practice of abortion among Buddhist women have slowly begun to be recognized as issues requiring attention by a small number within the Buddhist community within the past ten years,[52] they are still largely dismissed by the majority today (Spring 1996). Many believers in Seoul with whom my wife and I have spoken have never reflected on the topic. They accept abortion as no more than an act of discretionary, personal hygiene or emergency surgical relief, such as an appendectomy or first aid. While there are a small but growing number of Buddhists who are quite concerned about the common practice of abortion among their peers, they are not very visible in the general Buddhist populace. To date, there is no common or public practice of rites for aborted fetuses in Korea as is practised in Japan. There are no red-bibbed statues of Kṣitigarbha (Japanese: Jizō; Korean: Chijang) to be found on streets and cemeteries in Korea as they are in Japan. Nor are there commercial newspaper ads for *mizuko kuyō* ('water baby offering rites') as found in the Japanese press. Japan has thousands of temples where aborted fetuses are memorialized; Korea probably has no more

than ten or twelve sanctuaries where ceremonies for aborted babies
are performed. These rites are performed sporadically throughout
the year as the need arises, if at all. There are no traditionally fixed
dates on the annual ritual cycle for the ceremonies as there are for
other religious events. Nor are there temples or cemeteries like
Hase-dera or Purple Cloud Temple described by William LaFleur
in *Liquid Life,* where services for aborted fetuses are a major or
sole focus of religious activity.[53] For the great majority of Korean
Buddhist believers, if the spirits of aborted babies are remembered
at all, it is at the time of *Uranpun-jae-il* (*Ullambana*—Festival of
the Hungry Ghosts—15th day of the 7th lunar month) when some
Buddhists dedicate memorial tablets to the spirits of the aborted infant 'water child' or 'water babies' (*suja*—same Chinese characters
as Japanese *mizuko*) along with deceased family members in their
favourite temple. This, too, is only a recent trend. It is not a well
known or solicited practice, however. These tablets for the miscarried or aborted children of married women are displayed openly
and can be easily identified by family names, but are anonymously
attributed or absent for the unmarried. At this date, it can hardly be
characterized as a lucrative business. One must go out of one's way
to discover *suja* among thousands of paper memorial tablets dedicated to ancestors or the 'mature' dead, which are pasted on the
walls of the temple behind or near the altar for memorial services.

An awakening of concern for aborted fetuses occurred in Korea in early 1985 with the efforts of Venerable Sŏk Myogak, a
Chogye Order *pigu* (Skt: *bhikṣu*) now in his late fifties. Myogak,
formerly of famous Pulguksa Temple, incited great interest among
a group of *posallim* (devout female supporters) in Seoul when he
introduced them to parts of a first draft of his translation of a Japanese book on *mizuko*.[54] The book's depiction of the fears and suffering of the spirits of helpless, aborted children and their attempts
to seize the attention of their parents through dreams and interfer-
ence (misfortunes) in their daily lives resonated deeply among
these pious Buddhist women. It appears to have brought to the surface feelings of uneasiness and guilt they had experienced for years
but could not or would not identify. To quote a female supporter of
Myogak on a local radio broadcast this spring: 'We grieve over the

death of our pet animals and even bury them. How much more so a baby in the womb which is aborted? We cannot ignore them'.[55]

The *posallim* encouraged Myogak to continue his translation of the book which they eventually published as a paperback at their own expense in 1985. It is evocatively entitled *Aga-ya, yongsŏhaeda-o*, which can be translated as 'My Dear Baby, Please Forgive Me!' This volume was read eagerly among Ven. Myogak's followers and their circles of friends. The book's readership quickly spread from Seoul in the north to Taegu and Pusan in the Kyŏngsang provinces at the southern end of the country where, according to popular descriptions, 'there are many more devout Buddhists'. Readership quickly spread to other more rural parts of the country. News of the book also circulated in the *sangha*, and a number of clergy came personally to Myogak to purchase fifty or a hundred copies at a time to distribute among their followers. These monks began to offer rites for aborted fetuses on their own, modelling their rituals on what they learned from Myogak directly and through their reading and interpretation of his translation.

It appears that *Aga-ya* was a beginning, a first small step in the public expression of distress over the pain of abortion in Buddhist society. It remains an inspiration and catalyst for some monks and nuns to independently investigate the scriptures and innovate ritual practices they deem appropriate to the needs of their congregation. As the book has become more widely distributed, more and more people are asking to have *nak t'ae-a ch'ŏndo-jae* ('auspicious rebirth ceremony for aborted babies') performed at the ten or more temples which have initiated the rituals. It is difficult to estimate with any accuracy just how many more are performing or planning this unconventional rite.

Ven. Myogak claims that 'around 500 women have performed the ceremony at Kukch'ŏngsa'—his apartment style temple in Sadangdong, Seoul—since his book was published. 'Since those people aborted two babies on the average, about 1,000 spirits have benefited from the ceremonies.'[56] As of May 1992, he records in a later edition of his book, he had about 500 telephone consultations, 147 correspondences by letter and 300 personal consultations. 'Most people who consulted with me tried to rationalize their behaviour and put the blame on others. Whatever the reason or the situation was, they should acknowledge themselves as responsible for their actions, be very clear about this, and perform *ch'ŏndo-jae* offering for the little spirits with a very sincere heart', writes Venerable Myogak in the introduction of *Aga-ya!* (My Dear Baby!).

The people who come to Myogak share the belief that the act of abortion is unequivocally wrong, a grievous misdeed. One *posallim* said on radio, 'an old proverb says that if you "erase" your baby, you'll have no luck for three years. After I aborted my baby, nothing went well. I believe I was being personally punished for what I did.' Another mother revealed, 'I immediately got pregnant after my first baby was born. And I had an abortion. One day my elder sister bought a copy of *Aga-ya!* she found at a temple bazaar and lent it to me. After reading the book, I cried and cried and felt that I did a terrible thing. I went to see Venerable Myogak and performed *ch'ŏndo-jae* for relief.' Yet another lady testifies:

> I was too young and didn't know any better when I aborted my first baby. My second child died the day after she was born. I thought the baby was sleeping so I left her alone. My aunt came to visit but she didn't even want to see the baby. I was very upset. I assumed she acted that way because it was a girl. When I went in to change my baby's diaper, she was cold and stiff. Shocked out of my mind, I buried my baby with her soiled diaper on, with my father's help, on a small bank around a rice paddy (She begins to sob). It still breaks my heart that I left my baby like that, dead in a soiled diaper. I was foolish. I feel much better now after performing *ch'ŏndo-jae*.

The expression of repentance through confession and ritual offering undoubtedly had a healing effect for its performers.

Aga-ya! is mostly a recitation of many sad and shocking stories of abortion from both Korea and Japan. Although originally inspired by Japanese example, the sentiments expressed in the book well represent what I have experienced as the dominant Korean Buddhist 'pro-life' orientation toward abortion. It is concerned primarily with the suffering and neglect of aborted children and the deleterious effects of ignoring them in the unseen world.

Myogak's prologue first lays out a very simple and terse outline of the fundamental Buddhist understanding of existence—of past, present and future lives, of causality and the twelve links in the chain of dependent co-origination—and includes a diagram of

the six realms of (life and death) existence. There is a special nota-
tion that only in the human realm can one perform spiritual practice and experience realization of Buddha nature. Myogak then
presents his purpose with cultural and historical references (I
paraphrase):

> Like the solemn and complicated rites for the dying performed
> by Tibetan monks to assure that the spirit of the dead will not
> wander around in the other world or be restless, Koreans also
> perform *ch'ŏndo* for the spirit of the dead.
>
> Buddhist funeral rituals which were passed down from Koryŏ
> as indigenized custom were abolished by Chosŏn King Yejong
> and replaced with Confucian rituals. These Confucian rituals
> were merely a matter of form and procedure and not truly relig-
> ious in the sense of real concern for the spirits of the dead.
> Buddhist rituals were performed in temples with the understand-
> ing of dependent co-origination and *saṃsāra*. People reap the re-
> wards of their karma, consciously or unconsciously, therefore
> the families of the dead thinking of the karmic result the dead
> will receive in the next life sincerely pray that the dead will
> choose not to re-enter *saṃsāra* ...
>
> Whether Buddhist or not, people offered their entire hearts
> and minds for the spiritual rebirth of the dead. However, the
> young spirits that hadn't yet reached adulthood were neglected.
> For example, when children die in Korea they are usually cre-
> mated or buried without any funeral ritual. Those little lives
> which are aborted or miscarried without seeing the light of the
> world are treated as if they were vestigial organs (like an appen-
> dix) And, since many babies were conceived through immoral
> behavior, they are dispatched even more mechanically avoid dis-
> covery. If the baby is considered 'a problem' the parents' only
> thought is to rid themselves of it—they give no thought to the fe-
> tus at all. And, too, if the mother involuntarily miscarried, rela-
> tives and friends dote only on the woman's health and don't give
> a thought for the health or afterlife of the baby whose life was
> truncated abruptly. Yet when our pet animals die, we grieve for
> them so miserably.
>
> I believe something is wrong here when we are indifferent to
> the lives which grow in our own bodies. Babies who have been
> aborted through artificial means should be guided to a better re-
> birth. At the same time, we should consider the condition of
> many women who suffer in so many different ways, sometimes

inexplicably, and try to alleviate their anguish if even only slightly. More people should pay attention to the spirit of aborted fetuses. I hope many more women, especially those who have experienced miscarriage or abortion, will perform *ch'ŏndo* ceremonies for the spirit of these poor little ones. They should do it with devotion through chanting, recitation of names of the Buddhas and bodhisattvas, appropriate offerings and deep repentance of their cruel deeds in order to rid themselves of their karmic hindrances. And they should make greater efforts to nurture brighter and happier families for a brighter, happier society in the future.[57]

Myogak's call to repent for aborting babies as exemplified in Japan is echoed by other Korean Buddhist leaders since the publication of *Aga-ya!* in 1985. Cho Myŏng-nyŏl, a Japan-educated faculty member of Seoul's Central *Sangha* College, writes that 'the Japanese acknowledge abortion as an evil misdeed yet *mizuko* offerings allow the Japanese to dignify and revere life. The rituals provide an opportunity for people who committed abortion (all family members, sympathizers and doctors included) to rise above their suffering rather than be stigmatized as criminals. This practice is both rational and worldly-wise.' She notes that 'it seems that all religious groups in Korea except the Catholics are publicly silent on abortion. Rather than relying on government policy, the role of religion is to try to provide opportunity for people to raise above the problems of their daily lives through religious belief and to awaken them to an authentic ethics of life (bioethics?).'[58]

It is apparent that despite bitter memories of Japanese cruelty during the thirty-five year colonial period, and a well-founded fear of Japan's economic clout and cultural influence on Korea's youth today, Korean Buddhist leaders are still amenable to learning from their imposing neighbour. Many older Korean Buddhist scholars were educated in Japan during the colonial period. They were deeply influenced by Japanese scholarly values and comprehensive grasp of Buddhist traditions of East Asia and India. The younger Korean generation travels to Japan for graduate study and research at Buddhist universities. It is no surprise that they would respect Japanese traditions as worthy of serious consideration, yet emphatically affirm their own important Korean national heritage. This sentiment is expressed well by Professor Mok Jeong-bae,

Dean of the Graduate School of Buddhist Studies of Dongguk University when he suggests in the *Tabo* quarterly, an organ of the Korean Buddhism Promotion Foundation, that Koreans ought to 'find a way to transform Japanese *suja* belief into Korean form.'[59]

Proof that Korean Buddhists are not accepting Japanese innovation unquestioningly can be observed in matters of terminology, for instance. The term *mizuko* in Japanese is composed of two Sinitic logographs which are pronounced as *suja* in Korean. Koreans are not happy with this expression because it is not a Buddhist term; they say it has no scriptural reference and sounds foreign to their ears. It may be used for convenience by those who are not familiar with Buddhist terminology in Korea or by those who read Japanese materials and go back and forth between the two countries often. One Korean monk told us he thought it was an invention of a Japanese lay woman and not to be taken seriously! The *mizuko* concept is apparently deeply enmeshed in ancient Japanese folk belief,[60] however, and has been only recently revived in Japanese Buddhist ritual tradition.[61] It has not been picked up in popular Korean culture as a fashionable foreign trade name (yet)!

The Korean nun Venerable Sŏngdŏk who has been very committed to studying the abortion problem and leading ceremonies for her congregation over the past five years prefers to use the logographs which are pronounced *t'a-t'ae* in Korean. *T'a t'ae* is a Buddhist term for abortion which is found in Chinese Buddhist *sūtras*.[62] The most commonly used and medically and legally acceptable term for abortion in Korean is *nak t'ae*. The Japanese expression *mizuko kuyō*, or *suja kongyang* in Korean ('water-child offering'), is unfamiliar to Koreans. The term *nak t'ae-a ch'ŏndo-jae* is more readily identifiable as an 'auspicious rebirth offering ceremony for an aborted fetus.' It is a kind of new variant of the common expression *yŏng-ga ch'ŏndo-jae* which refers to 'an auspicious rebirth offering ceremony for spirits of the dead' which can be employed in both group and individual funerary occasions for adults. Another expression employed by Venerable Sŏngdŏk for her forty-nine-day-long group ceremonies for aborted fetuses is *T'a t'ae agi-ryŏng ch'ŏndo pŏphoe* which can be rendered as 'a Dharma meeting for the auspicious rebirth of aborted babies.'

Venerable Sŏngdŏk was born in 1950. She left home (*ch'ulga*) to begin *sŏn* (Zen) training at the famous *piguni* (Skt: *bhikṣuṇī*) monastery Unmunsa at age nineteen. She is also sometimes called by the respectful title *kŭn sŭṇim* (great master), an honorific title for revered elder clergy despite her relatively young age, and is also known by her lineage designation title *Pangsaeng* ('release of living creatures', 'protector, saviour, of all living beings'). Sŏng-dŏk is known for her devotion to social service and efforts in organizing the first Buddhist Volunteer Service Association in Seoul. She refrains from collecting offerings to use on expensive temple building projects but rather instructs her followers to use their time and money to help others. She has a vision to make Buddhism a visible, moral force in Korean society by engaging the energies of Buddhist laypeople who heretofore have had no Buddhist channels available to them to express their social commitment. She has studied Buddhism academically at Dongguk University and has done special study of Buddhist hospice care (*vihāra*) in Japan. She remembers being well warned by her Japanese teachers not to emulate the crassly greedy *mizuko* temples which operate there.

Sŏngdŏk has been leading long ceremonies for the spirits of aborted babies once a year since 1991. She began to lead similar rites before then on a case by case basis for individual mothers and families, much like the monk Myogak, but she found she could not accommodate all who asked for them. The magnitude of the abortion problem in Korea soon became clear, and as a consequence she and her family of nun disciples organized large group ceremonies in order to meet the requests of many women who felt they had to 'do something' about their abortions.

The ceremonies are more than just spectator events for lay believers. They are actually Buddhist consciousness-raising sessions in an active devotional and communitarian setting. Fifty to a hundred people have participated in the event every year since 1991. These ceremonies extend over forty-nine days, the same duration as the funeral service for adults. They are scheduled to begin in late May after Buddha's Birthday and to end in July, just before school lets out for summer recess. This allows mothers of young children to attend the services more freely. The majority of the participants are housewives and mothers; unmarried women would be too ashamed to attend. Husbands attend irregularly because of job demands.

Prayers are led for three hours every morning by Sŏngdŏk and her disciples. They are joined by lay participants who can make the time. Most believers try to attend every day. In 1995, over thirty out of a hundred participants had perfect attendance and most only missed a very few days. Those who must work away from home and far from the temple attend once a week, usually on Saturday, at seven-day intervals. (There are also normal Sunday morning Dharma services for the entire congregation in conformance with the solar calendar work week, like Christian services.)

A very modest fee is required for participation in 'auspicious rebirth ceremonies,' 49,000 *wŏn* or 1,000 *wŏn* ($1.35) a day for forty nine days, the price of a litre of milk in Seoul. This sum goes to cover expenses of printing, altar preparations, and food offerings which are consumed by the congregation after every service. Participants in *t'a t'ae agi-ryŏng chŏndo* Dharma meetings share responsibilities for preparing the temple for service, meal preparations and clean-up. The atmosphere at the temple is very solemn during prayers and prostrations, which require considerable exertion, concentration and self-reflection, but quite convivial at lunch after the three hour service.

In preparing reading materials which are distributed consecutively each week, Venerable Sŏngdŏk covers the gamut of teachings related to life, death and rebirth in the Buddhist canon as well as introducing ideas about the spiritual world from other religions in Korea. One year she even devoted space to Tibetan views on *bardo* and rebirth, a topic inspired by the long visit to Korea by the charismatic nine-year-old *tulku* Ling Rinpoche, the emanation (incarnation) of the present Dalai Lama's deceased head tutor. This is no doubt an innovative program in Korean Buddhism. Questions and answers about the nature of (re)birth and the beginning of human life in the womb at conception, why spirits of aborted babies cause troubles for the living, what are these troubles in fact, the best method of performing *ch'ŏndo*, and so forth, fill the weekly guidebooks.

The following translation of an article from one of Sŏngdok's *ch'ŏndo* guidebooks was reprinted in the monthly magazine *Ŏjin pŏt* (Good Friend) of the Buddhist Volunteer Service Association. It provides the names of the *sūtras* which are most often cited in Korea regarding abortion and briefly lists what must be done to prevent further suffering for both the aborted child and its family.

On the Spirits of Aborted Fetuses

Among the 84,000 Buddhist *sūtras*, *Agui-po-ŭng Kyŏng* (Ch: *E kuei pao ying ching*)[63], *Changsu myŏl-joe Kyŏng* (Ch: *Chang shou mieh tsui hu chu t'ung tzu t'o lo ni ching*),[64] *T'a T'ae Kyŏng*,[65] mention the karma caused by abortion.

1) The spirits of aborted fetuses (*t'a t'ae agi-ryŏng*) refers to the spirits of the fetuses who were intentionally, artificially aborted. All living beings including humans have Buddha nature created by the noble energy (*ki*) of the universe. To abort the precious life of the fetus conceived in the womb is against nature, undesirable morally, and very harmful to its mother medically. Besides, the life which is about to be born disappears from darkness to darkness without witnessing the light. It will become resentful and can cause harm and misfortune to the living who are related to the fetus.

2) Troubles or difficulties caused by aborted fetuses (*t'a t'ae-a ŭi t'al*)

   a) Why do they cause difficulties?
The spirits of fetuses who have been suddenly thrust into darkness without witnessing the light of the world (through birth) are too shocked by their evil karmic momentum to find the true dharma realm but instead find themselves besieged by unhappy phantoms. They strongly desire to be released quickly from wandering in the netherworld. They wish for spiritual peace, and to that end they insinuate themselves in the lives of people with whom they have a karmic connection by producing misfortunes. They cause troubles for their mother, father, brothers and sisters and other relatives. These troubles will become aggravated as time goes on unless *ch'ŏndo* rites are performed for them.

b) What are the troubles caused by the spirit of the aborted fetus?
The physical ailments caused by these spirits vary: chronic splenitis, breast cancer, uterine cancer, backache, hysteria, neurosis. Backaches, headaches and menstrual cramps are most common. Besides, 80 per cent of marital discord may be attributed to aborted spirits. Sometimes they are the root cause of bankruptcy or the destruction of families.
   c) Do Buddhists acknowledge the fetus as human?
According to Buddhism, rebirth in a particular realm among the six depends on one's accumulated karma. The parent-child relationship is a very important karmic connection. In Buddhism, life goes through four temporal states in the repeating cycle of *saṃsāra*:

1) Saeng-yu (*upapatti-bhava*)—the moment of conception;
2) Pon-yu (*pūrvakāla-bhava*)—from conception in the mother's body until the end of life;
3) Sa-yu (*maraṇa-bhava*)—the moment of death;
4) Chung-yu (*antara-bhava*)—from death until entering a body again according to karma.

Based on the aforementioned theory of four states of existences, receiving the human body is equivalent to *pon-yu*; the fetus is its beginning form. Therefore the fetus is duly recognized as a human being. In our Korean tradition, a child is considered a year old when it is born. A child in the womb for ten months is recognized as human. Since Buddhism encourages us to recognize the dignity of all life and regards killing the gravest evil of all, we Buddhists should protect the lives of fetuses at all costs. We should perform *ch'ŏndo-jae* for those aborted fetuses whose deaths could not be avoided in the past in order to brighten their future journeys.

4) Best Ways for Aborted Fetuses to Attain Auspicious Rebirth

a) Enshrine Chijang Posal (Kṣitigarbha Bodhisattva) in a temple and perform a *ch'ŏndo* ceremony;
b) Participate in temple activities in the name of the fetus—for example, donating temple rooftiles with the baby's name painted on them, merit-making in the name of the fetus;
c) Copy scriptures by hand and make Buddha statues;

d) Recite the names of the Buddhas and bodhisattvas according
to one's belief;
e) Make prayers of repentance regularly;

The most important of all is that the mother of the spirit of the
fetus should perform auspicious rebirth rites for all her aborted
babies so that they will be reborn in paradise (*wangsaeng gŭng-
nak*). She must offer deep, heart-felt apologies for the young
lives who are buried deep within darkness rather than be concerned for her own suffering.

A detailed analysis of the ritual proceedings which are enacted
during *ch'ŏndo* ceremonies will be described in a future study by
the author. It is necessary to note that there is considerable variation in terms of length and degree of engagement by the participants. Venerable Sŏk Myogak offers the service over a twenty-one
day period at his small temple. A younger monk, Venerable Hyŏnjang, offers weekend retreats and *ch'ŏndo* prayers for *sujaryŏng*
('water-baby spirits') over 100 days. He also installed what may be
Korea's first *Suja Chijangposal* monument—a statue of 'Kṣitigarbha of the Water-Babies' at his rural temple outside of Kwangju.
(Hyŏnjang was deeply impressed by his visit to Japan seven years
ago.) The traditional forty-nine day funeral period has been se-
lected by Venerable Kang Chawu who began offering aborted fetus
ch'ŏndo late this summer (1995) in conjunction with the publication of his new book.[66]

As at Venerable Sŏngdŏk's Temple of the Four Guardians (*Sa-
ch'ŏnwangsa*), Myogak's *shindo* (believers) in crowded Seoul
bring offerings of milk, fruit, cookies, baby clothes, toys and
candy. Since attendance is usually rather poor because of the busy
schedules of the participants and the time-consuming traffic, he
urges them to perform one-hundred-day repentance prayers privately at home. Psychologically innovative, Myogak has his laypeople draw pictures of the deceased infants on their infants'
tablets, as they may imagine them He also prescribes the ancient
Buddhist custom of copying *sūtras* by hand (*sa kyŏng*) and has the
repentant follower recite the prayer (*dhāraṇī*) while he or she is
copying it. Myogak also urges them to visit and contribute to

welfare facilities like orphanages in order to make merit for the spirits of the dead children.

Learning about these ritual activities for aborted victims in the past, and the consolation of perpetrators in the present, a concerned observer may remark, 'Fine! All well and good for the living and the dead as in Japan, but what about the doomed fetuses alive for moments today and those who will be conceived tomorrow? Granted Buddhist scriptures condemn abortion as killing, what are you doing to prevent it from happening now?' The Korean Buddhist leaders who have concerned themselves with the issue of abortion in Korea realize that they have very real challenges before them. They recognize that it is one thing to preach that abortion is murder and that Buddhism is unequivocally committed to protecting life: it is another thing to provide answers and alternatives to devout Buddhists who come to them with unexpected or unwanted pregnancies. Korean society in general, despite the relatively strong anti-abortion laws, is clearly pro-abortion and this attitude has been promoted with undeniable government support to the private medical establishment and national health programs for over thirty years. Abortion is easy in Korea and the general populace is nonchalant about it, despite its illegality. 'Pro-choice' advocates, as they are known in the Western world, do not have much to agitate about on a practical level in Korea. Since restrictive laws on the books are basically unenforced,[67] Korean women's groups apparently do not see abortion as an issue. (Abortion is also easy to obtain in neighbouring Buddhist Japan, but it is legal.)

The strongest anti-abortion voice in Korea is the Catholic establishment. Concerned Buddhists are well aware of its position but there has been very little dialogue or cooperation so far on any level on the abortion issue. The famous videotape 'Silent Scream' and others have been freely distributed in Korea by the Sisters of Mary (*Maria sunyŏ-hoe*) for years.[68] Most Buddhist leaders have viewed one or more films. Hyŏnjang even writes in *Yŏsŏng Pulgyo* ('Women's Buddhism'), that he saw 'Silent Scream' in Seoul ten years ago. 'I passed out when I saw the fetus's head being crushed by forceps. Perhaps I was an aborted fetus in a past life. After that video, I cultivated the seed thought in my mind, 'I'll save your poor suffering spirits'.[69] Catholics, however, were very surprised to learn that there was any interest at all in abortion

among Buddhists when I met them for background information at
the start of this research. They know that Buddhists 'vow to save
all sentient beings' and hold that 'even the lives of insects are to be
respected.' They just haven't seen much action among Buddhists to
prove they really mean it![70]

According to Kim Wan-ki, an editor of the Buddhist newspaper *Haedong Pulgyo:*

> There are only nine facilities specially designated for unwed
> mothers in Korea nationwide. Four of them are run by Catholics,
> three by Protestants, one by the Salvation Army and one by a
> private social welfare organization. Eight of these are Christian
> facilities. No one Buddhist facility! It is said there are a million
> and a half abortions per year in Korea. And over ten thousand
> new unwed mothers per year. No doubt there are many Bud-
> dhists among them. Is there any way for Buddhists to avoid kill-
> ing? Is there any way to help unwed mothers who are Buddhist?
> Must Buddhist women kill their babies or convert to other relig-
> ions, or observe their rituals, in order to live at or use facilities
> run by other religious groups?[71]

Buddhist temples have been homes for orphans, the aged, and
the unwanted from time immemorial in Korea, but they can no
longer easily be so now. The requirements of society are more
complex in recent times. But Buddhists can establish modern institutions to fill social needs. Venerable Myogak, for one, has raised
funds to purchase land for the first Buddhist home for unwed
mothers in Korea. It will be an important first step in providing an
alternative to abortion or foreign adoption for some Buddhist
women in Korea.

What other steps can Korean Buddhists take to be true to the
first precept of non-killing which they universally agree to be the
paramount virtue? As Professor Mok Jeong-bae has written, it is
not enough to be concerned with attaining the Pure Land in the future, as so many Buddhists in Korea pray for. The uncertainties,
contradictions and inconsistencies of traditional practices in modern Korean society have to be examined and dealt with. If there are
physical and mental ailments afflicting us, they must be corrected.
He has coined the term 'sattvaism' to represent the Buddhist view
of life, that 'the lives of all living beings are as precious as my

own. We have to practice *pohyŏnhaeng* ('Samantabhadra action') in the real world, not just in sermons or prayers. This will prevent "invisible killing" like abortion.' Professor Mok suggests six practical measures to awaken the moral conscience of Buddhists in Korea through 'expedient means' (*pangp'yŏn*, Skt: *upāya*) which may have universal applicability throughout the Buddhist world.

Briefly they are advice to:

1.   Curb the tendency to regard fetal life nonchalantly by developing more effective ways to propagate the idea and spirit of protecting life i.e. to present more public lectures, dharma talks and pertinent research to develop and refine a modern philosophy of respect for all life founded on Buddhist doctrine.
2.   Prepare abortion-prevention legislation from a Buddhist perspective and in Buddhist language and strongly recommend it to pertinent authorities.
3.   Explore ways to transform Japanese *suja* (*mizuko*) beliefs into Korean form.
4.   Educate people to understand that life in the womb is human. It wishes to live and go on living just as we do. Prepare video presentations to illustrate this fact.
5.   Hold more frequent special dharma practice assemblies dedicated to 'respect for fetal life' (*t'ae-a saengmyŏng chonjung*) similar to masses to accumulate (intensify) merit in advance of death (*yesu-jae*) and release of living creatures ceremonies (*paengsaeng pŏphoe*) practised in Mahāyāna countries[72]
6.   Produce and disseminate written literature which warns how today's immoral, unethical and conscience-less sexual indiscretion is correlated with the invisible murder of abortion.[73]

In May 1995, the radio narrator of 'Death without Resistance', a feature programme on abortion, suggested that Buddhism seemed to be developing a compromise between the 'pro-choice' stance of women who wish to trust their own conscience regarding a

decision to abort and that of the so-called 'pro-lifers' who emphasize compassion for the unborn child and its human rights. That
compromise was *ch'ŏndo-jae*, the auspicious rebirth ceremony for
the spirit of the aborted fetus wherein the parents repent their actions and the spirits are admonished to seek a higher plane of rebirth and be released of their anguish (*han*). Whether *ch'ŏndo-jae*
will serve as a call to conscience for those who have committed
abortion and will lead them to make greater efforts to avoid unwanted pregnancies in the future (and lead others to be scrupulously careful with their sexuality) or whether it will be an easy
way to assuage one's conscience and slide into the next facile decision to abort without guilt (rather than honour the first precept) is a
quandary Buddhists must face with courage and honesty. Supreme
Patriarch Most Venerable Wolha of the Chogye Order has taught,
'the value of life cannot be exchanged for the entire universe'
(*saengmyŏng-ui kach'i nŭn uju wado pakkulsu ŏpta*).[74] It remains
to be seen if Korean Buddhists will resonate with this message and
act in accord with it.

Notes

[1]   I acknowledge with thanks research funding for this chapter received from the Daeyang Research Fund of Sejong University,
Seoul, Korea in 1995.

[2]   Such as, for instance, very recently in the seminar proceedings
of the Planned Parent Federation of Korea (Seoul: Ministry of
Health and Welfare, 1995), 'Seminar on the Development of Strategy for the Prevention of Induced Abortion', and Cho, Nam-Hoon
(1993), *Demographic Transition: Changes in Determinants of Fertility Decline in the Republic of Korea*, Tokyo: Department of Demography and Health Statistics, Institute of Public Health, Japan.
There is, of course, the very important early work of Sung-bong
Hong and others. See Part IX Bibliography of Hong and Watson,
The Increasing Utilization of Induced Abortion in Korea (Seoul:
Korea University Press, 1976) 1161-162.

[3]   Shim, Young Hee (Shim Yŏng-hŭi) et al., *An Empirical Study
on Abortion in Korea: Focusing on the Extent and Attitude* (Seoul:
Korean Institute of Criminology 90-08, 1991) and Shin, Dong

Woon, *A Study on Adultery and Abortion from the Viewpoint of Criminal Law Reform in Korea* (Seoul: Korean Institute of Criminology 90-22, 1991).

[4] Eun-Shil Kim (Kim Ŭn-sil) (1993), 'The Making of the Modern Female Gender: The Politics of Gender in Reproductive Practices in Korea', doctoral dissertation in medical anthropology, University of California, San Francisco and Berkeley, and Suk Gyung Lee (Yi Suk-kyŏng) (1993), 'A Study of Unmarried Women's Sexuality: Focusing on Their Abortion Experience', Master's thesis, Department of Women's Studies, Graduate School, Ewha Womans University, Seoul.

[5] According to the Republic of Korea's National Statistical Office Social Statistics Survey in 1991, Buddhist adherents account for 51.2 per cent (nearly 12 million) of the religious populace (over 23 million). Buddhists leaders will commonly cite a figure of 20 million or more in news releases and public addresses. Social scientists generally agree that figures for religious affiliation in Korea are questionable at best. Buddhist temples generally do not register their membership although there is a recent move in that direction. I have excluded discussing Christian publications in this brief study.

[6] Especially as abortion directly pertains to the serious imbalance of the sexes among elementary school age children. September 24, 1995 *Korea Herald,* 3: 'Boys outnumber girls by some 200,000 in primary schools: education ministry.' Also *Korea Times*, March 26, 1995:3 'Survey Shows Current Population Policy Backfires: One in Two Housewives Has Abortion.'

[7] Frank Tedesco, 'Buddhist Social Welfare in Korea: What is it and where is it going?' Research paper presented at the First Buddhist Social Welfare and Modern Society conference (Taipei) January, 1994. Published in Chinese and English by Torch of Wisdom Press, Taipei, 1996.

[8] As demonstrated in many serious articles published in *Tabo* 'Many Treasures' of the Korean Buddhism Promotion Foundation since its first issue in 1991.

[9] Lack of available land for traditional Confucian style burial mounds is forcing many conservative Koreans to consider cremation as an alternative for the disposal of their dead. Lay Buddhists have generally not cremated in Korea, but there is a movement

arising to create columbaria for the ashes of the dead as in Japan. Young children and the unmarried have traditionally been cremated or buried without ceremony.

[10]   A severe labour shortage in Korea has led to the migration of labourers from so-called 'Third World' Asian and Pacific countries. They have had many problems with their Korean employers and have had to demonstrate their grievances publicly. The Catholic Church and Chogye Headquarters have supported them.

[11]   Frank Tedesco: *The Korea Times*, (Seoul) 'Crisis in Korean Buddhism,' Tuesday April 5, 1994, 1; 'The Buddhist Struggle Continues' 6, Saturday April 9, 1994. Also Jason Booth, *Far Eastern Economic Review* (Hong Kong) 'Bad Karma; Monks Fight for Control of Buddhist Order,' April 28, 1994, 22.

[12]   Frank Tedesco, 'Buddhist Social Welfare in Korea,' op cit. To quote Professor Venerable Im Songsan, *Pokji Pulgyo: Sasang-gwa sarye* (Buddhist Welfare: Thought and Examples) (Seoul: Popsu Publishing Co, 1983) 'Monks themselves have gotten into the habit of receiving, they do not care to take active responsibility for society or they are too theoretical and unaware of social problems, and, as a consequence, they haven't established Buddhist social welfare properly.' See Preface. Please note encouraging recent developments with the formation of the private Korean Buddhist Social Welfare Council which represents about 80 Buddhist facilities and the official Chogye Order For Social Welfare which has ambitious plans to promote social welfare in general throughout Korea by means of training programs, volunteer placement, extensive fundraising and co-operation with international social welfare organizations to implement assistance overseas.

[13]   Shim, Jae-ryong, 'Buddhist Responses to Modern Transformation of Society in Korea,' in *Korea Journal* (Seoul) 33:3 (Autumn, 1993) 54-55.

[14]   For family members and for the victims of such misfortunes as the Songsu Bridge disaster, gas explosions in Taegu and Seoul, the Sampoong Department Store collapse in the summer, 1995, etc.

[15]   Don Baker, 'Monks, Medicine, and Miracles: Health and Healing in the History of Korean Buddhism,' *Korean Studies* (Honolulu) 18 (1994), 63-64.

[16] Robert E. Buswell, Jr., *The Zen Monastic Experience* (Princeton: Princeton University Press, 1992).

[17] Eun Shil Kim (Kim Ŭn-shil) *The Making of the Modern Female Gender*, op cit., 73-89. See note 3.

[18] See note 4.

[19] Buddha's Birthday is an official national holiday which is celebrated in spring each year, the 8th day of the 4th lunar month. Pictures of the colorful celebration can be found everywhere but there is little explanation of its meaning in Korean belief and practice.

[20] Frank Tedesco, 'Sleeping Wisdom Awakens: Korean Buddhism in the 1990s' (Seoul: *Korea Journal* 33:3) 5-10.

[21] *Korea Herald*, (Seoul) September 15, 1995, 2.

[22] Robert Buswell, *The Zen Monastic Experience*, 23.

[23] Kwon, Kee-jong (Kwŏn Ki-chong), 'Buddhism undergoes Hardships: Buddhism in the Chosŏn Dynasty' in *The History and Culture of Buddhism in Korea* (Seoul: Dongguk University Press, 1993) 169-218. See also Martina Deuchler's analysis of the Confucian impact on Korea society in *The Confucian Transformation of Korea* (Cambridge, Mass.: Council on East Asian Studies, Harvard University, 1992).

[24] Mark Peterson, 'Women without Sons: A Measure of Social Change in Yi Dynasty Korea' in *Korean Women: View from the Inner Room* (New Haven: East Rock Press, 1983) 33-44.

[25] See the interesting discussion of 'population stagnation' in Japan in the late Edo period in William LaFleur, *Liquid Life*, (Princeton, 1992) especially Chapters 5-7. Also his exchange with George Tanabe regarding a review of *Liquid Life* in the *Japanese Journal of Religious Studies* 22 1-2 (1995). The review appears in *JJRS* 21:437-40.

[26] Roger L. Janelli and Dawnhee Yim Janelli, *Ancestor Worship and Korean Society*, (Stanford: Stanford University Press, 1982) 36.

[27] Cornelius Osgood, *The Koreans and Their Culture* (Tokyo: Charles Tuttle, 1951), 113.

[28] Informant interviews by the author. Popular lore has it that the mother of the assassinated dictator, President Pak Chung-hee (Pak Chŏng-hŭi), tried to abort the future president when he was a fetus by drinking nearly five gallons of soy sauce!

[29] Janelli and Janelli, *Ancestor Worship and Korean Society*, ibid.
[30] See Mark Peterson, note 23.
[31] Hong Sung-bong, *International Handbook on Abortion*, ed. Paul Sachdev (New York: Greenwood Press), 302.
[32] George Devereux, 'A Typological Study of Abortion in 350 Primitive, Ancient, and Pre-Industrial Societies' in *Abortion in America,* ed. H.Rosen (Boston: Beacon Press, 1967), 140,148.
[33] Nam-Hoon Cho, *Demographic Transition: Changes in the Determinants of Fertility Decline in the Republic of Korea* (Tokyo: Institute of Public Health, 1993), 2-3.
[34] The socioeconomic rationale for abortion was supported through government subsidies of menstrual regulation procedures for indigents beginning in 1974. Menstrual regulation is nothing but induced abortion in the very early stage of pregnancy. The number of MR recipients subsidized between 1974 and 1981, for instance, was reported to be about 327,000 and the number of birth averted as many as 236,000 according to a government publication.
[35] Hong Sung-bong, ibid., 303.
[36] Shim, Young Hee et al., *An Empirical Study on Abortion in Korea: Focusing on the Extent and Attitude* (Seoul: Korean Institute of Criminology 90-08, 1991), 241-242.
[37] A similar lucrative business has been noted for Japan.
[38] Cho Nam-hoon, *Demographic Transition*, 9.
[39] Ibid. 131.
[40] Hong citing Lim and Byun 308-309.
[41] Lee, Suk Gyung, *A Study of Unmarried Women's Sexuality, Focusing on Their Abortion Experience*, see note 3.
[42] My undergraduate students in Korea, both male and female, discuss the abortions of their mothers and relatives without compunction in the open classroom. As unmarried students, they are shy to discuss their own or their friends' abortions publicly, however. A middle-aged ob-gyn physician commented to me recently that unmarried women now visit his clinic without fear or subterfuge and without using false names as they did in the past before 1990.
[43] Chai Bin Park and Nam-Hoon Cho, *Consequences of Son Preference in a Low-Fertility Society: Imbalance of the Sex Ratio at Birth in Korea*, East-West Center Reprints, Population Series

No.311, 1995. Reprinted from Population and Development Review 21:1, March 1995, 73-74.

[44] Op cit. above.

[45] Ibid., 80.

[46] *Korea Herald* (Seoul) February 5, 1995, 'Doctors vow not to identify sex of fetus,' 3.

[47] Editorial page of *The Korea Times*, February 18, 1995, 'Female Fetal Abortions', 6.

[48] Nam-Hoon Cho, *Demographic Transition*, viii-ix.

[49] Trevor Ling (1969) 'Buddhist Factors in Population Growth and Control,' *Population Studies* 23: 58.

[50] Sung-bong Hong and Walter B. Watson, *The Increasing Use of Induced Abortion in Korea.* (Seoul: Korean Institute of Family Planning/Korea University Press, 1976), 'Buddhists are more likely to have abortions than Christians, and Christians more likely than the two thirds of Korean women who profess no religion. Among Christians, Catholics are a little more likely to have abortions than Protestants, but sample size is small. On the whole religious differences are not great and are probably associated with socioeconomic levels,' 12.

[51] Young Hee Shim et al. (1991) op cit., 158-159.

[52] The earliest Korean publication we are aware of to address abortion from the viewpoints of Korean Buddhist belief is Venerable Sŏk Myogak's *Aga-ya, yongsŏhaedao*, 'My Dear Baby! Please Forgive Me!' (Seoul: Ch'angusa, 1985). A 5th revised edition of 288 pages has been published, (Seoul: Kangyŏngdogam, 1995).

[53] William LaFleur, ibid, 3-10.

[54] Nakaoka Toshiya, *Mizuko rei no himitsu*, (Tokyo: Hutami Shobo, 1980).

[55] MBC Radio, Ch'ŏngju City, Ch'ungch'ŏngpukto, 'Yŏsŏng sitae t'ŭkjip pangsong' (Women's Age: Feature Program') Saturday May 13, 1995, 10:05-11:00 am.

[56] Ibid.

[57] Sŏk Myogak, *Aga-ya!*, ibid., 17-21.

[58] Cho Myŏng-nyŏl, 'Ilpon-ŭi suja kongyang-ŭl t'onghae pon chonggyo-wa saengmyŏng yulli' ('Religion, Life and Ethics Seen through Japanese Fetus Offering') in *Tabo* (Seoul) 1992: 4, 48.

[59] Mok Jeong-bae (Mok Chŏng-bae), 'Pulgyo-ŭi saengmyŏng chonjung undong-gwa t'ae-a ch'ŏndo' ('The Buddhist Respect for Life Movement and Auspicious Rebirth Ceremonies for Fetuses'), 55.

[60] See William LaFleur, *Liquid Life*, 22-29.

[61] Domyo Miura, *The Forgotten Child* (Henley-on-Thames, England: Aidan Ellis, 1983).

[62] See Han Pogwang, 'Pulgyogyŏngjon-ae nat'anan nak t'ae munjae' ('The Abortion Problem as it appears in the Buddhist Canon') in *Tabo* (Seoul) 1992: 4, 32-39.

[63] L.R. Lancaster, *The Korean Buddhist Canon: A Descriptive Catalogue* (Berkeley: University of California Press, 1979), 299, K 763; Taisho 2154-716c:27.

[64] Lancaster, op.cit, p.484, KS 11.

[65] A very short *sūtra* within the Chap Aham Kyŏng (*Samyuktāgamasūtra*).

[66] Kang Chawu, *Ŏdum-ŭi pich'ŭro ttŏnan t'ae-anŭn ŏdiro kanŭnga* ('Where is the Fetus Going, that which was a Light in Darkness?'), (Seoul: Miral, 1995).

[67] Except for recent cases of divulging the sex of the embryo to, in effect, solicit the abortion of female offspring.

[68] Dubbed into Korean and with an appeal for donations.

[69] Hyŏnjang sŭnim, 'Sujaryŏng ch'ŏndo-e taehaesŏ' ('On the auspicious rebirth of spirits of water-children') in *Yŏsŏng Pulgyo*, (Seoul: Tosŏnsa Women's Buddhist Association, 2539 BE: 7, July,1995 No.194, 18.

[70] Hugh MacMahon, 'Return, O Spirit of Confucius' in the Catholic *Kyŏng Hyang Magazine*. Reprinted in *Inculturation*, Korea, (Seoul: Columban Inculturation Center,V.5:3 Fall 1995), 5.

[71] Kim, Wan-ki, 'A-i rŭl natgo sip'ŭn mihon ŏdiro kaya hana' ('A Pregnant, Single Woman Who Wants to Bear Her Baby, Where Can She Go?') in *Yosŏng Pulgyo* 1995:7 No.194, 31.

[72] Venerable Myogak concludes the last day of his unique *ch'ŏndo* ritual with the release of fish into the Han River in Seoul. For more on interesting ritual, see Holmes Welch, *The Practice of Chinese Buddhism* 1900-1950 (Cambridge: Harvard University Press, 1967), 378-382.

[73] Mok, Jeong-bae, 'The Respect for Life Movement in Buddhism and the Auspicious Rebirth of Fetuses' in *Tabo* 1992:4, 55.

[74] Most Venerable Supreme Patriarch Wolha of T'ongdosa, the officially designated Buddha Jewel forest monastery of the Chogye Order. MBC broadcast in Korean, Ch'ŏngju, May 13, 1995.

8

Abortion in the Pāli Canon and Early Buddhist Thought

James P. McDermott

Introduction

Through the great Buddhist hell, Mahāniraya, there flows a great caustic river known as Vetaraṇī. Its waters are bitter and sharp as razors. Those who enter it are slashed up by swords and similar sharp weapons standing hidden along the river bank.[1] According to the *Saṃkicca Jātaka*, those who oppress the weak and those who are guilty of abortion (*gabbhapātiyo*) are reborn in this hell and cannot escape Vetaraṇī's cutting waters.[2]

While the karmic punishment referred to in this passage suggests the seriousness of abortion as an offence, there appears to be no clear, explicit, general prohibition of abortion in the Pāli Canon or its classical commentaries, in spite of the fact that killing itself is prohibited in the first precept. Nonetheless, a number of other Buddhist tales are also concerned with the karmic retribution which befalls abortionists, and a number of the monastic rules spelled out in the *Vinaya Piṭaka* of the Buddhist Pāli Canon aim at preventing involvement of monks and nuns in the performance of abortion. Further, there are passages both in the *Tipiṭaka* and in relatively early, authoritative, post-canonical writings, both in Pāli and Sanskrit, which discuss the processes of conception and fetal development in a manner relevant, at least in theory, to the issue of abortion. The purpose of this paper, then, is to study these texts with a view

toward understanding the early Buddhist attitude toward abortion
and its contribution to thought about the subject.

The *Dhammapada* Commentary

In a story of a previous rebirth of the Buddha recorded in the commentary to the *Dhammapada*,[3] we are told of a young man who is
married to two wives, one barren and the second fruitful. On learning that her rival has become pregnant, the barren wife, the senior
of the two, becomes concerned by the prospect that the birth of a
son will mean that the mother will become mistress of the entire
household. Wishing to prevent this eventuality, the barren woman
secretly administered an abortive drug to her rival along with her
food. The result was a miscarriage. A second time the fruitful wife
conceived, with the same results. Her neighbours called to her attention her rival's role in causing the miscarriage. A third time the
woman conceived, but this time kept her pregnancy a secret from
her rival. But eventually this pregnancy becomes obvious and a
third abortion is attempted, but because of the late stage of the
pregnancy, the child lodged across the neck of the womb. Immediately the mother suffered acute pain and realized she was dying
along with her child. Cursing her persecutor, she made an earnest
wish to be reborn as an ogress able to devour any children her rival
might bear. Dying, she was reborn in the same household as a cat.
Recognizing that his barren wife had been the cause of these
deaths, the husband beat her, as a result of which she too died, only
to be reborn in the same house as a hen. The hen laid eggs and the
cat ate them. This occurred three times. The third time, the hen recognized that the cat was likely to eat her too. Before she died, she
wished that upon rebirth she might be placed in a position to be
able to eat her enemy and her offspring. Expiring, the hen was reborn as a leopardess. When the cat died in turn, she was reborn as a
doe. Three times the doe brings forth offspring, only to have them
eaten by the female leopard. Wishing to get even, when she died
the doe was reborn as an ogress. When the leopardess too passed
on, she was reborn as a young woman named Sāvatthi. The ogress
devoured her first and second born sons. When Sāvatthi is about to
give birth to a third child, however, she manages to elude her enemy, until one day, sitting in a monastery with her child, she sees

the ogress approaching. Running to the Buddha for help, she gives him her child and pleads with him to spare her son. The ogress is brought into his presence. Upon learning the circumstances of the quarrel, the Buddha asks why they have been returning hatred for hatred. He cautions them: 'Hatred is never conquered by hatred. Rather, it is conquered by love. This is an eternal truth (*dhamma*).'[4] The ogress is converted by this lesson, and the two former enemies live from then on as friends.

Several observations may be made on the basis of this narrative. First is that the initial acts of abortion inaugurate a cycle of karmic retribution. Tit for tat, the destruction of the fetus leads to the guilty woman's loss of her own offspring, in the form of the hen's eggs, in her next existence. Although in this instance the abortionist does not end up in the caustic waters of the Vetaraṇī River as a result of her misdeed, the fact that she is reborn as an animal—and a chicken at that—which, furthermore, must suffer the loss of its own offspring, is indicative of the seriousness of the offence. Second, the parallel pattern of retributive blood revenge revealed through the course of the story suggests that the initial act of abortion is morally equivalent to the destruction of the hen's eggs, and that both of these acts in turn are to be considered morally equivalent to the eating of the new-born fauns by the leopardess and the ogress' meal of Sāvatthi's children. In short, the concept of the sanctity of life implied by this narrative extends as much to the unborn fetus and unhatched egg as to human children and animal young.

The *Petavatthu*

Another pair of stories concerning karmic retribution for abortion is related in the *Petavatthu* (Stories of the Departed). In these two similar stories, a jealous wife engages an abortionist to cause her rival co-wife to miscarry. When confronted by their husband and the victim's other relatives, the guilty wife protested her innocence and denied her involvement in causing the abortion. To prove her good faith, the guilty woman is asked to take an oath, which she falsely swears. Shortly thereafter she dies and is reborn as a naked, ugly, foul-smelling *petī* (i.e. unhappy ghost), covered with flies and doomed time after time to eat her own children. When asked the reason for her misfortune, she explains that her heart is scorched and smokes with hunger and thirst because she caused the miscarriage of her rival's unborn child. In verse she continues:

> I, even I, took the terrible oath falsely: 'May I eat the flesh of children if it was done by me.'
> In consequence of both the deed and the perjury, I devour the flesh of children, stained with the blood of the past.[5]

A significant difference exists between the similar stories at *Petavatthu* I.6 and I.7. In the version at Pv I.6 the abortion occurs in the second month of pregnancy. As a consequence, 'when the embryo was two months old just blood flowed forth.' In contrast, in the version at Pv I.7, the guilty *petī* describes her offence and its outcome as follows:

> Then my husband was angry and married another wife. And when she became with child, I meditated evil against her.
> And I with mind corrupted caused the fall of her unborn child. This fell in the third month, foul and bloody.[6]

As a result of her offence, she too is reborn as a suffering ghost doomed repeatedly to devour her own offspring. The significance lies in the fact that while both acts of abortion result in the same karmic retribution, the offences occur at different stages of embryonic development.

From these stories we can conclude that there is no difference in the moral status of the unborn at these two stages of development in the second and third months of the first trimester. Indeed, more generally, there is nothing in the early Buddhist texts to suggest that abortion was seen as less reprehensible at an earlier as opposed to a later stage of fetal development. This is consistent with evidence from the classical Hindu texts as well.[7] Peter Harvey and Trevor Ling to the contrary, however, purport to have found evidence to support the view that Buddhists consider the seriousness of an offence of abortion to increase with the size of the fetus.[8] Thus, Ling concludes that it would be 'less serious to terminate the life of a month-old fetus than of a child about to be born,' just as it would be less serious to destroy a mosquito than to kill a human being.[9] In his book, *Buddhism and Bioethics*, Damien Keown discusses this issue at length. He begins by quoting a key passage from Buddhaghosa's commentary to the *Majjhima Nikāya* which would seem to be a basis for the reading of Harvey and Ling:

> Taking life in the case of [beings such as] animals and so forth which are without virtue (*gunavirahita*) is a minor sin if they are small and a great sin if they are large. Why? Because of the greater effort required. In cases where the effort is identical, the offence may be worse due to greater size. Among [beings such as] humans and so forth who have virtue (*gunavant*), it is a minor sin to kill a being of small virtue but a great sin to kill a being of great virtue. Where both bodily size and virtue are the same, it is a minor sin if the wickedness (*kilesa*) involved and the assault itself are moderate, and a great sin if they are extreme.[10]

On the basis of a careful reading of this passage, Keown concludes that, with respect to abortion, 'the important point to note is that Buddhaghosa's discussion of size does not relate to human beings in any way.... [Rather,] size is a relevant factor in assessing the gravity of a breach of the first precept only when the victim is an animal.'[11] Thus, Keown's conclusions from this passage serve as confirmation of the inferences which I have drawn from the stories told at *Petavatthu* I.6 and I.7. In short, to reiterate, it would appear that, at least so far as the early Pāli texts and their commentaries are concerned, Harvey and Ling's conclusion that for the Buddhists abortion is a more serious offence in the later stages of pregnancy than it is in the earlier stages has no basis in fact.

Ethics and Embryology

Buddhist discipline is aimed at fostering moral conduct (*sīla*), concentration (*samādhi*), and wisdom (*paññā*). The kernel of this discipline is defined in the *Dhammapada* as 'to shun evil; to do good; and to purify one's mind—this is the teaching of the Buddha.'[12] This is to avoid doing anything harmful, whether to oneself or to any other creature. This applies even to the fetus during its period of gestation. Hence, discussing the suffering (*dukkha*) inherent with rebirth in his authoritative treatise *The Path of Purification* (*Visuddhimagga*), the fifth century C.E. commentator, Buddhaghosa, describes the experience of descent into the mother's womb and the ensuing gestation of the fetus as hellish in most vivid terms. According to Bhikkhu Nyanamoli's translation, he goes on to speak of the particular suffering which is 'rooted in abortion:'

> When the mother has an abortion [*mūḷhagabbhāya*],[13] the pain that arises in him [i.e. the fetus] through the cutting and rending in the place where the pain arises that is not fit to be seen even by friends and intimates and companions—this is the suffering rooted in abortion [*gabbhavipatti*]. [14]

More specifically, Buddhist moral training (*sikkhāpada*) is defined in terms of five precepts (*pañca sīla*) binding on all Buddhists, whether lay or monastic. These are to abstain (1) from killing any being, (2) from stealing, (3) from illicit sex—in the case of monks and nuns this is a requirement of total chastity, (4) from lying, as well as otherwise harmful speech, and finally (5) from the use of intoxicants.[15]

Members of the monastic community are further to be restrained according to the four principles of purification (*pārisuddhi sīla*). That is, they are to be restrained first in accordance with the principles of monastic code of discipline (*pāṭimokkha saṃvara sīla*). Second, their senses are to be restrained (*indriya saṃvara sīla*). Third, their livelihood should be befitting a member of the monastic community (*ājīva pārisuddhi sīla*). And finally, in their use of the four requisites (i.e. robes, alms food, dwelling, and medicine), they must be guided by a proper mental attitude. [16]

Respect for life is basic to Buddhism, underlying both the precepts and these principles of discipline. Indeed, in the authoritative post-canonical *Questions of King Milinda* (*Milindapañha*), the monk Nāgasena informs the pious King that the distinguishing mark of the Buddhist teaching, doctrine, or norm (*dhamma*) is non-injury (*ahiṃsā*). He further maintains that a verse from the *Cakkavāka Jātaka* to the effect that 'not injuring another in the world, you will be dear and beloved', is a teaching approved by all the Tathāgatas, and a statement of the very essence of the *dhamma*.[17]

The prose portions of several of the *Jātakas* refer to the observance of a rite of passage for the protection of the embryo (*gabbhaparihāra*) performed when a woman became pregnant.[18] It was considered proper, or in conformity to the *dhamma* (*dhammatā*), for a meritorious woman to be given such a ritual, and a result of bad kamma not to be given one.[19] While this may be taken as confirmation that Buddhists consider the sanctity of life to extend to the fetus, there is nothing to suggest that this particular ritual was uniquely Buddhist. That such observances were, rather, part of the broader pan-Indian culture can be inferred in part from the fact that references to this ceremony are lacking in the *Tipiṭaka* itself, though not uncommon in the various collections of *Jātakas* and in the Pāli commentaries.[20] More suggestive of this conclusion, perhaps, is the *Dasaratha Jātaka's* reference to the performance of the *gabbhaparihāra* on the conception of Prince Bharata, for this story, purportedly of a former birth of the Buddha, is but a highly condensed retelling of the narrative of the Hindu epic, *The Rāmāyana*, except that here Sītā is the hero's sister, rather than his wife.[21] It seems safe to assume, then, that the ritual for the protection of the fetus referred to in such passages is a Buddhist counterpart to such Hindu *saṃskāras* as the *garbhadhāna* (rite of conception; literally 'womb-placing') and, more specifically, the *puṃsavana* (third month blessing). The Hindu *garbhadhāna* is a purificatory rite performed to ensure not only conception but also the perfect development of the embryo. It is followed three months later by the *puṃsavana*, a rite intended to ensure that the child will be male. Concerning these rituals, a modern Śaivite commentator elaborates:

> Conception, pregnancy's crucial stages and birth itself are all sanctified through sacred ceremonies performed privately by the husband. In the rite of conception, *garbhadhāna*, physical union is consecrated through prayer, mantra and invocation with the conscious purpose of bringing a high soul into physical birth. At the first stirring of life in the womb, in the rite called *punsavana*, special prayers are intoned for the protection and safe development of child and mother.[22]

Vinaya Cases on Abortion

That abortion is prohibited by the precept against depriving a living being of life is made explicit in the *Mahākhandhaka* of the *Mahāvagga* of the *Vinaya Piṭaka*:

> An ordained monk should not deliberately deprive a living thing of life, even if it is only an ant. Whatever monk intentionally deprives a human being of life—even to the extent of causing an abortion—he becomes no longer a (true) recluse *(samaṇa)*, not a son of the Sakyans [that is, no longer a follower of the Buddha]. As a flat stone, broken apart, is something which cannot be put back together again, so a monk who has deliberately deprived a human being of life is no longer a (true) recluse, not a son of the Sakyans. This is something not to be done by you as long as life lasts.[23]

In commenting on another passage from the *Vinaya*, Buddhaghosa explains that deliberately depriving a human being of life refers to separating it from life, either at the first stage in the development of the embryo *(kalala)*—whether by scorching, by crushing, or by the use of drugs—or at some later stage of development by a similar kind of assault.[24] Thus, any monk who participates in performing an abortion is guilty of depriving a human being of life and loses his claim to being a follower of the Buddha.

The rules of monastic discipline, the *pātimokkha*, list four great categories of offences which entail defeat and warrant expulsion from the order for their commission. These are theft, murder, exaggeration of one's miraculous power and misconduct with women.

A number of specific cases relating to abortion are discussed in the *Vinaya Piṭaka* which help to demonstrate how this general principle applies in particular situations.[25] In the first such case, a woman whose husband was living away from home became pregnant by her lover. Seeking assistance, she turned to a monk who was dependent on her family for alms, and asked him to provide her with an abortive preparation. Acceding to her request, he gave her the abortive preparation. As a result, the child died. Although the monk was remorseful, he was guilty of an offence involving defeat for which the penalty was expulsion from the monastic order.

A similar case follows immediately. It concerns a man who had two wives, one barren and the other fertile. On learning that the fertile wife had become pregnant, the barren wife became jealous and afraid that her rival would become mistress of the entire household if she were successfully to produce an heir. To prevent this, she requested a monk to help her obtain an abortive preparation. He gave her one. Again the child died. In this case the text further explicitly specifies that the mother survived. The offence is still classified as one involving defeat and as punishable by expulsion from the monastic community.

Several further examples help to clarify the implications of these cases. Thus a case is cited which is identical to the one just referred to, except that in this instance the mother died but the child did not die. The resulting offence is not considered quite so serious. It is classified not as entailing defeat, but rather as a grave offence punishable by temporary suspension from the order.

Clearly the difference in these two cases is a matter of intent. There was no intent to kill the mother, who was the only victim in this example. This is consistent with the interpretation of a murder case elsewhere in the *Vinaya*, where it is said that 'there is no offence (involving defeat) if it was unintentional, if he did not know, if he were not meaning death.'[26]

The principles at work here may be analogous to the concept of complete action found elsewhere in the Buddhist literature. A fully developed theory of complete karma is spelled out for the first time in Vasubandhu's Sarvāstivādin treatise, the *Abhidharmakośa*[27] (although certain precursors to this theory can be found in the Pāli texts). First is the notion that for an act to have karmic consequences, it has to be done intentionally. Indeed, kamma is defined as an intentional impulse and the act that follows upon it. Related to this was the idea that for a deed to have the greatest possible effect, it has to be done with consideration, and not casually. Finally, in some instances it appears as if, to a certain extent, the ethical potential of a deed, whether good or bad, can be counteracted by repentance. In the abortion cases at hand, however, repentance does not play a mitigating role in determining the seriousness of the offence. In each instance we are told that the monk involved felt remorse, but this fact does not seem to impact on the level of offence.

Other cases in which both the mother and child succumb and in which both survive the attempt at abortion are considered together.[28] Where both survive, there is no defeat, but the offence is still considered grave, just as when the child survives but the mother does not. Where both survive, although the intent was present and serious steps were taken to complete the act of abortion, no actual killing occurs; hence no defeat is involved. The example where both the mother and child succumb is more difficult to understand, for here again the offence is classified as only a grave one (*thullaccaya*) involving no defeat. Reasonably, this is not the expected judgment, as there was intention to cause death and death resulted. The same judgment could hardly apply to two such different outcomes. Buddhaghosa's only comment on this case is: 'The case of the man with two wives is clear in meaning.' So clearly he saw nothing in need of explanation. In a personal communication, Damien Keown confirms me in my sense that if these two cases are read 'together as both getting a *thullaccaya* judgement then there clearly *is* something in need of explanation, so it is unlikely that they go together.' My suggestion is that, although we have two separate cases here, the judgment given relates to only one of them, namely the situation in which the outcome is the death of neither the mother nor the child. The judgment in the case where both die should have gone on to declare a *pārājika*, but this is swallowed up by an ellipsis indicated by the Pāli equivalent of a ditto (i.e. *pe*), referring back not only to the details of the earlier case where the child dies but the mother survives, but also to its judgment.

As Damien Keown notes in a personal communication, the same thing happens elsewhere, for instance in certain cases relating to medical treatment discussed at *Vinaya* III.83. In parallel cases, nasal treatment is given intending to cause the death of a monk. There are two ellipses indicated by the word *pe* in the passage. In the first instance the results are as planned and the victim dies. In the second instance he does not die. The decision is a *thullaccaya*. Once again, Buddhaghosa describes each of these cases as clear in meaning, in spite of the fact that it again seems impossible that two such diametrically opposed outcomes should result in the same judgment. Keown writes:

> Here again, my thought is that the first *pe* would include a judgment that it *was* a *pārājika* [in the instance where the monk died]. The alternative is impossible, namely that there was i) an intention to cause death, ii) death resulted, but iii) it was only a *thullaccaya*. [This] just doesn't add up, so my conclusion is ... that the decision about it being a *pārājika* has simply been omitted as part of the ellipsis and that this is a common practice in the text.

To return to the abortion cases considered at *Vin* III.83-84, another thing in favour of such a reading of the text is that it considers all possible permutations of the outcome, providing logical decisions for each situation. As Keown notes, the structure of this episode, then, would be:

1.   Child dies; mother lives— *pārājika*
2.   Child lives; mother dies—*thullaccaya*
3.   Both die (the missing judgment)—*pārājika*
4.   Neither dies— *thullaccaya*

The succeeding series of cases further clarifies the *Vinaya's* stance with respect to monks who participate in performing abortions. In two cases described at *Vinaya* III.84, a woman who is pregnant turns to a monk for help in procuring an abortive preparation. In these cases, however, instead of providing her with the requested drug, he suggests alternative methods of carrying out the abortion, in the first instance telling her to crush (*maddassu*) the fetus, and in the second telling her to scorch herself. In both instances the fetus is destroyed and, although the monk involved is remorseful, the offence is identified as *pārājika*. Thus, in keeping with the Buddhist Noble Eightfold Path's emphasis on right speech, the monk's role in merely counselling abortion, where the advice is taken, is considered as serious a violation of the monastic rule as would be the case had he actively participated in the physical act itself.

Two further cases not concerned with abortion can be used further to refine our understanding of the cases just discussed.[29] In the first a barren woman asks a monk to get her a fertility drug, which he does. As a result of taking the medicine, she dies. The second is identical, except that the woman is fertile and seeks help in procuring a contraceptive. As there was no intent to kill, as we might expect, theses offences are not classified as *pārājika*, rather they are identified as cases of wrongdoing (*dukkaṭa*), a level of offence less serious even than a *thullaccaya*. It is interesting to compare these cases with the case of attempted abortion considered above in which the child survived but the mother died. In that case the monk's offence was classified as *thullaccaya*. In each of these examples a drug is provided to a woman, with her death the unintended result. Since none of the cases involves intent to murder the eventual victim, there is no defeat punishable by permanent expulsion from the order. Where the cases differ is in intent and the resulting degree of culpability. Where there is malicious intent, even if not carried successfully to conclusion, the offence is more serious than where the intent is purely benevolent, as in the attempt to help a woman who desires a child to become fertile or in the case of the woman seeking a contraceptive. From these various cases, the following pattern becomes clear:

1.   Intended victim (only) dies—*pārājika*
2.   Intended victim dies & unintended victim dies—*pārājika*
3.   Unintended victim dies while intended victim
      survives—*thullaccaya*
4.   Intent but no victim (i.e. no unintended victim; intended
      victim survives)—*thullaccaya*
5.   Unintended victim dies where no victim is
      intended—*dukkaṭa*

A somewhat different case involving an abortion is considered in the *Cullavagga*.[30] Here a woman, who has become pregnant by her lover while her husband is absent, aborts her own fetus, and then asks a nun who is dependent on her for alms to become an accessory after the fact and dispose of the aborted fetus. Agreeing to help, the nun places the fetus in her alms bowl and covers it with her outer cloak. While carrying it away, she encounters a monk who has vowed not to eat his own alms food without first sharing it with another monk or nun. Three times he offers the nun a share of his meal; but each time she refuses, finally explaining the situation and begging him to keep her confidence. This he refused to do, criticizing her among his fellow monks. The more modest among them reported the matter to the Buddha who, in response decreed that a fetus should never be taken away in a bowl by a nun. A nun who violates this rule is guilty of an act of wrong doing (*dukkaṭa*). The Buddha further allowed monks the right to inspect the bowls of nuns whom they should encounter.

This case is one of a series of cases, otherwise unrelated to abortion, each of which is concerned with maintaining the purity of the monastic order and its reputation. In general, as Mohan Wijayaratna notes:

> The rules of the Community were established with ten intentions in mind (*Vin* III 21; IV 91, 120, 182, 299):
> 1. Protecting the Community
> 2. Insuring the Community's comfort
> 3. Warding off ill-meaning people
> 4. Helping well-behaved monks and nuns
> 5. Destroying present defilements
> 6. Preventing future defilements
> 7. Benefiting non-followers
> 8. Increasing the number of followers
> 9. Establishing discipline
> 10. Observing the rules of restraint.
>
> Eight out of the ten reasons given here deal with the relationship which is to exist between monks inside the Community, as well as between monks and society outside the Community .... The Community's regulations were thus for the most part motivated by the desire to safeguard the place of monks [and nuns] both in the Community and in the wider social and religious environment.[31]

Methods and Motives

Taken together these various cases related to abortion provide us with evidence both of the methods used to undertake abortions and of the reasons underlying their attempt. One common method was the use of an abortive preparation (*gabbhapātana*). While in certain contexts the term *gabbhapātana* may simply refer to the destruction of the embryo, that is, abortion, in other contexts it is explicitly connected with the term *bhesajja* (i.e. medicine).[32] Further, the *Vinaya* commentary, the *Samantapāsādikā*, without identifying the substance or drug involved, defines *gabbhapātana* as 'a medicine (*bhesajja*) of such a character by use of which the embryo falls.'[33] The texts provide cases where such medicine was provided by a monk and a wandering mendicant (*paribbājaka*),[34] while the abortionist in the story at *Petavatthu* I.7 is a physician. A second method used to cause abortions was by crushing or trampling on the womb. Heating or scorching was another method which was used.[35] In addition it was believed that charms and magic powers could be used to prevent a normal delivery. In this vein, Damien Keown cites a passage from Buddhaghosa where he writes:

> Moreover, monks, a religious wanderer (*samaṇa*) or a brahman who has achieved psychic control and mental mastery may direct evil thoughts toward the embryo in the womb of some woman with the wish that the embryo in the womb should not be delivered safely. In this way, monks, there is the slaying of [the heir to] an estate.[36]

Two primary reasons for the performance of an abortion appear in the examples provided by the Pāli texts. The first type involves married women who have illegitimately become pregnant by lovers, and seek abortions for themselves in order to protect their reputations, their family status, and to preempt the wrath of their husbands. In the second type, a jealous wife causes her co-wife to miscarry in an effort to maintain her own position in the family and the role of her sons, if any, as heirs. Clearly neither reason has ethical sanction. In the Pāli texts there appear to be no examples of abortions being performed for medical reasons.[37]

However, Vasubandhu's *Abhidharmakośa* considers one fascinating controversy concerning the termination of a pregnancy before term. The issue is:

> When the embryo (*kalala*) of a woman has issued out (*pratrutam*) and it is deposited in the womb (*yoniyā pītam*) of another woman, which of these two women is considered the mother

whose murder constitutes (matricide) entailing immediate retribution?[38]

The answer is that, although the second woman has taken up the duties of mother who nourishes and raises the child, the 'mother' is the woman from whose blood the child has been generated. It is thus her murder which constitutes matricide entailing immediate retribution.[39]

Although there is no evidence to suggest that this case represents anything but a hypothetical situation, certain implications of the example appear relevant. The term *kalala* used to refer to the embryo here refers specifically to the earliest stage of embryonic development. The *Yakkha Sutta* of the Pāli *Saṃyutta Nikāya* and the *Niddesa* provide the scriptural foundation for fully developed Buddhist embryology. They speak of five stages of fetal development. Quoting the *Yakkha Sutta*:

> How are you suspended in the womb-cavern (*gabbhara*)?
> First the *kalala* comes to exist. The *kalala* becomes the *abbuda*.
> From the *abbuda* the *pesī* is produced. The *ghana* comes into being from the *pesī*.
> The extremities (*pasākha*) arise from the *ghana*—the hair of the head (*kesi*), body hair (*loma*), nails, etc.[40]

Apart from these specific stages of fetal growth, prenatal development is counted by months, from one to ten.[41] The *Saṃyutta Nikāya* commentary, the *Sāratthapakāsinī*, expands on this treatment of fetal development.[42] It says that the *kalala*, which first appears as a drop of oil, develops into the *abbuda* after seven days. At this stage it takes on the colour of water which has been used to wash flesh. When seven additional days have lapsed, the *pesī* rises from it. This is a piece of flesh with the appearance of refined lead. It is said '*pesī* coagulates like a lump, produced from a crushed and heated bundle of black peppers, tied with a piece of cloth. After seven days of its existence, *pesī* becomes *ghana*' and takes on the appearance of a hen's egg.[43] The extremities develop from the *ghana*; the hands, feet, and head appearing during the fifth week of the embryo's existence. By the 154th day of its development, the embryo is said to be mature.

To return to Vasubandhu's hypothetical case, it is difficult to conceive how such a situation could arise, particularly at such an early stage of embryonic development, unless the process of premature delivery were intentionally induced. One could hardly imagine the serendipitous combination of so premature a natural delivery or accidental miscarriage, the coincidental presence of a suitable surrogate mother, and continued viability of the embryo as the alternative would require. Indeed, for precisely this reason, the Sthaviravādins would not admit the possibility of such a case, arguing: 'If the embryo is living, it does not fall; if it falls, it is because it is dead, because a living being cannot pass through all the filth.'[44] However, Saṃghabhadra counters that, according to the *sūtra*, this is precisely what occurred in the case of the birth of Kumāra Kaśyapa.[45] The Pāli versions of the story of Kumāra Kassapa found in the *Jātaka* and *Dhammapada* commentaries lack the motif of the embryo transplant, however,[46] as does the more detailed discussion of Kumāra Kassapa's conception in the *Questions of King Milinda (Milindapañha)*.[47] The latter follows a version of the story from the *Vinaya* which does not mention Kumāra Kassapa by name.[48]

When Does Life Begin?

Contemporary American debate concerning abortion includes discussion of the point at which the fetus becomes a person; that is, when does life begin? The issue of fetal development in relation to personhood is also of relevance in early Buddhist thought, though generally independent from the issue of abortion. The Buddhist discussion revolves around the issue of the processes of conception and rebirth, as well as the question of the existence of an 'intermediate-state being' (*gandhabba*). These discussions are found in their fully developed forms in such post-canonical texts as Buddhaghosa's *Visuddhimagga* and Vasubandhu's *Abhidharmakośa*.

As Damien Keown notes:

> A distinctive feature of Buddhist thought is that it does not postulate an initial starting point to the series of lives lived by an

individual. Instead, it regards the cyclic course of human existence as potentially eternal: it had no beginning and there is no
certainty it will ever have an end. What takes place at conception
is the rebirth of a previously existent individual. All conception
is thus reconception. The belief that each individual exists prior
to conception provides a distinctive perspective on the question
of when life begins.[49]

Further, teaching a doctrine of *anattā / anātman*, the Buddha denied the existence of a permanent soul.[50] Instead he taught that a
sentient being is made up of a body (i.e. form) and five mental constituents, namely consciousness, feelings, perceptions, and what is
variously translated as predispositions or karmic tendencies. Collectively these are referred to as the five *khandhas / skandhas*.
These are characterized by their impermanence. At any given time
an individual is but a temporary combination of these constituents.
An individual does not remain identically the same for any two
consecutive instants. The Buddhists deny that any of these constituents, whether individually or in combination is equivalent to a
soul or spirit.[51]

According to the canonical *Majjhima Nikāya*, three conjoined
factors are necessary for conception to occur: First, there must be
sexual intercourse between the parents. Second, the mother must be
in the proper phase of her menstrual cycle. And, finally, a *gandhabba* must be present.[52] In his translation of this passage, Damien
Keown translates the term *gandhabba* as 'intermediate being', apparently following the Tibetan interpretation based on the teachings of Vasubandhu's *Abhidharmakośa*.[53] However, the
implications of this third factor were open to broad debate among
various schools of Buddhist thought. In his interpretation of the
passage just quoted, Buddhaghosa, for example, explains the term
gandhabba as referring to a being about to enter the womb (*ta-
trūpakasatta*), ready to exist (*paccupaṭṭhito hoti*), driven on by the
force of karma.[54] This interpretation is not to be taken as implying
the existence of an intermediate-state being (*antarā bhava*) between one physical incarnation of a being and the next, however;
for elsewhere Buddhaghosa maintains that it is only those who are
confused about the process of death and rebirth who consider it to
involve a 'being's transmigration to another incarnation ... a

lasting being's manifestation in a new body.'[55] Theravāda Buddhism was vocal in its denial of the existence of an intermediate-state being between death and rebirth, as can be seen from the debate recorded in the *Points of Controversy* (*Kathāvatthu*) at VIII.2.[56] They were joined in this opinion by the Vibhajyavādins, Mahāsaṅghikas and Mahīśāsakas, who offered no clear alternative to the concept of the intermediate-state being which they rejected.[57] Buddhaghosa, however, elaborates on the process of rebirth in terms of a concept of 'rebirth-linking' (*paṭisandhi*).

As I have written elsewhere, Buddhaghosa maintains that in the normal state of human death, the body gradually withers away like a green leaf in the sun, the sense faculties cease, and the consciousness that remains is supported by the heart-basis alone. This last moment of consciousness before death is known as the *cuti viññāna*. Immediately on its cessation, contingent upon some kamma, conditioned by the *cuti viññāna*, and driven by craving and ignorance not yet abandoned, there arises in the mother's womb the first stirring of consciousness of the succeeding birth. It is known as the rebirth-linking consciousness (*paṭisandhi viññāna*). Not being carried over from the previous life, this rebirth-linking consciousness newly arises at the precise moment of conception. In other words, no transmigration of consciousness is being posited here, but rather a causally linked stream (*sota*) of discrete moments of consciousness. Buddhaghosa likens the relationship between *cuti viññāna* and *paṭisandhi viññāna* to that between a sound and its echo, or a signature-seal and its impression.[58]

A Buddhist controversy concerning the moment at which fetal consciousness develops is debated in the *Kathāvatthu* (*Points of Controversy*).[59] The issue concerns when the six sense mechanisms (*āyatana*; lit. 'spheres') arise. These consist of the five physical sense organs, with the mental base, consciousness, or—better—the coordinating organ (*manāyatana*) as sixth. The key point for our purposes is from the commentary's treatment of this controversy.[60] The commentator maintains that the sphere of touch and the mental coordinating organ alone of the sense mechanisms are reborn at precisely the moment of conception, with the remaining four taking seventy-seven days to develop.

An alternative interpretation of the rebirth process which, to the contrary, did posit the existence of an intermediate-state being (*antarā bhava*) between death and the succeeding rebirth was proposed by Vasubandhu. As he defines it in the auto-commentary to his *Abhidharmakośa*, the *antarā bhava* is a being which is found between two courses of existence (*gati*). It exists between the moment of death and the occurrence of the succeeding rebirth. It is made up of form and four mental factors, the so-called 'five aggregates' (*skandha*), but it exists without the support of any exterior element such as blood or semen.[61] Its existence is bracketed by the aggregates as they exist at the moment of death, on the one hand, and the aggregates as they exist at the moment of rebirth, on the other. Spatially, the intermediate-state being arises in the location where death takes place, from which it proceeds to the place of rebirth.[62] It has the power to act and the configuration of the being it is about to be born as. Vasubandhu goes on to suggest that it is precisely this intermediate-state being to which the term *gandharva*, the Sanskrit equivalent of the Pāli word *gandhabba*, refers.[63] It is, in short, the access (*sagamana*) through which a being reaches its proper course of existence in a new rebirth, rather than a separate course of existence (*gati*) in its own right.[64]

Given the existence of such an intermediate-state being, Vasubandhu proceeds to an explanation of how rebirth (*pratisaṃdhi*) takes place. The Oedipal character of his analysis would do justice to Freud: driven by karma, the intermediate-state being goes to the location where rebirth is to take place ... There it sees its father and its mother to be, united in intercourse. Finding the scene hospitable, its passions are stirred. If male, it is smitten with desire for its mother. If female, it is seized with desire for its father. And inversely, it hates either mother or father, which it comes to regard as a rival. Concupiscence and hatred thus arise in the *gandharva* as its driving passions. Stirred by these wrong thoughts, it attaches itself to the place where the sexual organs of the parents are united, imagining that it is there joined with the object of its passion. Taking pleasure in the impurity of the semen and blood in the womb, the *antarā bhava* establishes itself there. Thus do the *skandhas* arise in the womb. They harden; and the intermediate-state being perishes, to be replaced immediately by the birth existence (*pratisaṃdhi*) … Developing after it thus takes rebirth in the womb, the embryo then loses its mature sexual characteristics.[65]

As different as are their views concerning the existence of an intermediate-state being and the process of conception and rebirth, both Vasubandhu and the fully developed position of the Theravāda school as exemplified by Buddhaghosa and the *Kathāvatthu* agree in their rejection of a concept of a permanent soul (*ātman*) which transmigrates and defines one's identity across the cycle of rebirths. They also stand united in their opposition to those Buddhists collectively referred to as 'Personalists'[66] who believed that a personal entity (*puggala/pudgala*) exists and transmigrates from existence to existence, thereby defining one's individuality across the cycle of rebirths. If no such personal entity existed, they argued, the principle of karma could not operate, as there would be no connecting link between one life and the next. However, the Personalists nonetheless wanted to insist that their concept of such a personal entity is not to be taken as affirming the concept of a permanent soul (*attā/ātman*) in contradiction to the teachings of the Buddha. In a nice turn of phrase, Damien Keown describes this personal entity as 'a kind of pseudo-self.'[67] The Personalists further maintained the personal entity was neither different from nor identical with the *khandhas / skandhas* (i.e. changing pattern of form and mental factors) which constitute a living being. Unlike the *khandhas / skandhas*, this personal entity does not undergo constant change, dying and being reborn in each moment of consciousness. Nonetheless, it cannot be said to remain the same from moment to moment. How these two apparently contradictory claims can both hold true is considered ineffable (*avaktavya*), as is the relationship between the *puggala / pudgala* and the *khandhas / skandhas*.

Conclusion

From the above presentation it should be clear that while the Buddhists have contributed extensive consideration to the nature of the human 'person,' their approach consistently comes at the issue from a different perspective than do those treatments of the subject more familiar in the West.[68] These discussions, like the Buddhist concepts of karma and rebirth, and their understanding of the process of conception are all theoretically relevant to early Buddhist attitudes toward abortion. This is a conclusion that seems reinforced by observations in William R. LaFleur's masterful study, *Liquid Life: Abortion and Buddhism in Japan*.[69] Nonetheless, these issues are not explicitly connected with the matter of abortion either in the early Pāli texts, their commentaries, or in Vasubandhu's *Abhidharmakośa*. While the philosophical foundations for objection to abortion can in principle be derived from these texts, the explicit concern with abortion in the Pāli texts has two main types of focus. First, there are the references in the *Jātakas* and similar narratives. These deal with abortion instigated by a woman attempting to maintain her family status, either by aborting her own illegitimate fetus or by causing a rival co-wife to miscarry. Here the texts are at pains to show the karmic consequences of such misdeeds. Second, there are those references, from the *Vinaya* on the whole, focused primarily on the implications for monastic discipline of the involvement of monks and nuns in the actual practice of abortion.

Notes

[1] *SnA* ii. 482 (BUDSIR 29.312[680]. BUDSIR reads *vettaraṇī*). Thanks are due to Canisius College, Buffalo, New York, which supported research for this paper with a Summer Grant and Supplemental Research Grant from the Faculty Research Fund.

[2] *Jātaka* V. 269 (No.530) (JA BUDSIR 42.115[0]:17-18).

[3] *DhA* I.45-53 (BUDSIR 18.42[0]:5-49[0]:8).

[4] *Dh* 5 (BUDSIR 25.15[11]:16-17).

[5] *Pv* I.6 vss. 8-9 (BUDSIR 26.161[91]:13-16) as translated by H.S. Gehman, *The Minor Anthologies of the Pali Canon*, Part IV. *Petavatthu: Stories of the Departed* (London: Pali Text Society, 1974), p. 13. The two complete stories are *Pv* I.6 (BUDSIR 26.160[91]:17- 161:17) and I.7 (BUDSIR 26.161[92]:18-163:3).

[6] *Pv* I.7 vss. 7-8 (BUDSIR 26.162[92]:12-17) as translated by Gehman, Ibid., 14.

[7] For a thorough discussion of this issue as it applies to the Hindu texts, see Julius J. Lipner, 'On Abortion and the Moral Status of

the Unborn,' in *Hindu Ethics: Purity, Abortion, and Euthanasia* ed.
Harold G. Coward, et al. (Albany: State University of New York
Press, 1989), 53-57. For further consideration of the Buddhist un-
derstanding of embryonic/fetal development, see below.

[8]   Peter Harvey, *An Introduction to Buddhism: Teachings, history
and practices* (Cambridge: Cambridge University Press, 1990),
202 and Trevor Ling, 'Buddhist Factors in Population Growth and
Control,' *Population Studies*, Vol. 23, 58 as cited by Damien Keown, *Buddhism and Bioethics* (New York: St. Martin's Press,
1995), 96.

[9]   Ling as quoted by Keown, Ibid., 96 .

[10]   *MA* I.198 as translated by Keown, Ibid., 98.

[11]   Keown, Ibid., 99. Emphases Keown's; square brackets mine.

[12]   *Dh* 183 (BUDSIR 25.39[24]:19-40:1).

[13]   Literally: 'whose fetus has gone astray.'

[14]   Literally: 'false manifestation of the fetus.' *Vism* 500 (XVI.39)
= BUDSIR 59.85[0]:5-7, as translated by Bhikkhu Nyanamoli, *The
Path of Purification (Visuddhimagga) by Bhadantācariya*
Buddhaghosa (Colombo: A. Semage, 1964), 570. In his translation
of this text, Pe Maung Tin, *The Path of Purity* (London: Luzac for
the Pāli Text Society, 1971), 594, interprets this passage differently. He translates: 'And in the case of a miscarriage, pain comes
upon the child through the operations of cutting and splitting and
so forth at the seat of pain, which it is not proper even for the
mother's acquaintances and bosom friends to witness. This is ill
which has its root in miscarriage.' Dhammapāla's commentary, the
Paramatthamañjūsāṭīkā offers no help in choosing between seeing
this as a reference to 'suffering rooted in abortion' or suffering
'which has its root in miscarriage,' though the reference to cutting,
etc. seems to tilt the matter in favour of Bhikkhu Nyanamoli's interpretation. For text and commentary, see Dr. Rewatadhamma,
editor: *Buddhaghosācariya's Visuddhimaggo with Paramatthamañjūsāṭīkā of Bhadantācariya Dhammapāla* (Varanasi: Research
Institute, Varanaseya Sanskrit Vishwavidyalaya, 1969 [B.E.
2513]), Vol. II, 1126.

[15]   These five precepts are supplemented by five more rules binding on all monks, nuns and novices. The five precepts are also
sometimes expanded to a total of eight, often observed by laity on

full and new moon days, as well as on the days of the first and last quarters of the moon.

[16] See *Vism* I.42-130 (BUDSIR 57.19[0]:2-56:5) for a detailed exposition of this tetrad.

[17] *Miln* 185 (BUDSIR 56.257[0]). The Jātaka citation is from IV.71, vs. 9 (BUDSIR 27.296[1464]).

[18] *JA* 39.469[0]:19; 40.132[0]:17; 40.312[0]:2; 40.400[50]:19; 42.136[0]:3 and 43.3[0]:6.

[19] *ApA* 49.176[90]. I am grateful to Lance Cousins for this reference.

[20] BUDSIR lists 25 occurrences of the term *gabbhaparihāra* in its various forms in the Buddhist commentaries and related literature, including the prose portions of the *Jātakas*.

[21] *Jātaka* No.461 (BUDSIR 40.49[0]:1-58:18). E.B. Cowell, trans. *The Jātaka, or Stories of the Buddha's Former Births*, Vol. IV (London: Pali Text Society, 1981), 78-82. The reference to the *gabbhaparihāra* is on 79, where the translator has veiled the reference: 'In time she conceived, and all due attention having been given her [*gabbhaparihāra*], she brought forth a son...' Also see V. Fausböll, ed. and trans. *The Dasaratha Jātaka* (Copenhagen, 1871).

[22] Satguru Sivaya Subramuniyaswami, *Dancing with Śiva: Hinduism's Contemporary Catechism*, 4th edition (Concord, CA: Himalayan Academy, 1993), 269 [*Maṇḍala* 19, *śloka* 91, *bhāṣya*]. Cf. Margaret and James Stutley, *Harper's Dictionary of Hinduism* (New York: Harper & Row, 1977). I am grateful to Sadhunathan Nadesan and Srinivasan Pichumani for these references.

[23] *Vin* I.97 (BUDSIR 4.196[145]).

[24] *VinA* II.437f.

[25] A series of such cases is to be found at *Vin* III.83-84 (BUDSIR 1.158-159[214]).

[26] *Vin* III.78 (BUDSIR 1.147[203]:8-9).

[27] This is spelled out at *Kośa* IV.140-141. For a detailed treatment of this concept, see James P. McDermott, *Development in the Early Buddhist Concept of Kamma/Karma* (New Delhi: Munshiram Manoharlal, 1984), 141-142.

[28] *Vin* III.84 (BUDSIR 1.159[215]).

[29] These cases are again at *Vin* III.84 (BUDSIR 1.159 [215]:13-160:1).

[30] *Vin* II.267-268 (BUDSIR 7.349[561]:2-350:7).

[31] Mohan Wijayaratna, *Buddhist Monastic Life according to the texts of the Theravāda tradition*, translated by Claude Grangier and Steven Collins (Cambridge: Cambridge University Press, 1990), 122. Square brackets mine.

[32] At *DhA* I.47 (BUDSIR 18.43[0]:16 & 21), for example.

[33] *VinA* 1.573[0].

[34] *Vin* III.83-84 (BUDSIR 1.158-159[215]) and *Pv* I.6 (BUDSIR 26.160[91]:17-161:17) respectively.

[35] These three methods are all referred to at *VinA* II.437f.

[36] *VinA* II.441 as translated by Keown, *Buddhism and Bioethics*, 93.

[37] This is confirmed by Keown, Ibid., 92.

[38] *Kośa* IV.103. I have used the edition of Swami Dwarkidas Shastri, *Abhidharmakośa & Bhāṣya of Acharya Vasubandhu with Sphuṭārtha Commentary of Ācārya Yaśomitra*, 4 vols. Bauddha Bharati Series 5-7 & 9 (Varanasi: Bauddha Bharati, 1971), Part II, 730-731.

[39] *Kośa* IV. 103. Shastri, Ibid., 731.

[40] S I.206 = Kvu XIV.2 (BUDSIR 37.523[1557]-525[1560]). *Kalala* literally = soil. *Abbuda* literally = swelling. *Pesī* literally = lump. *Ghana* literally = swelling mass.

[41] *Vism* VIII.30 (BUDSIR 58.10[0]:15-11:1).

[42] *SA* I.301.

[43] J.R. Haldar, *Medical Science in Pali Literature* (Calcutta: Indian Museum, 1977), 29. Haldar outlines the entire process.

[44] Saṃghabhadra as quoted in Louis de la Vallée Poussin, *L'Abhidharmakośa de Vasubandhu*, Tome 3 (Paris: Paul Geuthner, 1924), 213-214, fn. 5 [translation mine].

[45] Saṃghabhadra, Ibid., 214. Cf Taisho XXIX 1562 xliii p. 588c, lines 9-15. I am indebted to Nobumi Iyanaga for the Taisho reference. Michael Sweet and Paul Dundas have pointed out to me the existence of a partial Jain parallel in the Śvetāmbara tradition of the transfer of Mahāvīra's embryo from a Brahmin woman to his Kṣatriya mother. Dundas notes (personal communication) that 'in the oldest Jain texts Mahāvīra is often called Kāśyapa.' Cf

Padmanabh S. Jaini, *The Jaina Path of Purification* (Berkeley: University of California Press, 1979), 7-9.

[46] *Jātaka* No.12 (I.145ff) and *DhA* Book XII, story 4a (III. 144-149). Cf *AA* I. 283F and *AA* I.311.

[47] *Miln* 124-125 (BUDSIR 56.175[0]:11-177:9).

[48] *Vin* III.205f.

[49] Keown, *Buddhism and Bioethics*, 65.

[50] Pāli: *attā*; Sanskrit: *ātman*.

[51] For a detailed treatment of this and related ideas, see Steven Collins, *Selfless Persons: Imagery and Thought in Theravāda Buddhism* (Cambridge: Cambridge University Press, 1982).

[52] *M* I.265-266.

[53] Keown, *Buddhism and Bioethics*, 69.

[54] *MA* II.310. On the concept of the *gandhabba*, see O.H. De A. Wijesekera, 'Vedic Gandharva and Pali Gandhabba,' *University of Ceylon Review*, Vol. III (April, 1945), 73-107.

[55] *Vism* XVII.113-114 (BUDSIR 59.145[0]:7-12).

[56] Cf. *KvuA* VIII.2 (BUDSIR 55.233[1177]-234[1180]). On the intermediate-state dispute, see Alex Wayman, 'The Intermediate-State Dispute in Buddhism,' *Buddhist Studies in Honour of I.B. Horner* (Dordrecht: D. Reidel, 1974), 227-237.

[57] See André Bareau, *Les Sectes Bouddhiques du Petit Véhicule* (Paris: École Française d'Extrême-Orient, 1955), 283.

[58] James P. McDermott, 'Karma and Rebirth in Early Buddhism,' in Wendy Doniger O'Flaherty, editor, *Karma and Rebirth in Classical Indian Traditions* (Berkeley: University of California Press, 1980), 169.

[59] *Kvu* XIV.2 (BUDSIR 37.523[1557]-525[1560]).

[60] *KvuA* XIV.2 (BUDSIR 55.273-274[1363]).

[61] *Kośa* III.40.

[62] *Kośa* III.4 & 10.

[63] *Kośa* III.13-14.

[64] *Kośa* III.4.

[65] McDermott, 'Karma and Rebirth,' 171-172, following *Kośa* III.15.

[66] I.e. Puggalavādins (Pāli) or Pudgalavādins (Sanskrit). The Puggalavādins constituted one of eighteen early school of Buddhist

thought. No longer extant, they were frequently attacked as unorthodox by other schools. For detailed refutations of the *puggala / pudgala* and *attā / ātman* theories see the appendix to Chap. VIII (sometimes cited as Chap. IX) of the *Kośa*; as well as *Kvu* I.1 (BUDSIR 37.1[1]-83[189]).

[67] Keown, *Buddhism and Bioethics*, 30.

[68] For more detailed treatment of this issue, see Keown, ibid., 21-37; and Collins, *Selfless Persons*.

[69] LaFleur, *Liquid Life* (Princeton: Princeton University Press, 1992).

9

Buddhism and Abortion: A Western Approach

James Hughes

Introduction

I once believed it important to determine the 'Buddhist view' on many social and political questions. Today I'm much more circumspect. Buddhist texts offer few coherent views outside of the core doctrinal elements. Consequently, Buddhists, to an even greater degree than most religionists, are required to address contemporary problems in the spirit of their teachings, rather than according to the letter of their law.

In the case of abortion, classical Buddhist texts, from the Pali canon through the Mahāyāna *sūtras*, offer no specific guidance. Even if there was a specific, classical Buddhist text addressing the moral status of the fetus and the act of abortion, it would not be consistent with 'Buddhism' to accept this teaching uncritically. Buddhism encodes with its teachings a reflexive, dynamic, self-critical element, beginning with the *Kālāma Sūtra*, which encourages Buddhists not to simply follow scriptures, but to continually adapt the Dharma to new audiences.

Consequently, a Buddhist approach to abortion has more to do with approaching the issue with a characteristic set of concerns, and in dialogue with a vast body of texts and teachers. It therefore comes as little surprise that most Western and Japanese Buddhists come away believing in the permissibility of abortion, while many other Buddhists believe abortion to be murder.[1] In this essay I would like to sketch some of the reasons why most Western

Buddhists accept abortion as an unfortunate but necessary part of women's reproductive health care.

Buddhism and Reproduction

First, it is important to note that Buddhism, unlike many other religions, does not hold that humans have a responsibility to procreate, and forbids the consecration of marriage or birth by Buddhist monks and nuns. The religions most opposed to abortion, notably Catholicism, believe that sex is for procreation, and that procreation is a duty and gift from God. In these theistic traditions, an abortion is an usurpation of God's will.[2]

In Buddhism however, the monastic life is of a higher order than the householder life. Unlike the pro-procreative religions, in Buddhism masturbation and homosexuality were seen as morally equivalent to heterosexuality.[3] One entire book of the Pali canon, the *Therīgāthā*,[4] is devoted to the description of the misfortunes of maidens, married women and mothers, and the joyous liberation they discovered in the nuns' order.[5] This radical indifference to family life was one of the principal sources of Confucian hostility to Buddhism in China.[6] The late Trevor Ling[7] pointed out that the Sinhalese embrace of contraception and abortion was so enthusiastic in the 1960s, compared to Sri Lanka's Muslims, Catholics and Hindus, that racialist monks began to argue, with little success, that Buddhists had an obligation to 'race-religion-nation' to reproduce.

In itself, a denigration of sexuality and reproduction does not lead to the condoning of abortion, and these attitudes do not explain Western Buddhists' views on abortion. On the contrary, Western Buddhists have been drawn to the strains of Buddhism more tolerant of sexuality, principally Japanese Buddhism and Tibetan Tantra.[8] Even Western Theravādin communities tend to de-emphasize anti-carnality.[9]

Of course, in Asia and in Asian Buddhist immigrant communities in the West, monks often do officiate in marriages and birth blessings, and Buddhism has developed a 'pro-family' lay theology. In these communities the sexual mores are not that different from Christianity. Nonetheless, the core images and ethos of Buddhism do not sacralize family and reproduction, and this in itself is probably part of the attraction for Western counterculture

Buddhists, and part of the explanation of our attitudes towards abortion.

Buddhist Ethics of Abortion

Buddhists in Asia and in the West have adopted many different moral logics.[10] All of these logics can be used to argue both for and against the permissibility of abortion. Some are more consistent with the textual and historical record of Buddhism, but authentic Buddhist ethicists could hold any of these positions.

For instance, the most simple-minded approach to morality is the letter of the law, and one of the top five precepts of the Buddhist is not to kill. Asserts one American Theravādin Buddhist:

> Abortion is the intentional taking of human life, an extremely bad and unwholesome act which is not to be done. For the devout, traditional Buddhist, that is the end of the matter.[11]

Similarly, David Stott, the British student of Tibetan Buddhism asserts:

> The performance of abortion or fatality-causing experiments on the unborn child constitute the taking of life, just as surely as the taking of life at any other point in the continuum of conception to death...[12]

While it may sound like sophistry, the question that this precept leaves unanswered is whether an embryo or fetus is alive. While there was a minority tradition in classical Hindu embryology that held that incarnation does not occur till as late as the seventh month,[13] most Buddhist commentators have adopted classical Hindu teachings that the transmigration of consciousness occurs at conception, and therefore that all abortion incurs the karmic burden of killing. Before modern embryology, however, in both Buddhist countries and the West,[14] ideas about conception were scientifically inaccurate, and often associated the beginning of life with events in the third or fourth month of pregnancy. The medieval descriptions of the incarnation of the *skandhas* in the fetal body do not discuss the fusing of sperm and egg, the growth of a central nervous system and so on.[15] Therefore, not only do their writings lack canonical weight, but they lack convincing relevance.

Another problem in early Buddhists' embryology is their assumption that the transmigration of consciousness is sudden rather than gradual. Based on the findings of modern neuro-embryology, Buddhists today might maintain that the fetus does not fully embody all five *skandhas* (the 'aggregates', or factors of individuality) and the illusion of personhood until after birth. Gradual embodiment of personhood is the argument developed by most Western ethicists to defend abortion.[16] If the fetus is not yet a fully embodied person, then the karmic consequences of abortion would be even less than the killing of animals, which Buddhism clearly teaches do have moral status. This neurological interpretation of the *skandhas* may be more consistent with Western Buddhism, which often sees the doctrine of rebirth as peripheral or interprets rebirth metaphorically rather than literally.[17]

Another popular, and probably the dominant, interpretation of Buddhist ethics in the West is utilitarian;[18] that the Buddhist should seek the greatest happiness for the greatest number. Under a utilitarian ethics, a particular abortion, and legal abortion in general, can be ethical so long as the suffering of all beings is lessened. The factors that a utilitarian Buddhist would take into account are the relative amounts of suffering experienced by mothers of unwanted children versus women who have abortions; the suffering of unwanted children versus the 'suffering' experienced by a fetus during abortion; the suffering of societies that permit abortion, versus the suffering of societies that don't. Utilitarian Buddhists would consider abortions more moral if the child will be disabled, or lead a painful, unhappy life for some other reason such as poverty; if the mother's life or health is endangered; and if the society or world is threatened by over-population or famine. In a consequentialist, utilitarian ethics, abortion may be ethical in some cases and not others, and for some societies and not others.

As critics are quick to point out, utilitarianism can legitimate many repugnant actions, murder among them, and most utilitarians add two modifications to address this 'yuck factor': general rules of thumb and a hierarchy of happiness. Since the estimation of the consequences of every action is impossible, most utilitarians accept general principles that will lead to greater happiness in the long run, among them freedom of speech, 'a right to life,' and so on. For these rule utilitarians, the abortion question returns to whether a fetus is a moral person with a right to life, or more precisely, whether suffering will be less if we treat fetuses as moral persons. Even if the fetus is not a person, permitting abortion may create a cognitive slippery slope to the murder of infants, and then mentally disabled children, and then adults. On the other hand, if clear and defensible distinctions can be made between fetuses and other human life, then it makes more sense to have two separate rules to apply to them.

This clear, defensible line is derived, I believe, from the second utilitarian caveat, the hierarchy of pleasures. This refinement of utilitarianism was articulated by John Stuart Mill in reaction to Bentham's version of utilitarianism which held that a life spent in an opiated stupor was just as moral as a life spent in creative endeavour. Instead, Mill posited the very Buddhist idea that there were higher states of mind which should be factored into any utilitarian calculus as more important than simple pleasures. To the extent that the fetal nervous system exists at all, its 'sufferings' and 'pleasures' are clearly of a rudimentary order compared to those of the pregnant woman. In other words, the suffering experienced by a self-conscious child when murdered is qualitatively different from that experienced by an infant when aborted, and thus the first can and should be forbidden, while the latter may be acceptable.[19] In reference to the slippery slope argument, LaFleur notes:

> The Japanese history of abortion offers an example of moral practices going the other way. In the seventeenth and eighteenth centuries, the Japanese practiced birth control almost entirely through infanticide, when there was no other real option. In the twentieth century, the Japanese have virtually eliminated infanticide, substituting it with abortion. Now, more and more, abortion is being supplanted by contraception.[20]

Within both modern Buddhist ethics and Western bioethics the 'sentience' of a being is considered in evaluating the morality of ending its life; not all life is equal and therefore not all killing is equal. Most Western bioethicists believe that human beings and animals take on ethical significance, a 'right to life,' to the extent that they are 'persons.' Some Western ethicists[21] would set a standard which would exclude almost all animals, newborns and the severely retarded or demented. When they specify which elements of sentience and neurological integrity create the illusion of personhood, Western bioethicists begin to sound remarkably Buddhistic: 'the awareness of the difference between self and other; the ability to be conscious of oneself over time; the ability to engage in purposive actions'.[22]

Buddhist psychological analysis is consistent with an ethical distinction between three kinds of beings: those that do not feel pain, those that feel pain, and those with individuated consciousness, i.e. 'persons.' The insensate are considered by almost all Western philosophers, except the 'deep ecologists,' some of whom are also Buddhists[23], and the Catholics, to be morally inconsequential. The deep ecologists would extend a right to life to viruses, plants and eco-systems, while the Catholics would extend it to the embryo.

The significance of pain is more universally recognized, leading to the establishment of organizations and laws protecting animals from unnecessary cruelty as domestic pets or in research. Similarly, pediatricians have become increasingly sensitive to the sensitivities of infants receiving shots or circumcision. Buddhism and bioethics would clearly argue for respecting the extent to which the fetus is sensate in the carrying out of abortion, though the end is obviously quick.

The moral significance of murder, however, comes with the development of the illusion of self some time after birth. A Buddhist ethics that tied the significance of killing to the sentience of the being would, in turn, be consistent with laws such as the U.S. Supreme Court's Roe v. Wade decision, and the laws of many European nations, which allow unrestricted abortion in the first trimester of a pregnancy and more restricted abortion rights in latter stages of pregnancy.

A third ethical logic, and the one argued for by Damien Keown,[24] is a virtue-ethics interpretation of Buddhism. Virtue-oriented Buddhists view the intentions and psychological state of the actor as determining the morality, and karmic consequences, of an act. In this case the mental attitude and motivations of the pregnant woman and her collaborators would determine the ethics of an abortion.

Along this line, Tworkov[25] argues that the karmic skilfulness of an abortion is related to whether the woman became pregnant and made her decision to abort with serious mindfulness. From this perspective, aborting a fetus conceived without an effort at contraception or without serious moral reflection would be more karmically significant, in fact a breaking of the precept against sexual misconduct, than an abortion necessitated in spite of contraception, and undertaken without moral reflection. Tworkov argues that while hardening the heart against fetal life may appear to make the abortion choice easier, in the long run it is important to keep an open heart to the painfulness of the choice. Similarly, in her description of an abortion after she began practising Zen Buddhism, Margot Milliken says:

> A wise friend encouraged me to love this new being, accept it for what it was, send it loving thoughts, and if I decided to have the abortion, to also wish the being a peaceful journey. The other advice was to send myself healing and loving thoughts, and to be completely accepting of the many reactions and feelings I was experiencing. Finally I reached a point of balance and understanding. I had the abortion, and now, four years later, I still have questions. My questions are not about whether I did the right thing; I'm sure I did.[26]

In fact, I believe that most Western Buddhists employ both utilitarian and virtue ethics, in the paradoxical unity of compassion and wisdom. On the one hand, our personal karmic clarity is most related to our cultivation of compassionate intention, but on the other hand we also need to develop penetrating insight into the most effective means to the ends. We do not believe that the person who helps others without any intention of doing so has accrued merit, while we look upon the person who causes others suffering with the best intentions a hapless fool. Similarly, in approaching the abortion decision, both the mindset of the actors and the utilitarian consequences are important.

The Difference Between Social Ethics and Personal Ethics

This distinction between the personal karmic consequences of abortion, and the general social consequences, are yet another cause of Western Buddhists' tolerance toward abortion. While many Buddhists feel conflict about the moral status of the act for themselves, they fear dire consequences for women and society if abortion were to be re-criminalized. These concerns are in line with those of liberal democracy, but they are also unwittingly in line with a Buddhist tradition of a liberal state.[27]

Western Buddhists are only slowly becoming aware of the social and political ethics of the Buddhist canon. The early Pali canon's image of traditional monarchs was of arrogant egotists pursuing imperialistic, unjust policies, guided solely by greed, hatred and ignorance. When Siddhartha Gautama was born it was predicted that he would either be a world-conqueror or a world-saviour, in line with the Great Man mythos. Though his father tried to steer him toward conquest of the world, Siddhartha conquered himself instead. The symbol of secular power was the wheel of the war chariot, 'the wheel of power,' but the symbol of the Buddha's awakening was 'the wheel of Truth' (*dharmacakra*) of which he was the 'wheel-turner' (*cakravartin*).

Subsequently Buddhists found that radical disjuncture between dharma and power untenable, and a concept of the righteous king developed. If the king could be converted and brought under the sway of the *Sangha*, he could be taught to rule with compassion, selflessness and wisdom. Such a qualitatively transformed monarch was called a *dharmarāja*, or dharma-king. By subordinating himself to the way of truth, the *dharmarāja* allows the *dharmacakra* to turn the wheel of power. A *dharmarāja*, as portrayed most significantly in the *The Lion's Roar of the Wheel-Turning Monarch Sūtra*, provides for all the people and animals of the realm, listens to the counsel of the wise, controls his passions and, most importantly, makes sure that there is no poverty in his kingdom. The first Buddhist emperor, Aśoka, attempted to fulfill these obligations of righteous governance by setting out edicts on stone posts throughout India, proclaiming social welfare measures, amnesty for sacrificial animals and encouragement for lay people to practice meditation.[28]

While the *dharmarāja*/Aśoka tradition has inspired many Buddhists to take an active role as a moral force in governance, this model is also one of tolerance. The *dharmarāja* texts and Aśoka himself were tolerant and respectful of non-Buddhist religious groups. The *Vajjian Sūtra* suggests in fact that the support and free movement of religious mendicants of all kinds is a precondition for social health. Internally, the Buddhist order was not to establish a 'true' faith, but simply to schism when major disagreements developed.

Asian Buddhists have often shown a less tolerant side when Buddhism was made the state religion, Western Buddhists have evinced no interest in evangelism or the institutionalization of Buddhist moral edicts as state policy.[29] In other words, the Western liberal moral stance that 'I personally disagree with abortion, but I believe it should be legal,' is a common stance among Western Buddhists as well, and is consistent with the general moral tolerance of Buddhist governance.[30] Again in the words of Margot Milliken:

> Given the present political and social climate, we are in danger of losing the legal right to choose abortion. While I do not believe abortion is something that should be legislated against, I do feel it is an option that should not be taken lightly. Even if it seems that the best choice is to terminate a pregnancy, we must acknowledge we are ending a potential life. This seems more honest than acting as if our 'pro-choice' stance does not involve taking life, even though we may assume that that life is not fully realized, conscious or developed.[31]

And in a pamphlet from the Japanese-American Buddhist Churches of America:

> It is the woman carrying the fetus, and no one else, who must in the end make this most difficult decision and live with it for the rest of her life. As Buddhists, we can only encourage her to make a decision that is both thoughtful and compassionate.[32]

This stance has its limits. Few Buddhists would say 'I'm personally opposed to slavery and torture, but I think they should be legal'. That many Buddhists are politically tolerant of abortion despite personal reservations suggests their recognition that their discomfort with abortion is not a fundamental moral objection, as with slavery or torture, but a personal and emotional one. In most

Buddhist societies the occupation of butcher is considered unclean, but no Buddhist society has ever imprisoned or executed butchers. In Buddhist law as well as ethics, abortion is more of the status of killing animals, a matter of personal karmic consequences not state-imposed punishment.

It is certainly possible for a Buddhist to legitimate authoritarian and non-democratic forms of government, and many have, especially in the twentieth century in reaction to, and in support of, communism. In the West, however, this Buddhist spirit of tolerance has entered into dialogue with the liberal democratic tradition to develop a model of enlightened citizenship in some Buddhist groups. The liberal democratic model of citizenship, consistent with Buddhism, implies that the citizens of a society will develop the greater wisdom and insight when they have the freedom to make mistakes.

Acknowledging the Sadness of the Choice

What happens to the consciousness of a baby that is aborted, or dies very young? What can the parents do to help the baby? Dilgo Khyentse Rinpoche explained:

> The consciousness of those who die before birth, at birth, or in infancy will travel once again through the *bardo* states, and take on another existence. The same meritorious practices and actions can be done for them as are usually performed for the dead: the purification practice and mantra recitation of Vajrasattva, offering of lights, purification of the ashes, and so on.
>
> In the case of an abortion, in addition to these usual practices, if the parents feel remorse they can help by acknowledging it, asking for forgiveness, and performing ardently the purification practice of Vajrasattva. They can also offer lights, and save lives, or help others, or sponsor some humanitarian or spiritual project, dedicating it to the well-being and future enlightenment of the baby's consciousness.[33]

Despite Sogyal Rinpoche's recent and welcome suggestion, Japan is apparently the only society in the world that has developed a ritual, the *mizuko kuyō*, for the blessing of the aborted fetus's spirit, and the expiation of the guilt of the reluctant parents. The *mizuko kuyō* is performed by Buddhist priests, who then place a small statue, a Jizō, in the Buddhist cemetery to represent these good wishes. William La Fleur[34] is thus far the principal interpolator of this practice to the West, and he suggests that the practice may be a model for a Western moral approach to abortion.

Robert Aitken Roshi, a successor of the Japanese Zen teacher Yasutani Roshi, took up this challenge in his Hawaiian Zen community, the Diamond Sangha. Adapting and translating the *mizuko kuyō* ceremony, the Diamond Sangha uses the following ceremony:

The Diamond Sangha Ceremony on the Death of an Unborn Child[35]

1. Three full bows
2. The Three Refuges
3. *Enmei Jikku Kannon Gyo* or other short *sūtra* in Japanese or English
   Leader :
   > We gather today to express our love and support for (names of parents) and to say farewell to a child unborn, a bit of being we have named (name of child), who appeared just as we all do, from the undifferentiated mind, and who passed away after a few moments of flickering life, just as we all do.
   >
   > In our culture, we place great emphasis upon maintaining life, but truly death is not a fundamental matter, but an incident, another wave. Bassui Zenji speaks of it as clouds fading in the sky. Mind essence, Bassui says, is not subject to birth or death. It is neither being nor nothingness, neither emptiness nor form and colour.
   >
   > It is, as Yamada Koun Roshi has said, infinite emptiness, full of possibilities, at once altogether at rest and also charged with countless tendencies awaiting the fullness of karma. Here (name of child) is in complete repose, at one with the mystery that is our own birth and death, our own no-birth and no-death.

5. *Heart Sūtra* in Japanese and English, as parents, leader and friends offer incense.
6. Leader:
   > Buddha nature pervades the whole universe,
   > existing right here and now;

with our reciting of Enmei Jikku Kannon Gyo
let us unite with
the Ancient Seven Buddhas,
Fully Realized Shakyamuni Buddha,
Great Compassion Avalokiteshvara Bodhisattva,
all Founding Teachers, past, present, future.

We especially dedicate our love and our prayerful thoughts to
you (name of child)
May you rest in peace

Let true Dharma continue—
Sangha relations become complete
All:
All Buddhas throughout space and time,
all Bodhisattvas, Mahasattvas,
the Great Prajna Paramita.

7. Great Vows for All in English
8. Three full bows

Western Buddhists could make quite a contribution to the abortion
conflict by offering these sentiments, reflections and rituals for adaptation by our Christian and secular neighbours.

Notes

[1] For an introduction to the range of Buddhist attitudes on abortion see Robert Florida, 'Buddhist Approaches to Abortion', *Asian
Philosophy* 1991 1:39–50.

[2] Geoffrey Parrinder, *Sex in the World's Religions* (London:
Sheldon Press, 1980).

[3] Leonard Zwilling, 'Homosexuality as seen in Indian Buddhist
texts', *Buddhism, Sexuality and Gender* ed. Jose Ignacio Cabezon
(NY: SUNY Press, 1992). Kate Wheeler, 'Vinaya Vignettes: or,
why the buddha had to make some rules', *Tricycle*, Summer 1994:
84–89.

[4] On the role of women in Buddhism see Lenore Friedman,
Daughters of Lion's Yawn: Women Teachers of Buddhism in

America (Boulder, CO: Shambhala, 1987). Rita M. Gross, *Buddhism after Patriarchy: A Feminist History, Analysis and Reconstruction of Buddhism*, (NY: SUNY, 1992); James Hughes, 'Buddhist Feminism,' *Spring Wind* (Toronto), 1986: 36–45; Anne Klein, *Meeting the Great Bliss Queen: Buddhists, Feminists and the Art of the Self* (Boston: Beacon, 1994).

[5] Pali Text Society, trans. *Therīgāthā* (London: Pali Text Society, 1980).

[6] Kenneth Chen, *The Chinese Transformation of Buddhism* (Princeton, NJ: Princeton University Press, 1973)

[7] Trevor Ling, 'Buddhist Factors in Population Growth and Control', *Population Studies* 23 1969:53–60.

[8] See especially Sallie Tisdale's essay in *Tricycle* (Winter 1994: 44–48) 'Nothing Special: The Buddhist Sex Quandary'.

[9] The principal exception to this appears to be the British Friends of Western Buddhist Order, directed by the British monk Sangharakshita, though even in this case sexuality itself is not seen as problematic, but rather sex roles and behaviour patterns.

[10] I refer here to the work of Lawrence Kohlberg, *The Philosophy of Moral Development* (New York: Harper and Row, 1981), though the ethical logics I discuss do not correspond to his schema directly.

[11] Leonard Price 'A Buddhist View of Abortion', *Washington Buddhist* 16, 4, 1985: 3–13.

[12] David Stott, *A Circle of Protection for the Unborn.* (Bristol: Ganesha Press, 1985).

[13] Julius J.Lipner, 'The Classical Hindu View on Abortion and the Moral Status of the Unborn,' in *Hindu Ethics*, ed. H. G. Coward, J. J. Lipner, and K. K. Young, 41–69. (Albany, New York: State University of New York Press, 1989)

[14] See for instance Luker's investigation of beliefs about the onset of pregnancy in American history (Kristin Luker, *Abortion and the Politics of Motherhood*, University of California Press, 1984).

[15] For a discussion of traditional Tibetan embryology, see Yeshe Dhonden 'Embryology in Tibetan Medicine', in *Tibetan Medicine* (Dharamsala: Library of Tibetan Works and Archives, 1980); and Philip A. Lecso, 'A Buddhist View of Abortion', *Journal of Religion and Health* 26 1987:214–18.

[16]   See for instance Michael Tooley, *Abortion and Infanticide*. (Oxford: Oxford University Press, 1984); Michael J. Flower 'Neuromaturation of the human fetus', *Journal of Medicine and Philosophy* 10, 1985:237–251; Michael Bennett, 'Personhood from a Neuroscientific Perspective', pp. 83–86 in *Abortion Rights and Fetal Personhood*, eds. Ed Doer and James Prescott, (Centerline Press, 1989). On no-self and personhood see Derek Parfit, *Reasons and Persons*, (Oxford: Oxford University Press, 1984).

[17]   See for instance Stephen Batchelor, 'Rebirth: A Case for Buddhist Agnosticism', *Tricycle* 1992: 16–23; Winston King, 'A Buddhist Ethics Without Karmic Rebirth?' *Journal of Buddhist Ethics* 1, 1994:33–44.

[18]   Damien Keown, *The Nature of Buddhist Ethics*, (New York: St. Martins Press, 1992).

[19]   Of course, this raises the question of the painless death, which leads to another rule of thumb, that we'll all be happier if we know we are protected from murder, no matter how humane our assassins.

[20]   William LaFleur, 'The Cult of Jizo: Abortion Practices in Japan and What They Can Teach the West', *Tricycle*, Summer 1995: 41–44.

[21]   See for instance Tooley, *Abortion and Infanticide*.

[22]   See for instance, Joseph Fletcher, *Humanhood: Essays in Biomedical Ethics* (Buffalo: Prometheus Books, 1979).

[23]   See for instance John Seed, Joanna Macy, Pat Fleming, Arne Naess, *Thinking Like a Mountain: Towards a Council of All Beings* (New Society Publishers, 1988).

[24]   Keown, *The Nature of Buddhist Ethics*.

[25]   Helen Tworkov, 'Anti-abortion/pro-choice: taking both sides', *Tricycle* 1992: 60–69.

[26]   Margot Wallach Milliken, *Not Mixing Up Buddhism: Essays on Women and Buddhist Practice*. eds. Kahawai Collective (Fredonia, NY: White Pine Press, 1986), 74–77.

[27]   My thoughts on Buddhist social and political ethics are drawn largely from Trevor Ling's *The Buddha* (London: Pelican, 1973).

[28]   See especially Robert Thurman's radical interpretation of the ideal Buddhist state ('Nagarjuna's Guidelines for Buddhist Social

Activism', in F. Eppsteiner, ed. *The Path of Compassion: writings on socially engaged Buddhism* (Berkeley: Parallax Press, 1988). Also Thurman 'The Politics of Enlightenment', *Tricycle*, Fall 1992: 28–33.

[29] See Stuart Smithers, 'Freedom's just another word', *Tricycle,* Fall 1992: 34–39 for an interesting discussion of the historical tension between the precepts and antinomian freedom in Buddhism, and the parallel tension between morality and liberalism in the United States.

[30] See for instance, Ryo Imamura, 'The Shin Buddhist Stance on Abortion,' *Buddhist Peace Fellowship Newsletter* 6 1984: 6–7, and Lecso, 1987.

[31] Margot Wallach Milliken, *Not Mixing Up Buddhism: Essays on Women and Buddhist Practice.* eds. Kahawai Collective (Fredonia, NY: White Pine Press, 1986: 74–77), 76.

[32] Anonymous. *A Shin Buddhist Stance on Abortion.* San Francisco: Buddhist Churches of America.

[33] Sogyal Rinpoche *The Tibetan Book of Living and Dying* (Harper Collins, 1992), 376.

[34] William LaFleur, 'Contestation and Confrontation: The Morality of Abortion in Japan', *Philosophy East and West* 40 1990:529–42; *Liquid Life: Abortion and Buddhism in Japan* (Princeton: Princeton University Press, 1992); 'Silences and Censures: Abortion, History, and Buddhism in Japan. A Rejoinder to George Tanabe', *Japanese Journal of Religious Studies* 22/1–2 1995:185–196; 'The Cult of Jizo: Abortion Practices in Japan and What They Can Teach the West', 1995; Anne Page Brooks, 'Mizuko Kuyo and Japanese Buddhism' *Japanese Journal of Religious Studies* 8 1991:119–47; Hoshino Eiki and Takeda Dosho 'Indebtedness and comfort: the undercurrents of mizuko kuyo in contemporary Japan', *Japanese Journal of Religious Studies* 14 1987:305–20; Bardwell Smith, 'Buddhism and Abortion in Contemporary Japan: Mizuko Kuyō and the Confrontation with Death', *Japanese Journal of Religious Studies* 15 1988:3–24; Z. Werblowsky, 'Mizuko Kuyō; Notulae on the most important "New Religion" of Japan', *Japanese Journal of Religious Studies* 18 1984: 295–354.

[35] Robert Aitken, *The Mind of Clover: Essays on Zen Buddhist Ethics* (San Francisco: North Point Press, 1984), 22.

10

Buddhism and Abortion: Is There a 'Middle Way'?[1]

Damien Keown

Introduction

In this final chapter I would like to address directly a question which will have occurred to many readers while perusing this volume. The question is: Does Buddhism have the answer to the abortion question which has so far eluded the West? It will be clear from the preceding chapters that there are those who think that it might, or that it may at least provide new insights which will help to move the Western debate forward. Indeed, there seem to be a number of general reasons why Buddhism might be thought well placed to make a contribution to the Western debate.

First, as a third party, it may be possible for Buddhism to mediate between the two sides and create an area of common ground. Second, the presence of a new participant may in itself change the nature of the debate, in the way that the introduction of a single new element can sometimes change the entire chemistry of a compound. Third, Buddhism has come to the Western debate late and has the advantage of hindsight in being able to survey the fallout from battles which have already been fought. Fourth, Buddhism brings with it a philosophy and world-view which in important respects differ from the intellectual and cultural framework which underpins present positions. By broadening the context of the debate, Buddhism may create space which is not gained at the expense of either side. In deadlocked disputes sometimes just a little clear water can be enough to break the logjam.

In recent years a number of Buddhist teachers, writers and academics have expressed dissatisfaction with the state of the Western debate over abortion and suggested that Buddhism may be able to offer a way forward. The respected American Zen *roshi* Robert Aitken has criticised 'Over-simplified positions of pro-life and pro-choice' which, in his view, fail to 'touch the depths of the dilemma'.[2] Helen Tworkov, editor of the popular Buddhist magazine *Tricycle*, has suggested that a Buddhist position can be developed by 'taking both sides'.[3] In this volume Professor William LaFleur commends for consideration a Japanese approach to abortion through which 'A third option—perhaps a middle way between the others—is opened',[4] while Pinit Ratanakul refers to 'the Thai "middle way" in the abortion issues' which negotiates a way 'between the extreme positions found in different Western views'.[5] The position advocated by these writers may be summarised broadly as follows:

1.   Buddhism calls itself the 'Middle Way' and traditionally seeks to steer a course between extreme or opposing views
2.   The 'pro-choice' and 'pro-life' positions represent two such extremes with respect to abortion
3.   The Buddhist position on abortion, therefore, should be one which occupies the middle ground between these extremes.

As regards point 3, there seems to be a convergence of opinion to the effect that a new and distinctive position on abortion can be arrived at which acknowledges the truth of opposing views while holding them together in creative tension within a Buddhist philosophical and, perhaps also, liturgical framework. The acknowledgment that abortion *is* taking human life seems to be one of the key elements in the proposal. In not seeking to minimise the seriousness of what is done it moves away from one of the Western 'extremes', namely the view that fetal life lacks moral status, and is simply a 'cluster of cells', 'fetal tissue', a 'potential' human life and so forth. At the same time, by regarding abortion as permissible, it moves away from the other extreme, the pro-life end of the spectrum, which holds that abortion is almost without exception wrong. What this proposal amounts to in practice, however, is not entirely clear. We know what advocates of the middle way on abortion are *against* (extremes), but not what they are *for*. The moral and legal implications of the middle way have yet to be spelt out and defended in terms of Buddhist doctrine.

One attempt at mapping the centre ground on this issue was made by Ken Jones in his popular book *The Social Face of Buddhism*. There, he describes abortion as a moral 'dilemma',[6] which arises from the fact that Buddhism is on the one hand 'profoundly compassionate' and yet on the other 'counsels against all killing'.[7] In the book, the views of American Zen teachers are quoted to the effect that this dilemma can only be resolved by the pregnant woman herself. In reaching a decision on whether to have an abortion, the practice of meditation is commended as a way of directly and intuitively apprehending the correct course of action in that situation. It might be said that abortion is seen as a kind of moral *kōan*. Whatever decision the woman reaches, it is felt, is then justified by what in the West would be called her 'conscience'.[8] Other parties, meanwhile, are encouraged to adopt an attitude of compassion towards both mother and child.

The position Ken Jones sets out is not without its attractions. For certain Western Buddhists it seems to offer an appealing synthesis of Buddhist and liberal values. It adopts a 'non-judgemental' stance which may be thought at the same time both to express the central Buddhist virtue of compassion and support the principle of 'a woman's right to choose'.

This position also seems to have an appeal outside of Buddhism. Indeed I was struck recently by the similarity between what is proposed here as a Buddhist view and the position adopted by the feminist Naomi Wolf in 1995 in a controversial article in the *New Republic*. 'When I was four months pregnant, sick as a dog', she was quoted as saying, 'I realised I could no longer tolerate the foetus-is-nothing paradigm of the pro-choice movement'. A newspaper report summed up her position as follows:

> She has not joined the ranks of the anti-abortionists, but stakes out what she claims to be the moral high ground between the two extremes, defending the right of a woman to have an abortion, but attacking those who view the procedure as a simple act of convenience lacking moral consequences.[9]

Naomi Wolf is not a Buddhist, so far as I am aware, but the views expressed—and in particular the reference to the 'two extremes'—seem remarkably similar to those currently being advanced as a Buddhist middle way. In an interview in the same newspaper a week later Wolf made an explicit reference to Buddhism. The report states:

> She cited Buddhist concepts of self-forgiveness: 'The Buddhists say you should do the best you can, alleviate as much suffering as you can, and it seems to me that we still need the right to safe and legal abortion. So in that world view the best we can do is minimise the times abortions happen, and when they do happen the best we can do is be conscious about it and try to make the world better in memory of that'.[10]

There is no reason, of course, why Buddhism and Naomi Wolf—or, indeed, anybody—cannot arrive at the same conclusions on abortion. That such similar views should be expressed by a Western liberal feminist however, gives us cause to ask what, if anything, is distinctly or uniquely Buddhist about the proposed middle way? A further question which suggests itself is whether it is an authentic *Buddhist* middle way, or simply Western liberalism in Buddhist clothes?

Based on his research in Japan, LaFleur summarises what he feels is distinctive in the new position:

> The Buddhist orientation is rather distinctive on a couple of points that are worthy of note. For instance, the Buddhist posture permits—and even encourages—language about the fetus as human life in some sense but refuses to draw the conclusion that, therefore, abortion is disallowed. It avoids the dualizing dilemma often found in the American and European abortion polemics: namely, that of feeling compelled either to think of the fetus as life equivalent to that of a fully formed young child or, alternatively, as so much inert matter or 'tissue'. On the one hand it is not 'LIFE!' and on the other it is not just 'AN UNWANTED PREGNANCY!'[11]

It is not immediately clear, however, how the position described above 'avoids the dualizing dilemma'. To use language about the fetus as human life, and yet to condone abortion, seems to sharpen the dilemma rather than reduce it. In the circumstances described above it seems fairer to say that the moral dilemma is put to one side rather than resolved. There is little to suggest that Japanese women resort to abortions with the confidence that their distinctive attitude towards their unborn child has resolved a moral dilemma. On the contrary, they seem to do so reluctantly in the knowledge that they are being forced by circumstances to do what they intuitively feel to be morally wrong. As one respondent who had undergone an abortion confessed movingly to Elizabeth Harrison: 'all I can do is move my feet towards *mizuko kuyō*'.[12]

Lafleur goes on a little later to describe what he sees as the advantages of the new position:

> Some advantages in this should be clear. This view makes abortion permissible but, at the same time, makes unnecessary any denial of strong emotions a woman might have about her fetus as life and even as a child. In short, there is no need to reduce the options to 'inviolable life' or 'an unwanted pregnancy'. A third option—perhaps a middle way between the others—is opened. That is, a woman is free to acknowledge any feelings of bonding that have developed within herself. Such feelings need not bar her from deciding to have an abortion.[13]

What LaFleur appears to be suggesting here is that the abortion dilemma can be resolved by allowing a woman to acknowledge her feelings of bonding. However, this does not resolve the moral aspect of the dilemma but merely reframes the problem as essentially a psychological one. The references to 'emotions', 'feelings', and 'bonding' make clear that what is being ameliorated is a psychological condition. By acknowledging her feelings toward the child the woman may indeed feel better, and the rite of *mizuko kuyō* may assist greatly in the grieving and healing process. The *morality* of abortion, however, is a separate matter from how a woman *feels* about an abortion, and it is difficult to see how the non-denial of 'strong emotions' offers a solution to the underlying moral dilemma of intentionally taking what one knows to be human life.

The Middle Way

The phrase 'middle way' has been used freely so far and since it may well be misunderstood it is worth pausing at this point to consider its meaning in more detail. The idea of the middle way is ancient and well-established in Buddhism. The original sense derives from the Buddha's own experience in rejecting the extremes of sensual indulgence and self-mortification. As is well known, the two extremes are represented in his early life by princely self-indulgence followed by six years of penance and mortification in the forest. When he renounced both and adopted a balanced and moderate lifestyle he quickly gained enlightenment. The primary sense of the 'middle way', then, is as a principle of moderation governing the body and its appetites. As such, it has no direct connection with Buddhist ethical precepts.

Based on his own experience, the Buddha went on to formulate and teach the Eightfold Path, which itself is referred to as the 'Middle Way' (*majjhimā paṭipadā*). It is worth noting, however, that the course the Middle Way steers is directly *away* from evil, not midway between good and evil (M.i.15f). The notion of a middle way is also used in other contexts in Buddhism: it denotes emotional balance between the extremes of greed and hatred and is also used in connection with certain doctrines.[14]

The concept of the 'middle way' thus has a distinguished pedigree in Buddhist thought. But how successfully can it be applied to abortion? It would seem, as noted, that the middle way makes most sense with reference to extremes which lie in a continuum. Thus indulgence and self mortification lie at opposite ends of the spectrum of sensuality. Greed and hatred lie at opposite ends of an emotional spectrum. Are the pro-life and pro-choice positions extremes which are related in this sense? At first sight they seem to be, but we may have cause to wonder whether moral positions are susceptible to analysis in this way.

Buddhist sources nowhere suggest, for example, that moral precepts are to be understood through the principle of the middle way. It is not hard to see why when we reflect on what this would mean in practice. With respect to the Five Precepts, for example, would it be wrong to kill someone, but alright to beat them half to death? Wrong to steal £1 or £100 but alright to steal £50? Wrong to commit adultery to excess, but alright to do it in moderation? Wrong to tell lies but alright to tell half-truths? Wrong to take hard drugs but alright to take soft ones?

The concept of the middle way makes little sense in these contexts, and the reason seems to be that the wrongness of the things mentioned does not depend upon the *degree* to which they are done. Acts such as killing and adultery are intrinsically immoral—there is no 'right' way to do them. Aristotle, who also propounded a middle way of a kind in his famous 'doctrine of the mean'[15] was careful to point this out. He wrote:

> But not every action or feeling admits of a mean; because some have names that directly connote depravity, such as malice, shamelessness and envy, and among actions adultery, theft and murder. All these, and more like them, are so called as being evil in themselves; it is not the excess or deficiency of them that is evil. In their case, then, it is impossible to act rightly; one is always wrong. Nor does acting rightly or wrongly in such cases depend on circumstances—whether a man commits adultery with the right woman or at the right time or in the right way, because to do anything of that kind is simply wrong.[16]

A principle such as the 'middle way' or 'golden mean' can be applied profitably in many contexts, but not, it would seem, in all.

But perhaps this oversimplifies what the call for a middle way entails. Perhaps what is meant is that Buddhism can offer a solution which somehow encompasses, rather than bisects, the two 'extremes' represented by the pro-life and pro-choice positions. The subtitle to Tworkov's article on abortion—'taking both sides'—suggests something more complex than a simple bifurcation of positions is envisaged. What is on offer seems to be not so much a middle way—in the traditional Buddhist sense of a course between the two extremes—as a pragmatic compromise which combines them, shorn of their more radical elements.

Buddhist Doctrine

This brings us to the question of the moral implications of the compromise embodied in the proposed middle way *vis-à-vis* traditional Buddhist ethical teachings. It is here the proposal seems to encounter its major obstacle, in that it represents a significant departure from the teachings on abortion which have been handed down from the earliest times. With only minor variations, the mainstream position (the idea is so well established there seems no reason not to describe it as the 'orthodox' position) in Buddhism is similar to that known in the West as the 'sanctity of life'. The argument against abortion on this view can be set out as follows:

> **Premise One**: It is wrong to take innocent human life
> **Premise Two**: from conception onwards the embryo or fetus is innocent, human and alive
> **Conclusion**: it is wrong to take the life of an embryo or fetus.[17]

In Buddhism, premise one is supplied by the First Precept, while premise two is supplied from Buddhist teachings on rebirth and embryology. The conclusion follows as a matter of formal logic, so if the premises are accepted the conclusion must be also.

Those in the West who think abortion is permissible have generally tended to attack the second premise of the argument, suggesting that a new human life comes into being not at conception but at some point between conception and birth. The time when the fetus becomes viable outside the womb at around twenty-eight weeks, is sometimes seen as one such point, as for example by the US Supreme Court in *Roe v Wade*. Buddhists generally, however, seem to accept the second premise. In his 1991 paper 'Buddhist Approaches to Abortion', Robert Florida sums up as follows:

> In short, what all this boils down to is that Buddhists traditionally have understood that the human being begins at the instant of conception when sperm, egg, and *vijñāna* come together ... Therefore, the precept against taking life applies in the case of abortion.[18]

I think it is uncontroversial to say that the high tradition has consistently taught that conception marks the start of a gradual process of development leading to birth, childhood and maturity.[19] In adopting this view Buddhist thinking was ahead of the West, and its views on embryological development, although not accurate in all respects, are broadly in line with the discoveries of modern science.

Western thinking on the matter followed Aristotle for almost two thousand years, and its understanding of embryology was hampered by his theory of progressive animation through the sequence of vegetative, animal and rational souls.[20]

Since Buddhism believes in rebirth, it regards all conception as reconception. The new life which comes into being at conception is in fact an older one being recycled. Buddhist embryology gives a very clear account of fetal development as beginning at conception[21] when the spirit of a deceased person unites with the biological substrate which will constitute its physical nature.[22] The early embryo then evolves through four or five main stages within the first twenty-eight days.[23] None of these stages is singled out as having any particular importance from a moral perspective.

But what about the Japanese concept of the *mizuko*,[24] and other such ideas? It seems that few Japanese take this notion seriously enough to offer it as a justification for abortion. LaFleur writes:

> ... Japanese are for the most part much less ready than persons in the West to refer to an unborn fetus in terms that suggest it is something less than human or even less than sentient. The Japanese tend to avoid terms like 'unwanted pregnancy' or 'fetal tissue.' That which develops in the uterus is often referred to as a 'child'—even when there are plans to abort it.[25]

No doubt the *mizuko* concept has more significance than Western folk-tales about childbearing—such as that babies are brought by a stork—but perhaps not *that* much more.[26] One prominent Japanese Buddhist—Domyo Miura, a priest of the Enmanin temple near Kyoto and first Chairman of the Japan Buddhist Society—has written a book in which he rejects the concept of the *mizuko* as justifying abortion.[27] Other commentators have also pointed out that there is very little firm evidence that Buddhists in Japan ever condoned abortion or, indeed, that they do so today.[28]

We might note in passing that ideas such as that of the *mizuko* are not unique to Japan. A similar belief concerning the *khwan* exists in Thailand, as reported by Trevor Ling.[29] The same notion also appears to be found in Vietnam: Tworkov recounts how 'some Buddhist women in the Vietnamese community in Boston explained to me that during the first couple of months of pregnancy, the fetus has no consciousness, no spirit and therefore, first trimester abortion is not the taking of life'.[30] These widely dispersed folk beliefs (to which, perhaps, the Western notion of 'quickening' is related) may be survivals of animistic beliefs which have their origin in prehistory. It should be noted, however, that while Buddhism is not hostile to views of this kind, it regards them neither as true nor as part of its orthodox teachings.[31]

Returning to the formal argument set out above, since few Buddhists (and this includes both Western proponents of the middle way and Japanese Buddhists) seem disposed to challenge the second premise, a Buddhist argument for allowing abortion must aim to rebut the first premise, that it is always wrong to take innocent human life.

So far as I am aware, no formal or systematic arguments to this effect have yet been made. It can be deduced from the positions adopted by certain Western Buddhists, however, that two possible lines of argument are under consideration. The First Precept is formulated in general terms and forbids causing 'injury to living creatures' (*pāṇātipāta*).[32] Doubts are sometimes raised as to whether this precept should be taken at face value, since its scope seems unclear. It is suggested, for example, that the Buddhist treatment of animals shows that breaking the First Precept is inevitable in the course of everyday life (for instance by killing animals for food), and therefore the precept stands in need of 'interpretation'. On this basis Tworkov suggests that it may be wrong to insist on a 'literal' application of the precept, and therefore abortion may be permissible.[33]

Many, myself included, would agree that there is genuine uncertainty about the requirements of the precepts in certain contexts. This is largely due to the fact that Buddhism has invested very little effort in what in the West is known as 'moral philosophy', the discipline which seeks to clarify moral obligations and develop a system of internally consistent ethical principles which can be applied to the complex situations encountered in daily life. There is certainly an urgent need for research, reflection and debate regarding both the theoretical and applied aspects of Buddhist ethics, and for Buddhism to provide an explicit and consistent rationale for its views. However, that there may be doubt on some matters does not preclude there being certainty on others, and there is surely no doubt that the First Precept applies to human beings. There is considerable textual evidence—including an explicit prohibition on abortion in the monastic code—to confirm that abortion at any stage of pregnancy from conception onwards is the intentional killing of a human being and gravely wrong.[34] Nor is there any textual basis for the view sometimes suggested that the seriousness of an abortion varies according to the gestational phase of the pregnancy.[35]

Tworkov offers no specific reason why abortion should be an exception from the precept against taking human life, and it is extremely difficult to find support for the view that killing human beings in any situation—even in self-defence—is condoned in Buddhism.[36] It would appear that the execution of criminals by the state, and killing in the course of a 'just war' are also impermissible, and if so Buddhism may be regarded as holding what is known as a 'consistent' (i.e. exceptionless) pro-life position.

The second line of argument—the one which seems most relevant to the proposed middle way—does not challenge the view that abortion is prohibited by the First Precept. Instead it takes a different tack and suggests that killing in certain circumstances may be justifiable because compassion requires it. Although not spelt out in detail, the likely direction this argument would take would be to suggest that the rule against taking human life is of a *prima facie* nature and can be overridden when circumstances require. An appeal to the concept of 'skilful means' (*upāya-kauśalya*) would almost certainly be made, and some kind of utilitarian-style computation invoked to determine in which situations taking life is allowed.[37] Since this argument has yet to be made at any length it is difficult to comment further at this stage. Suffice it to say for now that such a reading would be a departure from the mainstream moral tradition. It is, moreover, an argument which proceeds not by invoking the middle way, but by reframing the problem as a conflict between two principles: on the one hand the duty not to take life, and on the other the obligation to be compassionate.

The 'Middle Way' Revisited

The attempts made so far to establish a Buddhist middle way which will allow abortion face major problems and it is difficult to see how they can be sustained. I wish to conclude by suggesting that there is no need to search for a Buddhist middle way on this issue since the tradition has already presented us with one, namely the teachings on abortion set out from the earliest times. The traditional prohibition on abortion is itself a middle way in that it embodies a mean between two philosophical extremes which Buddhism rejects. The first extreme is the doctrine of vitalism, which holds that life is an absolute value to be preserved at all costs. Vitalism may also hold, as does Jainism, that even unintentional killing is morally wrong. According to vitalism, not only is it always wrong to kill, but it is also necessary to go to extreme lengths if necessary to preserve the spark of life. In the context of euthanasia, for example, vitalism requires that dying patients be kept alive as long as possible and that the full range of medical resources be deployed in all circumstances to preserve life.

The other extreme is the 'quality of life' position, which is commonly embedded in a utilitarian ethical framework. On this view, life has no intrinsic value and moral decisions are to be taken by weighing up the prospective amount of pleasure or other pre-moral good to be produced by alternative courses of action. Thus if an abortion produces greater happiness (or yields less suffering) for all concerned than allowing a pregnancy to continue, it is morally justifiable. Life is regarded as a commodity which can be traded off against other goods (such as a reduction in suffering), although utilitarians have never been able to explain satisfactorily how the weighing is to be carried out. As well as allowing abortion, a utilitarian ethics would permit other breaches of the Five Precepts such as murder, lying, stealing, sexual immorality and the taking of intoxicants, if they lead to greater happiness than observing the precepts.

I wish to suggest that the middle way between the two extremes described above is the doctrine of the sanctity of life. To avoid possible problematic theological associations, in a Buddhist context we might refer to it as the doctrine of the 'inviolability' of life. This doctrine is the foundation of traditional Western law and ethics and also forms the basis of the ethics of many Indian traditions. Respect for life is fundamental to Buddhism, as can be seen from the prominence given to the principle of 'non-harming' (*ahiṃsā*). This acknowledges both the inviolability and the fragility of human life, and holds that while intentional killing is always wrong there is no obligation to preserve life at all costs. Thus, for example, a patient who is beyond medical help may be allowed to die without intrusive and burdensome medical intervention. The strict and consistent prohibitions on the taking of life found in Buddhist scriptures and commentaries down the centuries make it extremely difficult to see how abortion—a paradigm case of premeditated intentional killing—could be justified in terms of Buddhist ethics. Desperate though many situations may be, to condone abortion as a compassionate means to reducing suffering is not to follow the middle way but to abandon it and move to the extreme of utilitarianism. Once that step is taken it is hard to see why other breaches of the First Precept, such as infanticide, should be immoral, since the arguments used to justify abortion can also be used to justify the killing of children already born, as has sometimes been the practice in Japan on a large scale.[38]

Conclusion

What conclusions, then, can be drawn regarding the proposed middle way and the Buddhist contribution to the Western debate? First, I think whatever contribution Buddhism does make to the debate is likely to be a peaceful one; injuring or killing those who do not share one's views is not the Buddhist way, and there are as yet no signs of Buddhists resorting to violent action over this issue.

Second, there is no doubt that the compromise proposed in the middle way has its attractions. One of the features of the Japanese experience which strikes observers is that a consensus on abortion appears to have been reached without society tearing itself apart over the issue. LaFleur makes this point when commending the Japanese approach to abortion to the West. Appealing to the spirit of American pragmatism he writes:

> The gain to us in looking hard at how the Japanese have dealt with this problem could come, perhaps, in the form of a stimulus

to us to reappreciate the importance of pragmatism. In some
sense it is the Buddhist position that articulates a kind of societal
pragmatism. It forefronts the need for a solution but, importantly, one that does not tear the social fabric apart. Community
matters.[39]

Community indeed matters, but one wonders how much the Japanese solution owes to the distinctive nature of Japanese society
rather than to the intrinsic merits of the consensus itself. As many
observers have noted, in Japan the group takes precedence over the
individual. A Japanese proverb is often quoted in this context: 'The
nail that stands up gets knocked down'. The West, on the other
hand, has a very different cultural tradition, one which encourages
freedom of expression. Given the contrasting socio-cultural contexts, how confident can we be that a solution which is right for Japan is right for the West? And while community matters, surely
what matters more is the sort of community which is being preserved and the values it holds.

A third point is that the solution offered by the proposed middle way is not really a new position in terms of the spectrum of
views on abortion already on offer in the West. Liberal Christians
or Jews, for example, or even those with no religious convictions,
might adopt a similar position in seeing abortion as regrettable, but
nevertheless justifiable.[40]

Fourth, it is hard to see the proposed middle way as an authentic
application of this traditional Buddhist concept. On certain matters
our instincts tell us there can be no middle way. Would making
slaves into second-class citizens be the appropriate middle way on
slavery?[41]

Fifth, it is clear that the proposed middle way has a problem in
reconciling itself with long-established doctrinal and ethical positions. Belief in rebirth effectively rules out the view that a fetus is
not entitled to the same moral protection as an adult since, for Buddhism, a fetus is simply an adult who died some time ago.

Sixth, the ritual of *mizuko kuyō* seems worthy of further consideration by Western laity and clergy. LaFleur certainly seems right
in his suggestion that 'there is an appreciable level of psychological and spiritual sanity in the practices of *mizuko kuyō* and that aspects of these practices should be introduced into Western society

and the ambit of the West's religious modalities'.[42] Bringing abortion within the framework of religious liturgy provides a mechanism for those who have lived through one to come to terms with any unfinished business the experience leaves in its wake. The service can also be held in cases of spontaneous miscarriage.

Seventh, a more appropriate understanding of the Buddhist middle way on abortion is to see it as holding not a permissive position on abortion but adhering to the principle of the inviolability of life and occupying a middle position between the extremes of vitalism and 'quality of life' utilitarianism.

Finally, LaFleur is correct to describe abortion as a 'panhuman' problem.[43] As the world continues to shrink we stand poised to enter an era of transcultural ethics. A dialogue with other cultures can help us appreciate the dimensions of these questions as human universals. Nevertheless, Buddhism does not, in my view, hold the key to the much-sought consensus on this issue which has so far eluded the West. Buddhism cannot offer a middle way on abortion because it has already taken sides.

Notes

[1] Earlier drafts of this paper were read at seminars at Bristol University, Department of Theology on 31st October 1995, and Penn State University, Religious Studies Program, on 22nd November 1995. I am grateful to all who offered comments and suggestions on those occasions.

[2] *The Mind of Clover: essays in Zen Buddhist ethics* (San Francisco: North Point, 1984), quoted in R. Florida 'Buddhist Approaches to Abortion', *Asian Philosophy* 1, 1 1991:46.

[3] Helen Tworkov 'Anti-abortion/pro-choice: taking both sides', *Tricycle,* Spring 1992:60–69.

[4] *Infra* p.89, cf. *Liquid Life*, p.213. See also William LaFleur 'Abortion Practices in Japan and What They Can Teach the West', *Tricycle* Summer 1995:41–44.

[5] *Infra* p.63.

[6] Thus Ken Jones *The Social Face of Buddhism* (London: Wisdom, 1989), 176.

[7] Ibid.

[8]   Robert Aitken writes, 'Once the decision is made, there is no blame' (quoted in Jones, *The Social face of Buddhism*, 177).

[9]   *The Sunday Times* (London), 8 October 1995, 'Abortion Heretic Outrages Feminists', by Nick Peters and Kirsty Lang, World News, Section 1 p.19.

[10] *The Sunday Times* (London), 15 October 1995, 'Mother Knows Best', interview by Tony Allen-Mills, News Review, Section 3 p.1.

[11] LaFleur (1992:196).

[12] See chapter six.

[13] LaFleur (1992:213).

[14] With respect to nirvana, for example, the views of eternalism or annihilationism are seen as extremes. One school of Buddhist philosophy, the Madhyamaka or 'Middle School' virtually made a career out of this idea and used it to great effect as a critique to undermine extreme views and opinions of all kinds.

[15] The 'doctrine of the mean' (discussed in Book II of the *Nicomachean Ethics*) holds that virtue lies in a mean between two extremes. For example, courage is the mean between rashness and cowardice, and generosity is the mean between prodigality and miserliness.

[16] *Nicomachean Ethics*, Book II, c.1107a1-27, J.A.K. Thomson et al *Aristotle: Ethics* (Penguin Classics, London, 1976), p.102.

[17] This formulation of the argument is taken from Peter Singer, *Rethinking Life and Death* (Oxford: OUP, 1995), p.100.

[18] R. Florida 'Buddhist Approaches to Abortion', *Asian Philosophy* 1, 1 1991:41. The matter is well settled. 'Thus, in Buddhism, abortion is regarded as an act of taking the life of a human being', Shoyu Taniguchi 'Biomedical Ethics from a Buddhist Perspective', *Pacific World* 3 Fall 1987:76. 'Hence, there is no doubt about the unequivocal attitude of the Buddha's teaching in respect of life from the very inception of conception, i.e., from the moment of penetration of the ovum by the spermatazoon, thereby placing artificial and intentional abortion in the same category as wilful murder' (*Encyclopaedia of Buddhism*, s.v. 'Abortion').

[19] For further details of Buddhist embryology see Damien Keown *Buddhism & Bioethics* (London: Macmillan, 1995), Ch.2.

[20] A useful account of Aristotle's views on embryology and their influence may be found in Norman M. Ford *When did I begin?* (Cambridge: Cambridge University Press, 1991).

[21] *Vin*.iii.73; *VA*.ii.437f

[22] This information is based primarily on the literature of the Theravāda school, although I believe it holds for the Indo-Tibetan tradition and possibly beyond. On Tibetan embryology see Yeshi Dhonden 'Embryology in Tibetan Medicine', in *Tibetan Medicine* (Dharamsala: Library of Tibetan Works and Archives, 1980), 43-48; Lati Rinboche and Jeffrey Hopkins *Death, Intermediate State and Rebirth in Tibetan Buddhism* (Ithaca, NY: Snow Lion Publications, 1980).

[23] On these pre-natal stages see *S*.i.206, *Kvu*.494, *Nd*.I.120, *SA*.i.300, *Vism* 236. The stages of fetal growth as understood by Tibetan medicine are depicted in the 'Blue Beryl' paintings. See Plate 5 on embryology in *The Middle Way* vol.67,4, February 1993 p.228ff. On the correspondence with Āyurvedic embryology, Jyotir Mitra *A Critical Appraisal of Ayurvedic Materials in Buddhist Literature (with special reference to Tripiṭika)* (Varanasi: The Jyotirlok Prakashan, 1985), 296ff.

[24] I am grateful to Elizabeth Harrison for enlightening me on the history of this term. It seems that in the Heian period (794-1185) 'it referred to a young child and had no connection with death. It was not until relatively recently, in the Tokugawa period (1603-1868), that the word came to be defined in relation to a dead child, and then only to a child that had died after being born. This included young children who died of any cause as well as those who were killed immediately after birth. I recall a Buddhist definition from this time as any child that died at too young an age to have heard the teachings of the Buddha. Unborn children did not warrant much, if any, attention; only with the popularization of the modern practice of *mizuko kuyō* does the word, and the *kuyō* ritual (which I call a memorial service) become associated with dead unborn children as well' (personal communication, 8th November 1995).

[25] LaFleur (1992:11).

[26] Indigenous ideas about fetal life will typically form part of a more complex network of beliefs about the supernatural than the example of the stork. Such ideas, however, have no more of a place

in a philosophical assessment of the morality of abortion than does the medieval notion of 'quickening'.

[27] Domyo Miura *The Forgotten Child* (Henley-on-Thames, England: Aidan Ellis, 1983). Although he refuses to allow the *mizuko* concept as in any way justifying abortion, Miura has been a great advocate of the *mizuko kuyō* service.

[28] See, for example, George Tanabe 'Sounds and Silence: A Counterresponse', *Japanese Journal of Religious Studies* 22 1995: 197-200.

[29] Tevor Ling 'Buddhist Factors in Population Growth and Control. A Survey based on Thailand and Ceylon', *Population Studies* 23 1969:214.

[30] Helen Tworkov 'Anti-abortion/pro-choice: taking both sides', *Tricycle,* Spring 1992:65.

[31] They are also difficult to reconcile with the findings of modern embryology.

[32] It might be noted that the Sixth Commandment 'Thou Shalt not Kill' (Deut. 5,17) is equally unspecific.

[33] Helen Tworkov 'Anti-abortion/pro-choice: taking both sides', *Tricycle* Spring 1992:65.

[34] *Vin.* i.97. According to the Dalai Lama the precept is understood the same way in Tibet. 'Abortion is considered an ill deed of killing a living being. With respect to monks and nuns, there are four types of ill deeds that bring about a defeat of the vow itself; one of them is to kill a human being or something forming as a human being'. Jeffrey Hopkins ed. *The Dalai Lama at Harvard* (Ithaca, NY: Snow Lion Publications, n.d.), 91.

[35] See my *Buddhism & Bioethics*, p.96ff.

[36] It may be suggested that abortion is a form of self-defence by which the pregnant woman defends her body against 'invasion' by the fetus. However, this line of argument faces two problems: as noted, it is unclear that Buddhism permits killing even in self-defence, and it is extremely strained to cast an unborn baby in the role of aggressor.

[37] The concept of 'skilful means' is sometimes held to justify the performance of acts prohibited by the precepts. Although there are some Mahāyāna sources which seem to support this position, such an interpretation lacks any foundation in the earlier teachings.

Furthermore, in those small number of contexts where killing arises, the victim is rarely innocent and the fatal deed may be justifiable as, for example, when done in defence of other lives. In a religious tradition as complex and diverse as Buddhism it would not be surprising to find a variety of views, including even overtly antinomian teachings, as in some Tantric sources. However, even if taken at face value, these variants rarely offer a complete justification for breaking the precepts (often only minor monastic precepts are envisaged) and often impose qualifications it would be impossible for most people to meet (such as that the agent is an enlightened bodhisattva). Furthermore, the sources require careful analysis and interpretation (which they have yet to receive) before any normative conclusions are drawn from them. The prospect of justifying abortion through skilful means therefore seems remote. On the concept of skilful means (*upāya-kauśalya*) see Michael Pye *Skilful Means: A Concept in Mahāyāna Buddhism* (London: Duckworth, 1978); on the interpretation of Tantric texts which apparently condone breaking the precepts see Michael M. Broido 'Killing, Lying, Stealing and Adultery: A problem of interpretation in the Tantras', in *Buddhist Hermeneutics*, ed. D. Lopez, (Kuroda Institute Studies in East Asian Buddhism, 6, Honolulu: University of Hawaii Press, 1988), 71–118. The relationship between skilful means and ethics in Mahāyāna Buddhism is considered in chapter six of Damien Keown *The Nature of Buddhist Ethics* (London: Macmillan, 1992).

[38] For references see 'infanticide' in the index to LaFleur (1992).

[39] LaFleur (1992:212).

[40] A liberal Jewish view on abortion suggests we must: ' ... allow the individual the full force of her agony in having to make a decision that for thousands of years we were lucky enough to leave "in the hands of God". We allow her the dignity of her struggle, offering neither ethical niceties nor moral judgements, but rather honest compassion and support. We respect her as a maker of decisions and help her weigh the alternatives and deal with their consequences.' Rami M. Shapiro 'Blessing and Curse: Towards a Liberal Jewish Ethic' in S. Cromwell Crawford, ed. *World Religions and Global Ethics* (New York: Paragon House, 1989), 183.

[41] The example is taken from Ronald Dworkin *Life's Dominion* (London: HarperCollins, 1995), 10.

[42] LaFleur (1992:216).

[43] LaFleur (1992:219).

Glossary

Abhidhamma	The Scholastic Treatises; the division of the Pali canon dealing with scholastic philosophy
Arahat	One who gains enlightenment by following the teachings of a Buddha
Aśoka	Indian Buddhist emperor of the third century BC
Āyurveda	Traditional Indian medicine ('science of life')
Bodhisattva	One who seeks enlightenment in order to assist others
Brahmanism	The early classical phase of Hinduism
Brahmin	A member of the highest of the four castes
Buddha	Honorific title of Siddhattha Gotama who lived in north India and died around 410 BC.
Buddhaghosa	A famous scholar and commentator of the Theravada tradition (fifth century AD)
Dependent Origination	The doctrine that all phenomena originate from pre-existing conditions.
Dhamma	Pali for *Dharma* (q.v.)
Dharma	Natural law; Buddhist doctrine
Dukkha	Suffering, unsatisfactoriness
Five Precepts	The prohibitions on taking life, stealing, sexual misconduct, lying, and taking intoxicants
Hīnayāna	A derogatory term implying inferiority in doctrine and practice, applied by the Mahayana to schools such as the Theravada
Kalala	Embryo, zygote

219

Karma	Moral actions from which good or bad consequences will inevitably flow.
Karuṇā	Compassion
Mahāyāna	A broadly-based movement which appears around the time of Christ, characterized by more liberal attitudes to doctrine and some aspects of practice. Traditionally prominent in North Asia
Mizuko	Japanese notion of the fetus as 'water child'.
Mizuko kuyō	Religious service held following abortions in Japan
Monastic Rule	The section of the Pali canon dealing with monastic discipline
Nirvana	The summum bonum; the end of cyclic existence
Pali canon	The canon of the Theravada school, written in the Pali language. It contains three main divisions: the Discourses, the Monastic Rule, and the Scholastic Treatises
Paññā	Intuitive wisdom, *sophia*
Pārājika	'Defeat'. The most serious category of offence in the monastic Rule, punished by expulsion from the Order.
Prajñā	The Sanskrit equivalent of *Paññā*
Prāṇa	Breath, life; the bodily 'humour' regulating the vital functions of life
Saṃsāra	Cyclic existence
Saṅgha	The Buddhist monastic Order
Sutta	A religious discourse
Theravāda	The oldest surviving school of Buddhism, prominent today in south-east Asia.
Vinaya	The Monastic Rule
Viññana	Consciousness

Index